Consumption and Public Life

Series Editors: **Frank Trentmann** and **Richard Wilk**

Titles include:

Harold Wilhite
CONSUMPTION AND THE TRANSFORMATION OF EVERYDAY LIFE
A View from South India

Consumption and Public Life
Series Standing Order ISBN 978–1–4039–9983–2 Hardback
978–1–4039–9984–9 Paperback
(outside North America only)

You can receive future titles in this series as they are published by placing a standing order. Please contact your bookseller or, in case of difficulty, write to us at the address below with your name and address, the title of the series and one of the ISBNs quoted above.

Customer Services Department, Macmillan Distribution Ltd, Houndmills, Basingstoke, Hampshire RG21 6XS, England

The European Consumer Citizen in Law and Policy

Jim Davies
University of Northampton, UK

First published 2011 by
PALGRAVE MACMILLAN

Palgrave Macmillan in the UK is an imprint of Macmillan Publishers Limited, registered in England, company number 785998, of Houndmills, Basingstoke, Hampshire RG21 6XS.

Palgrave Macmillan in the US is a division of St Martin's Press LLC, 175 Fifth Avenue, New York, NY 10010.

Palgrave Macmillan is the global academic imprint of the above companies and has companies and representatives throughout the world.

Palgrave® and Macmillan® are registered trademarks in the United States, the United Kingdom, Europe and other countries.

ISBN: 978–0–230–30028–6

This book is printed on paper suitable for recycling and made from fully managed and sustained forest sources. Logging, pulping and manufacturing processes are expected to conform to the environmental regulations of the country of origin.

A catalogue record for this book is available from the British Library.

Library of Congress Cataloging-in-Publication Data

Davies, Jim, 1952–
    The European consumer citizen in law and policy / Jim Davies.
        p. cm.
    Includes bibliographical references and index.
    ISBN 978–0–230–30028–6
        1. Consumer behavior – European Economic Union. 2. Consumption (Economics) – Government policy – European Economic Union. I. Title.
HC240.9.C6D38 2011
339.4'7094—dc23   2011020952

10 9 8 7 6 5 4 3 2 1
20 19 18 17 16 15 14 13 12 11

Printed and bound in the United States of America

To my wife Chris
for the journey of a lifetime

Contents

Figures

Abbreviations

ACER	Agency for the Co-operation of Energy Regulators
ADR	Alternative Dispute Resolution
ANEC	European Association for the Co-ordination of Consumer Representation in Standardisation
BEUC	Bureau Européen des Unions des Consommateurs
CEER	Council of European Energy Regulators
CEO	Chief Executive Officer
CRM	Customer Relationship Management
Defra	Department for Environment Food and Rural Affairs (UK)
DTI	Department of Trade and Industry
EC	European Community
ECCG	European Consumer Consultative Group
ECC-Net	European Consumer Centres Network
ECJ	European Court of Justice
EEA	European Economic Area
EEC	European Economic Community
EESC	European Economic and Social Committee
EFTA	European Free Trade Association
ERASMUS	European Community Action Scheme for the Mobility of University Students
ERGEG	European Regulators Group for Electricity and Gas
EU	European Union
FIN-Net	Financial Dispute Resolution Network
GDP	Gross Domestic Product
GMO	Genetically Modified Organism
IMAG	Industry Metering Advisory Group (UK)
NGO	Non-Governmental Organisation
NHS	National Health System (UK)
NRA	National Regulatory Authorities
OFT	Office of Fair Trading (UK)
TEU	Treaty on European Union
TFEU	Treaty on the Functioning of the European Union
VAT	Value Added Tax

Acknowledgements

There are a number of people to whom I am indebted. First, I very much wish to thank Professor Hanz W Micklitz for instilling in me the confidence that this was a worthwhile project to pursue. His encouragement came in the form of an invitation to present a paper at the EUI in Florence. That paper constituted the basis of a journal article 'Entrenchment of New Governance in Consumer Policy Formulation: A Platform for European Consumer Citizenship Practice?' originally published in the *Journal of Consumer Policy* 32 (2009) 245, DOI 10.1007/s10603-009-9108-7, and for which I would wish to acknowledge the kind permission of Springer Science + Business Media B.V. for allowing me to reproduce an updated version that, with various refinements, has now emerged as the main focus of Chapter 3 in this book.

I would also wish to thank Punch Magazine for their permission to reproduce the extract from Patrick Barrington's poem *I want to be a Consumer*, published in *Punch* on 25 April 1934.

I am also very much indebted to the anonymous referee whose report on my proposal for this book contained valuable advice and suggestions which I hope I have acted on as they would have wished.

On a much more personal level, for her belief in me, and in my pursuit of the research that eventually led to the completion of this book, I thank my wife Chris. Her unerring support, encouragement, love and patience have played a significant role in the fulfilment of this project. I would also thank her and my friend Duncan for accepting the daunting task of proof reading many earlier drafts. Special heartfelt thanks must also go to my colleague Professor Erika Szyszczak for her support, encouragement and guidance, and for her friendship. A final special thank you must also go to my mother Shirley who sadly died shortly before this book went to press. Many years ago during my schooldays she recognised an academic capability in me that eluded my teachers; she fought for me to be given the opportunity to advance my education and succeeded.

Table of Cases

European Court of Justice (numeric)

Case 139/85 *R H Kempf* v *Staatssecretaris van Justitie* [1986] ECR 1741, 122
Case 234/85 *Keller* [1986] ECR 2897, 85
Case 158/86 *Warner Brothers* v *Erik Viuff Christiansen* [1988] ECR 2605, 33
Case 236/86 *Humbel* [1988] ECR 5365, 120
Joined Cases, 154 and 155/87, *RSVZ* v *Heinrich Wolf* [1988] ECR 3897, 83
Case 382/87 *R Buet and EBS SARL* v *Ministère Public* [1989] ECR 1235, 33
Case C-18/88 *Régie des télégraphes et des téléphones* v *GB-Inno-BM SA* [1991] ECR I-5941, 129
Case C-362/88 *GB-INNO-BM* v *Confédération du Commerce Luxembourgeois* [1990] ECR I-667, 33, 133, 190, 191
Case C-230/89 *Commission* v *Greece* [1991] ECR I-1909, 27
Case C-238/89 *Pall Corp.* v *P. J. Dahihausen & Co. Ltd.* [1990] ECR I-4827, 33, 190, 191
Case C-361/89 *Di Pinto* [1991] ECR I-1189, 72
Case C-159/90 *SPUC* v *Grogan* [1991] ECR I-4685, 120
Case C-89/91 *Shearson Lehmann Hutton Inc.* v *TVB Treuhandgesellschaft für Vermögensverwaltung und Beteiligungen mbH.* [1993] ECR I-139, 73
Case C-126/91 *Yves Rocher* [1993] ECR I-2361, 190, 191
Case C-320/91 *Procureur du Roi* v *Paul Corbeau* [1993] ECR I-2533, 130
Case C-315/92 *Verband Sozialer Wettbewerb eV* v *Clinique Laboratoires SNC* [1994] ECR I-317, 33, 190, 191
Case C-456/93 *Langguth* [1995] ECR I-1737, 190, 191
Case C-470/93 *Mars* [1995] ECR I-1923, 190, 191
Case C-84/94 *United Kingdom* v *Council (Working Time)* [1996] ECR I-5755, 86
Case C-120/95 *Decker* [1998] ECR I-1831, 120, 126
Case C-269/95 *Francesco Benincasa* v *Dentalkit Srl.* [1997] ECR I-3767, 73
Case C-158/96 *Kohll* [1998] ECR I-1931, 126
Case C-184/96 *Commission* v *French Republic* [1998] ECR I-6197, 56
Case C-210/96 *Gut Springenheide GmbH* v *Oberkreisdirektor des Kreises Steinfurt* [1998] ECR I-4657, 34, 70, 191
Case C-224/98 *D'Hoop* [2002] ECR I-6191, 123
Case C-368/98 *Vanbraekel* [2001] ECR I-5363, 126
Case C-376/98 *Germany* v *European Parliament and Council of the European Union* [2000] ECR I-8419, 29
Case C-74/99 *The Queen* v *Secretary of State for Health and Others ex parte Imperial Tobacco Ltd. and Others* [2000] ECR I-8419, 29
Case C-157/99 *Smits & Peerbooms* [2001] ECR I-5473, 126

Court of First Instance

World Trade Organisation (WTO)

Table of Legislation

Treaties and Conventions

Brussels Convention on Jurisdiction and the Enforcement of Judgments in Civil and Commercial Matters

Convention on the Law applicable to Contractual Obligations (Rome 1)

EU Charter of Fundamental Rights

Single European Act (SEA)

Treaty establishing the European Community (EEC/EC)

Treaty of Lisbon

Treaty on European Union (TEU)

Treaty on the Functioning of the European Union (TFEU)

Directives

Directive (EEC) 84/450 relating to the approximation of the laws, regulations and administrative provisions of the Member States concerning misleading advertising [1984] OJ L 250/17, 33

Directive (EEC) 85/374 concerning liability for defective products [1988] OJ L 307/54, 189

Directive (EEC) 85/577 to protect the consumer in respect of contracts negotiated away from business premises [1985] OJ L 372/31, 32, 189, 191

Directive (EEC) 87/102 for the approximation of the laws, regulations and administrative provisions of the Member States concerning consumer credit [1987] OJ L42/48, 189, 191

Directive (EEC) 89/622 on the approximation of the laws, regulations and administrative provisions of the Member States concerning the labelling of tobacco products [1989] OJ L359/1, 29

Directive (EEC) 90/219 on the contained use of genetically modified micro-organisms [1990] OJ L 117/1, 61

Directive (EEC) 90/220 on the deliberate release into the environment of genetically modified organisms [1990] OJ L 7/39, 61, 62

Directive (EEC) 90/314 on package travel, package holidays and package tours, [1990] OJ L 158/59, 71, 191

Regulations

EU Decisions

I Want to Be a Consumer

"And what do you mean to be?"
The kind old Bishop said
As he took the boy on his ample knee
And patted his curly head.
"We should all of us choose a calling
To help society's plan;
Then what do you mean to be, my boy,
When you grow to be a man?"

"I want to be a consumer,"
The bright-haired lad replied
As he gazed up into the Bishop's face
In innocence open-eyed.
"I've never had aims of a selfish sort,
For that, as I know is wrong,
I want to be a Consumer, Sir,
And help the world along."

"I want to be a Consumer
And live in a useful way;
For that is the thing that's needed most,
I've heard Economists say.
There are too many people working
And too many things are made.
I want to be a Consumer, Sir,
And help to further trade."

"I want to be a Consumer
And work both night and day,
For that is the thing that's needed most,
I've heard Economists say.
I won't just be a Producer
Like Bobby and James and John;
I want to be a Consumer, Sir,
And help the nation on."

"I want to be a Consumer
And do my duty well,
For that is the thing that's needed most,
I've heard Economists tell.
I've made up my mind,"
The lad was heard … to say;
"I want to be a Consumer, Sir,
And I want to begin today."

(Patrick Barrington, *I want to be a Consumer,*
Punch, 25th April 1934, p. 467)

1
Introduction: European Consumer Citizenship Practice

Consumer power and political influence

Both Kathleen Donohue and Frank Trentmann used extracts from Barrington's rhyme to introduce discussions on changing ideas of the consumer. For Donohue, the focus was on the changing place of the consumer in political economy of the United States (Donohue, 2003), whilst for Trentmann the rhyme offered a 'convenient entry' into his enquiry into the 'increasingly powerful vocabulary of "the consumer" as a self-evident category or ontological essence [that] has…distracted attention from the historical emergence of this creature…and the different positions it has occupied in politics and society' (Trentmann, 2006b, p. 2). The rhyme clearly indicates that consumer behaviour has been considered, at least for the past seventy-five years, to have a depth to it; that it can embrace self-lessness and economic agency linked to national membership and belonging. Yet the optimistic goal of Barrington's 'curly headed boy' has, and had, proved elusive, with structural and cognitive barriers identified as early as 1920 by co-operative theorist Percy Redfern, who suggested that

[i]n our common everyday needs the great industries of the world take their rise. We – the mass of common men and women in all countries – also compose the world's market. To sell to us is the ultimate aim of the world's business. Hence it is ourselves as consumers who stand in a central relation to all the economies of the world, like the king in his kingdom…as consumers we are set by nature thus to give leadership, aim and purpose to the whole economic world. That we are not kings, but serfs in the mass, is due to our failure to think and act together as consumers and so to realise our true position and power. (Redfern, 1920, pp. 11–12)

This book does not pursue Redfern's notion that 'we are set *by nature* thus to give leadership' but examines the proposition that, within an EU context, the *opportunity* for the consumer to *realise* his or her *true position and power* has never been greater; that there exists a coherent, tangible and relevant, albeit perhaps narrow, concept of citizenship that can be associated with the notion of the *consumer citizen*. This notion has been reflected in the literature of the social sciences over the past thirty years and has seen the development of a 'new orthodoxy' in defining the agency of the *active consumer* within a limiting framework of markets, choice and point of purchase (Trentmann, 2006b, p. 3). From a legal perspective, concepts and definitions of the consumer and of citizenship are individually complex and contentious and the idea of conflating these concepts particularly problematic. However, the notion of the consumer citizen has not been confined to the literature of political and historical science but has emerged in the legal scholarship concerned with aspects of both citizenship and consumer law (for example, Everson, 1995; Shaw, 1997a; Howells and Weatherill, 2005; Everson and Joerges, 2006). This book is concerned with what we might mean by the notional term consumer citizen and introduces, through empirical and theoretical research, both the behavioural attributes and the normative processes that we can associate with the idea of a *consumer citizenship practice*. The originality in this research arises from its specific investigation into how as individuals we may assume, through the exercise of particular market-related behaviours, an identity and ascribable category consistent with the concept of consumer citizenship and its legal relevance within the EU.

This introductory chapter outlines the problems and the complexity associated with this research and introduces arguments for a hierarchy of normative influences and consequential behaviours that define a model of consumer citizenship practice. It briefly discusses the methodology that has been used in tracing the development of this consumer citizenship practice before providing an overview of the chapters that follow.

Issues and questions: the research problem

The hypothesis

This book examines the developing relationship between *individuals* and the EU as a polity, a polity deeply rooted in economic ambition and the establishment of the internal market. This economic focus has developed a form of citizenship practice based on individual rights and obligations that operate within this EU 'space'. Under the narrowest of definitions this is a citizenship practice that may attach merely to the Union citizen of Article 20 of the Treaty on the Functioning of the European Union (TFEU) and therefore exclusively to the nationals of the Member States. But, given a broader definition, in which the spatial boundary component of citizenship is defined by market access, the concept can apply to all individuals engaging with the internal market. The exclusionary nature of citizenship is, in this context, defined by the rules of the internal market as they vary from sector to sector and by an individual's capacity to access the market – not by the individual's citizenship status *vis à vis* the Member State.

The model of a developing consumer citizenship practice presented in this book is derived from the study of the changing status of *individuals* in relation to their *access* and *choice rights* and to their *duties* and *obligations* as market actors. The purpose of this examination, which to a large degree focuses on secondary legislation, the case law of the European Court of Justice (the Court) and the contribution made in the literature of the political sciences, is threefold. Firstly, the primary objective is to introduce an explanatory model or framework definition of what we may mean by the terms consumer citizen and consumer citizenship practice. Secondly, there is the underlying objective to contribute to the understanding of a developing EU post-national citizenship through a study of the changing relationship between individuals and the internal market. This relationship will be shown to be shaped by the institutions of the EU within a policy objective that increasingly seeks to involve the consumer as an effective market actor through the provision of channels for *voice* and *influence*: a process influenced by structures of new governance, the globalisation of trade, technological development and later twentieth-century economic theory. To that particular end, this book examines arguments and observations based on an analysis of the conflicting notions of citizenship and the emergence of the politicised consumer in a globalised market: arguments and observations that will identify consumer citizenship practice as an increasingly influential role played by individuals in a developing framework of EU law and policy. The third purpose of this book is to bring a study of new governance, or at least certain characteristics of newer forms of governance (see Scott and Trubek, 2002), and a broader understanding of the politics of European consumer law into the mainstream of European consumer law scholarship (see Davies, 2009). This book begins by exploring and developing an argument that seeks to validate the notion of a consumer dimension to citizenship, or, perhaps better, a citizenship dimension to consumerism, through an analysis of the complex, practical and theoretical development of the two concepts.

Complex notions of the citizen and the consumer

Although the goal of a European citizenship had existed 'since even before the earliest days of the European Coal and Steel Community in the 1950's' (Maas, 2007, p. 61) it was not until 1993 that all *nationals* of the Member States were declared *Citizens* of the Union. Article 20 TFEU is clear; it establishes Citizenship of the Union for every person holding the nationality of a Member State, a status that complements rather than replaces national citizenship.[1] In doing so, it provides that citizens of the Union shall enjoy the rights conferred by the Treaty and shall be subject to duties imposed thereby. The simplicity of the provision, however, belies the paradox that contested modern concepts of European citizenship, varying from 'thick' to 'thin', and depending on the degree to which rights and obligations affect individuals, are dominated by the notion that citizenship operates within the context of the *state*. Further, no complete or elaborate theory of citizenship exists (Wiener, 1998, pp. 3–4), and those who drafted Article 20 TFEU were careful to associate Union citizenship with the more certain criteria of Member State nationality.

This new post-national citizenship did, however, significantly add to the complexity of elaborating a definition of citizenship and 'instantly provoked debates over its political and conceptual implications' (Wiener, 1998, pp. 3–4). Citizenship and notions of the state have traditionally been both interrelated and contingent concepts, the one on the other: both are evolving concepts and the establishment of the 'institutionalised link between the citizens of the Union and the EU as a polity differs in many ways from the familiar citizen-polity relation that had been established in nation-states over the past two centuries' (Wiener, 1998). What the introduction of Union Citizenship did accomplish, at least according to French President François Mitterrand, was the turning of 'the whole of Europe into one space' (Tiersky, 2003, p. 115, cited in Trentmann, 2006b, p. 61).

Initially, the focus of this book is on the development of this 'one space' through the completion of the internal market; through the corresponding development of the role played by, and expected of, the individual as a consumer, and the development of new organisational structures of governance in an expanding EU. The arguments propounded suggest that the role of the individual as an influential market actor is continuing, albeit slowly, to gain ground within the ambit of the behavioural attributes of a European consumer citizenship practice. The process may be incomplete but this book argues that there is a discernible trend in which the individual can increasingly be found to be serving the public interest, as an influential actor, across the EU internal market. For the purposes of this book, this EU internal market is construed broadly, stretching from the general private sector retail markets for goods and services to the increasingly marketised components of the social welfare sector: a market that can be associated with free movement rights in the consumption of welfare benefits; with the modernisation of public sector service delivery; with the privatisation and liberalisation of services of general interest and with the purchasing of commodified goods and services in the general retail market.

These arguments are developed from an evaluation of the contested and developing concepts of citizenship, an analysis of the background to modern market dynamics and a review of the changing political and economic environments that have influenced a thickening conception of post-national Union citizenship. The Union itself, as a political entity, has provided the necessary collective component to the notion of citizenship that, from the early days of limited rights for the coal and steel *worker-citizen* (Olsen, 2006, pp. 2 and 5; see also Szyszczak, 2000, pp. 176–179), has developed into a wide range of rights that, whilst notably still primarily of economic interest, have now attained a fundamental status in case law.[2]

This book, suggests that there is validity in the notion of the consumer citizen. It recognises that such a narrow construction of citizenship is based on a membership dimension of consumer rights and eligibility that at one extreme is about defined *access rights*, of a type perhaps more readily associated with state-based concepts of citizenship, and at the other is more about the *choice rights* typically associated with selection of goods and services in a competitive market. Such a membership dimension for consumer citizenship needs to accommodate the different eligibility criteria encountered by individuals acting within different sectors of the market. This is identified through a discussion of the emergence of consumer rights and duties within a citizenship context that recognises the impact of a developing global openness in both trade and technology.

Such a discussion is, however, not straightforward and even the definition of consumer varies within the secondary legislation of the EU's consumer *acquis* (Schulte-Nölke and others, 2008, p. 713 *et seq.*). These definitional variances are further compounded by issues of translation and different national conceptions of 'consumer' where EU law has been transposed into the national systems. There is, however, a common core to these definitions, identified in the Consumer Law Compendium, and adopted for the purposes of this book, that 'all provide that a consumer is: a natural person; who is acting for purposes which are outside some kind of business, commercial or trade activity' (Schulte-Nölke and others, 2008, p. 715).

Introducing the duty dimension in consumer citizenship practice

On the 'duty' side of the citizenship paradigm, this book suggests that in the model of consumer citizenship practice, we can expect to find new duties or obligations attached to *choice* rights in the substantive development of a 'thicker' *market* citizenship; that it is in the effective exercise of these duties that we may identify the political and economic agent identified by Redfern. In considering such novel notions, Balibar has suggested that the history of citizenship 'is open to new, non-predetermined developments', and that

> questions of citizenship can *only* be posed in terms of process and access. [That] [w]e are not 'citizens' but we can '*become*' citizens; we can enter into one or several processes of creation of citizenship. And we enter all the more deeply into them the more numerous and more different we are. (Balibar, 2004, pp. 198–199, emphasis added)

This is an approach that reflects Breton's depiction of systems of collective organisation, such as the EU, in which identity in a multi-level system is contingent, in part, on a utilitarian identity derived from 'a network of opportunities and constraints that impinge on people's interests and partly determine their life chances'; in part on 'pragmatic solidarities', or 'communities of fate' identities derived from identification with the system of organised interdependence based on reciprocity, joint investments, participation in collective achievements and on the perceived fairness of the distribution of costs and benefits; and in part on the common heritage derived from a sense of 'people-hood' that can develop in all levels of social organisation, whether sub-national, national, or transnational (Breton, 1995, from Shaw, 1997a, text associated with fns 96–101).

Shaw highlighted Breton's contribution in her paper on EU citizenship and her discussion of 'the duty problem' (Shaw, 1997a, text associated with fns 96–101). In particular, she draws attention to Everson's contention that the figure of the 'market citizen' is the 'most pressing concern' at the present time (Everson, 1995, p. 89, text associated with fns 441–442) and Breton's discussion of the exercise of citizenship in which the focus is on the role of citizens input into decisions, and the breaking down of the distance between the citizen and the formal political institutions at the transnational level. Based on this literature, the duty problem as expressed in general terms by Breton is adopted as the basis for the discussion of the duty dimension in this book, and is defined as 'the willingness to and possibility of helping with the construction, maintenance, and improvement of the collectivity' (Breton, 1995, cited in Shaw, 1997a, text associated with fn. 439).

Methodology

European integration and Europeanisation

European integration develops manifold, complex and at times contradictory relationships that exist between the economic and political levels and the legal sphere of structures, institutions and norms. This book traces the development of norm creation in the consumer area where, as with other areas, legal elements play a dual role in which 'they are both the object and the agent of integration' (Dehousse and Weiler, 1990, pp. 242–243). It follows the gradual conceptual development by the Commission and the Court of both vulnerable and active consumers, the fusing of citizenship characteristics with those of the consumer and the development within the legal sphere of institutional structures through which European integration may be progressed by the gradual removal of differentiated treatment across the Member States. This provides a sectoral analysis of the integration process that formed the main objective of the Community's programme for the completion of the internal market from the mid 1980s (Commission, 1985). An analysis that now provides for an aggregate of the consumer interest in which an essentially 'top down' inspired complex of organisational structures has created channels for 'bottom up' consumer voice and influence and co-operative development of regulatory and 'consumer watchdog' processes at the Member State level.

Dehouse and Weiler asserted that there was a general acceptance that 'integration must be regarded as a *process*, leading gradually, with the passage of time, to an increase in the exchanges between the various societies concerned and to a more centralized form of government' (Dehousse and Weiler, 1990, p. 246). As such, legal development of the status, rights and duties that are associated with the concept of the consumer citizen, or more particularly with individual behaviours that can be identified with a consumer citizenship practice, are generally described in terms of their *evolutionary development* within this book. Where law, by its nature, has a tendency to 'provide a fixed and relatively rigid image of the situations it takes into consideration' (Dehousse and Weiler, 1990, p. 246) its evolutionary development in the field of consumer law is seen, and seen increasingly with the passing of time, to be smoothed out with interventions of soft law and institutional elements of new governance. This is a smoothing out that corresponds with the model of multi-level constitutionalism described by Pernice, and that, within the scope of this book, is identified with the space that links society to the political institutions and in which society has become involved with the decision-making process (Pernice, 2002, pp. 511–522).

That legal and institutional factors largely condition the evolution of the integration process, through an influence that is often indirect, was pointed out by Dehousse and Weiler who identified that the institutional framework can directly affect the substance of the policies pursued by the various actors. They assert that any attempt to review the legal patterns of integration 'should encompass the relationships between all actors interested by this phenomenon', both public and private actors, and that 'private actors can play a semi-normative role in drafting integration instruments' (Dehousse and Weiler, 1990, pp. 247–249). In this book I argue that both formal and informal channels now exist for such public and private actors to influence the development of centralised consumer policy and that the individual consumer can be included amongst these actors through the exercise of behaviours that define consumer citizenship practice. To that end, and in that context, the extent of any discussion of European political and market integration through law is specifically confined to the consumer policy sector and its developing network of coalitions and actors.

Even within the sectoral confines of consumer policy, the broader issues and complexities of European integration, associated with geographic and functional expansion, (see Weatherill, 1997) have produced systemic inconsistency at the Member State level that challenge any traditional notion of a Kelsenian or Hartian legal order as a hierarchical structure of norms (Walker, 2005, p. 592). Instead, at the state level, new governance techniques of *inter alia* benchmarking, identification of 'best practice' and non-binding co-operation are employed to promote the integration process and add to the policymaking process (Majone, 2005, citing Scott and Trubek, 2002). The exponential growth in the number of Member States acceding to the EU since the 1990s has seen the theoretical debates over European integration develop into an analysis of the process of Europeanisation, raising questions of how the EU's supranational institutions have affected the institutions of the Member States and how the policies of the EU affect national policy through the process of Europeanisation (Schmidt, 2009, p. 194).

In examining the notion of consumer citizenship practice this book addresses the top down integrationist measures of harmonisation in the consumer *acquis* and provides a description of the institutional structures of consumer policy formulation. These are institutions and channels for agency that reflect movements in decision-making power away from the Member States and, upwards towards the EU, outwards towards independent regulatory agencies and enforcement authorities, and downwards towards individual consumers. Schmidt argues, in particular, that the move to regulatory agencies, 'whether EU-related or the result of internal dynamics, has produced a weakening of the state-*qua*-central actor although at the same time it could be seen as a strengthening of public action and effective governance *for* the people' (Schmidt, 2009, p. 205). These are agencies *and* regulatory authorities that are forming networks of self-supporting epistemic communities for the sharing of new ideas and best practice that, whilst strengthening governance *for* the people and providing consumer citizenship practice with the channels for voice and influence, may also be increasing the 'power position' of the Commission *vis à vis* national government (Coen and Thatcher, 2005, p. 335).

Aspects of constitutionalism and sovereignty in a fast changing union

Early scholarly analysis identified the Court as a 'champion of the integration process' in a new legal framework within a new legal order for a new political order that was 'part international, part national, and crucially, part supranational' (Hunt and Shaw, 2009, p. 93). Also, as outlined above, there has since the 1990s been a move away from the initial integrationist approach towards one of Europeanisation: an accompaniment to the political focus on expansion. The consequence is that doctrinal analysis in EU legal scholarship has, suggests Walker, 'strained to keep up with the flow of new law, and, not unsurprisingly, the effort required has restricted broad-ranging theoretical reflection to modest proportions' (Walker, 2005, p. 582).

The pace and diversity of change that has accompanied the processes of integration and Europeanisation has given EU legal studies an event-sensitive, or problem-centred, approach at both the systemic level and in sectoral research (Walker, 2005, pp. 590–591). From a methodological perspective, the sectoral focus of this book sticks to this approach as it addresses a series of problems associated with the basic hypothesis that the notion of a consumer citizenship practice has a definable validity. The individually problematic development of conceptions of the consumer and the citizen are reviewed before the narrower but equally problematic notion of the consumer citizen is considered. The potential for a new constitutionalised democracy of individual and representative involvement in policy formulation, and its consequential input to law making, are then exposed through a study of the structures of 'new governance' in the consumer domain. It is an approach that seeks to identify an internal coherence within a poly-centred structure of political authority: an authority that embraces the notion of a fragmented sovereignty and provides a possibility for developing the sectoral aspect of sovereignty that concerned Percy Redfern.[3] In setting out the parameters for locating consumer citizenship practice within an internally coherent poly-centred structure of political authority this book identifies, within the confines of the consumer sector, what Walker suggests should be encouraged: that is,

> a new commitment to a bottom-up democratic experimentalism...in which coherence is...a...matter of forward-looking mutual learning and synergy between different problem-solving micro-communities in which the norm-application distinction dissolves in a process of continuous reflection, adaptation and recognition. (Walker, 2005, p. 594, citing *inter alia*, Cohen and Sabel, 1997)

Beyond functionalism and output legitimacy: complexity and new paradigms

To conclude this section on the methodological framework adopted for this book, attention is drawn to the complex, process-based reality of EU governance. The approach to European integration that had endured from the 1950s through to the late 1990s had been accompanied by a perception of citizens granting a 'permissive consensus' to European policy making in which societal participation was analysed 'from a functional, output-orientated point of view investigating interest groups' contribution to effective problem-solving and governance "for the people"' (Finke, 2007, p. 4). The Maastricht Treaty 1993 provoked an EU legitimacy crisis in which societal participation in European governance faced the fundamental democratic dilemma of a choice for national citizens and their political leaders, between, on the one hand, the preservation of authority within a smaller political (national) unit, but, one that, on some important matters, may not have the capacity to deal with them effectively and, on the other hand, the larger political unit (the EU) that could deal more effectively with such matters but, with a significantly reduced capacity for the citizen to democratically influence governmental decision-making (Dahl, 1994, pp. 23–24).

By the end of the 1990s attention had shifted towards an input-oriented dimension of democratic legitimacy. It was the Commission, in particular, that focussed on civil society and participation as a remedy for the perceived legitimacy crisis (Commission, 2001b). It is a focus that has been described as 'the transnational channel of EU democracy' with procedures that lack the formality and binding quality of European and national parliamentary democratic processes (Hurrelmann and DeBardeleben, 2009, p. 232). This book examines this transnational channel of democracy in the context of consumer policy formulation – a channel through which 'a number of authors see a considerable democratic potential in its mechanisms of policy-specific, functional representation, which seek to identify and consult relevant stakeholders in early stages of the decision making process' (Hurrelmann and DeBardeleben, 2009, citing Ruzza, 2004; Greenwood, 2007, pp. 177–194; Steffek and others, 2007). Hurrelmann and DeBardeleben, however, question whether civil society participation can ultimately secure an unbiased connection between the preferences of citizens and the outcome of EU decision-making. They identify that

> [f]irst, the stakeholder representatives consulted by the Commission are usually professional lobbyists, whose positions need not reflect the preferences that exist in society. Second, it is ultimately up to the Commission how it reacts to the positions voiced in the consultative process, and there is little the consulted groups can do if the Commission fails to listen to them. (Hurrelmann and DeBardeleben, 2009, p. 233)

These are elitist contingencies that impinge on the effectiveness of the developing participatory dimension of the consumer citizenship practice that this book seeks to define, and through which diffuse interests present a barrier that, in Olson's utilitarian analysis, preclude the incentives necessary for individuals to organise and engage in the sort of collective consumer action discussed by Redfern (see Finke, 2007, citing Olson, 1965). They are contingencies that may be challenged by new paradigms in which the EU's concern for the participation of *individuals* and civil society in the consumer arena is identified through the input-oriented legitimacy created by the Commission's long-standing consumer education and information programmes.

The European consumer citizen

Development of the consumer concept

Chapter 2 provides a critical review of the range of descriptions that have been applied to the word 'consumer' in European Union law and policy and analyses the 'consumer' taxonomy used by both the Court and the European legislature. It also acknowledges the academic legal discussion that has identified, within these various definitions, a basic common core that identifies the 'consumer' as the final, individual, purchaser, of goods and services. Whilst, for the purposes of this book, such legal clarification helps to bring a focus to the defining characteristics of the consumer as an individual, natural person, acting as the final purchaser of goods and services in the internal market Chapter 2 also introduces a range of sub-categories of 'the consumer' that, to a large degree, have appeared in the political and economic analysis of neo-liberal economic theory over the last quarter of the twentieth century associated with the consumer.

The development of these sub-categories in the consumer lexicon reflects the changing status of the individual market citizen who has come from obscurity to gain recognition, and some legal re-definition as a market agent. The chapter discusses the importance of this agency role to the economic performance of the internal market and argues that with the identification of both capable and vulnerable sub-categories of the consumer there emerge behaviours that can equally be associated with concepts of citizenship.

The notional 'consumer citizen' is not an exclusive class of individual to which a particular section of the population belongs. It is a term that better reflects the individual exercise of civic duty, public-spiritedness and self-education within a politicised consumer society: an aspirational and behavioural concept to which *all* can belong. The reasons that we do not all belong, or that we should not expect any of us to belong in *all* of our consumer activities are introduced in Chapter 2 through a discussion of the barriers that bring about consumer detriment. It is a discussion of those characteristics of both the market and of individual consumers that are likely to militate against consumer empowerment or consumer activism such that '*any* consumer can be vulnerable in certain circumstances' (Europe Economics, 2007, p. 4, emphasis in the original). This is an incursion into the realm of behavioural economics that identifies both cognitive and structural barriers to the exercise of choice, and that harks back to the issues raised by Redfern. These are barriers that the Community institutions have sought to reduce through the adoption of policies founded on the model of the 'rational consumer' who could benefit from education and information. What emerges is the concept of a consumer citizenship practice in which all individuals *can* engage when acting as consumers, but a practice that is limited by the level of consumer detriment present.

The discussion on consumer detriment makes it clear that such categories as 'vulnerable', or 'capable', consumers apply not to the consumer as an individual *per se* but rather to the nature of the role adopted by an individual in a given consumer transaction. These are archetypal categories associated with the emergence of consumer protection as a policy focus built on a set of rights aimed at restoring or maintaining market efficiency. The chapter follows the policy developments that have encouraged consumer empowerment and activism, and touches on the consequential doctrinal overlap between, on the one hand, the traditional private law aspects of the consumer transaction and contract privity and, on the other hand, the more public law areas, broadly construed, of consumer protection and the responsibilities of citizenship linked to economic agency.

Theory and coherency: modelling consumer citizenship practice

The coherency of a theoretical model for consumer citizenship is introduced in Chapter 3. It builds on the behavioural model for a consumer citizenship practice established in Chapter 2 through a discussion of the difficulties in defining the concept of the consumer in European law and the consequential fragmentation of the consumer protection rules. The chapter explores the thematic notion of the consumer in its private law setting and the rationales behind the range of characterisations it attracts; it identifies, surprisingly positively, a construction of the consumer as both a chooser *and* a citizen, capable of individual and collective political and economic action.

The first part of the chapter briefly examines the traditions of the consumer and the citizen before concluding that it is not unreasonable to conflate aspects of the two theoretically distinct traditions to provide a framework for accommodating the notion of a consumer citizenship practice. The remainder of the chapter takes this developed model and considers it in a constitutional setting before discussing the organisational structures and networks that provide the practical platform for an effective consumer citizenship practice.[4]

The conceptual tradition of the 'consumer' identifies that it is something that the law has a limited capacity to define in anything other than the stereotype of the *average consumer* – a conclusion drawn from analysis of the case law of the Court and from statutory, procedural and regulatory law. If a broader perspective is pursued, the political and social science literature provides legitimacy for the individual and collective conceptions of the consumer and identifies that a comparison between the consumer and the citizen shows them as contingent universal concepts, sharing both similar boundaries and conceptual constraints.

When the focus switches to citizenship in Chapter 3 it is clear that, even at a basic level, the concept of citizenship remains contested: it means different things in different contexts, although Wiener does suggest that even within these contextual tensions 'it is possible to state that citizenship is about rights, access and belonging' (Wiener, 1998, pp. 3–4). Despite the difficulties in locating a consensus on the meaning of citizenship, the rise of neo-liberal economic thinking saw ideas of individualism reflected in a growing importance for the citizen's role in the market: a development that was matched by the introduction of the combined notion of the consumer citizen into the literature since the 1990s: although overtones of such a conception are clearly evident in the duty aspect of Barrington's rhyme from the 1930s and Redfern's lament from the 1920s.

Bringing together the contentious nature of conceptions of both the consumer and the citizen may be seen as factoring in a multiplication of the controversies: Chapter 3 argues that need not be the case. Rather, that this synthesis can be seen to facilitate a coherent theoretical definition for the consumer citizen that complements and extends the practical model considered in Chapter 2. The final sections of the chapter take the definitional model of consumer citizenship and consider its constitutional standing. Beginning with a discussion of whether consumers can constitute a Demos and hold constituent power, these issues are considered in the context of a developing network of new governance structures and organisations that appear to be increasingly entrenched in the process of consumer policy formulation. Structures and organisations that, together with consumer rights, provide a platform for voice and influence in consumer citizenship practice: a consumer citizenship practice that is being reinforced through EU-wide consumer citizenship education in schools and monitored through the Commission's, metrics-based, Consumer Markets Scoreboard initiative.

The chapter concludes that although the consumer collective may not constitute the conventional notion of a Demos, the consumer citizen, both individually and collectively, has voice, rights and expertise that have the potential to be exercised through a developing national and EU-level network in a modern form of constituent power.

Spatial boundaries of European consumer citizenship practice

Starting from the position that the concept of consumer citizenship, or at least the exercise of a consumer citizenship practice, has both validity and coherence Chapter 4 explores the spatial and membership dimensions that can be associated with such a European consumer citizenship. It considers a segmented model of the internal market and identifies the boundaries in which consumer citizenship practice has a tangible presence within four distinct market sectors. These are market sectors that have seen the individual benefit from the evolution of access rights across broad aspects of common daily activity: in work and the consumption of associated welfare benefits; in the modernisation of public sector services; in the liberalisation of services of general interest and, lastly, in the general retail market for commodified goods and services.

The chapter then discusses aspects of modernisation across each of these four broad market sectors. It identifies the development of entitlement rights to social welfare in a hitherto public sector that has seen the changes of privatisation, marketisation, competition and de-centralisation identified with new governance and the operation of social policy. These are terms that describe aspects of change which have introduced new issues of choice, quality and consumerisation into a modernised public sector, and a social dimension into the internal market: changes that have generated questions of citizenship associated with process and access. The effects of privatisation, together with those of liberalisation, are then discussed in the context of Services of General Interest. This chapter identifies the changing approach of the Community institutions towards the liberalised Services of General Interest in consequence of an increasingly assertive consumer approach in the exercise of rights and in demands for more in terms of choice, quality and price. The key issue highlighted by this change of attitude to services of general interest is that the *value of citizenship* has a growing legitimacy in this sector of the market where services are themselves developing as essential expressions of European citizenship rights, specifically through the introduction of public and universal service obligations.

Chapter 4 concludes its analysis of the spatial boundaries of European consumer citizenship practice with a study of the relevance to consumer citizenship practice of the increased consumer *choice* that has accompanied market modernisation. It deals with issues of both individualistic and more communitarian aspects of consumer choice that identify a spectrum of participatory behaviours and help provide a definition for consumer citizenship practice. It also considers the market-based origins of the consumer citizen concept from two perspectives rooted in individual choice. Firstly, the transformation of the *citizen* into the consumer citizen, made possible through the choice exercise of political consumption; through ethical and ecological buying and a vision of the market politic assisted by product labelling. Secondly, the transformation of the *consumer* into the consumer citizen as a consequence of the hybridisation of public and private law and the introduction of regulatory agencies into the contractual arrangements associated with services of general interest. This is an area of the market where public service obligations limit the contractual freedom of some service providers, but not all, and where liberalised markets introduce competition and *choice* of service provider as an element of consumer citizenship practice. The final section of the chapter identifies that the essential nature of the marketisation of services of general interest has attracted an amalgam of developing normative processes through sector-specific regulation, and in which there appears to be an ambition by the Commission for an active and participatory consumer citizenship practice.

The relevance of European consumer citizenship practice: applying the model

In its final substantive chapter, this book builds on the discussions of the origins of the consumer citizenship concept and the model of consumer citizenship practice that will emerge. It draws together the normative components that provide a justification for this model of consumer citizenship practice and assembles them into a hierarchical framework. It is a framework that strengthens the *theoretical relevance* of the consumer citizenship concept as a tool for assessing the functioning of any particular market sector, but it is also a framework in which the inherent barriers of the model highlight its practical limitations and give context to the idea of consumer citizenship practice.

This hierarchical framework of normative components is then applied to a short case study of the European energy sector. The energy sector is chosen as a focus for a case study because of its particular relevance to many of the issues that are raised in this book. It is a network industry that falls within the ambit of a service of general economic interest and attracts universal service obligations. As such, it belongs to that sector of the market that has been identified with the origins of the consumer citizen concept and in which consumer agency is encouraged. It is also a key sector in the ongoing modernisation of network service provision that will see a rapid expansion of consumer involvement through technological innovation and the imminent introduction of smart metering in its distribution network. These are technological developments that are recognised in the EU's third energy package[5] and that require Member States to ensure the implementation of intelligent metering systems[6] with the objective of increasing the consumer's role in the reduction of energy consumption, linked to global concerns over climate change and 'green' energy production.

In its concluding chapter this book draws together the major concepts it has sought to develop. It reflects on the multiple identities of the consumer that have developed in law and policy since 1975: identities that extend beyond the mere transactional aspects of consumerism and that embrace attributes associated with somewhat similarly contentious notions of citizenship. It also revisits the arguments for conflating conceptual aspects of the consumer and citizen before concluding that the theoretical model of consumer citizenship practice developed in this book helps to provide an understanding of the relationships and limitations of the normative processes it outlines. What emerges is the new paradigm of a consumer citizenship practice that has the potential to be used in assessing the functioning of the internal market: a potential that may prove useful to policy-and law-makers as well as making a contribution to the scholarly literature. This notion of a consumer citizenship practice provides the central theme of the book although it is addressed from various perspectives in the following chapters. At this stage, however, rather than in the concluding chapter, it is appropriate to introduce a definition of consumer citizenship practice to better set the detailed discussion into an appropriate context for the reader.

A definition for consumer citizenship practice

Participation and influence: processes of input

Firstly I should make clear that there is no explicit use of the term 'consumer citizen' in the legislation or case law of the EU, or of its alternative configurations, but there is explicit recognition of the essential nature of the *attributes* of the consumer citizen that are to be found when the individual, acting in the role of the consumer, actively participates in developing and improving society by considering ethical issues, diversity of perspectives, global processes and future conditions (see Thoresen, 2003, p. 12). Reflections on the traditions of the consumer and the citizen in the academic literature have also identified a social dimension to the consumer that has the consumer and citizen as contingent figures (Trentmann, 2001, p. 6) with a political constituency that belongs to everyone, but begins with the individual (Fine, 2006, pp. 304–305). Recognition of the significant parallels between the two distinct traditions of the consumer and the citizen have been argued to give a legitimacy to the concept of a consumer citizenship rooted in the convergence of political ideology from both the left and the right: a convergence in which the motivated and capable consumer becomes a politicised citizen with the potential to engage in influential transactional, post-transactional and extra-transactional dimensions of consumer citizenship practice. That is in the choices we exercise when buying goods and services, or in choosing not to buy; in the demands and complaints we make for faulty or wrong goods and services, when exercising our consumer rights; and in the ethical standpoints we may adopt and/or may campaign for, or against, in respect of specific goods or services.

This definition of a developing consumer citizenship practice, based on the idea of individuals acting, alone or collectively, places politicised consumers within a market characterised within four broad sectors: a market that provides for a post-national boundary dimension in which the consumer enjoys access and choice rights infused with a duty requirement that embraces notions of solidarity and sustainability, of ethical decision-making and of participating in market shaping activities. These aspects of belonging, rights and duty are more readily associated with citizenship.

The blurred boundary between citizenship and consumerism has been brought together by EU consumer policy in a way that embraces the essential nature of the economic and social aspects of a consumer citizenship practice that is reflected in the importance attached to the monitoring of consumer outcomes. Consumer policy is now influenced by data that measures the degree to which individuals exercise their consumer rights, complain and switch, and pursue enforcement actions (Decision (EC) 2006/1926, and specifically Recital 5). Such scoreboard data acts passively as a tool of soft governance, it carries a normative influence in which consumer behaviour highlights market malfunctioning and failure of economic efficiency. As a tool of soft governance, market monitoring and analyses is complemented by the Commission's encouragement of policy-shaping networks and structures of new governance that provide a platform for the consumer to exercise his/her voice and expertise in a form of constituent power.

The emphasis in such ideas of governance is concerned with relationships, processes networks and organisation of collective action: it is about multi-level regimes with many centres of competing authority that have emerged, or are emerging, as a consequence of ending the monopoly of traditional power mechanisms. These new ways of organisation are founded on a pluralism of forces of new associations in civil society (Hirst, 1997, from Della Sala, 2001, p. 6) and through which legislation, for example the Ecodesign Directive (Directive (EC) 2009/125, Article 18), is now beginning to provide for consumer input into the policy process. Where networks and structures of EU consumer policy governance have been shown to provide channels for consumer input into policy decisions, more direct, sector-specific, market shaping through consumer organisations has been extended to include the definition and review of implementing measures, the examination of the effectiveness of market surveillance mechanisms and the assessment of voluntary agreements and other self-regulation measures.

Market spaces and consumer relevance

The focus on four broad and overlapping sectors that define the internal market will be argued to lend some legitimacy to the notion of the consumer citizen. It has provided a new rudimentary model of the boundaries and spaces of EU consumer citizenship with membership boundaries defined by market sectors and an EU post-national territorial dimension. The model reflects the transformation in the market that has seen some commodification, and private sector delivery, of public services; public and private investment in the public sector; and social rights de-coupled from national citizenship. It is a transformation in which the Court's development of EU citizenship in the social welfare sector has been engaged with the tension that exists between aspects of social solidarity and the individualism associated with the internal market and freedom of movement. A tension highlighted in the context of consumer access to public sector services by *Lawrie-Blum* (Case 66/85) and the development of individual rights through the involvement of individuals in the social dimensions of the internal market.

Privatisation and liberalisation, associated with services and networks of general interest, have been identified by Micklitz as the source of a new area of hybridised public and private law that provides a legal basis for the consumer citizen concept (2009, p. 9) although it is acknowledged that he uses the reversed and hyphenated term citizen-consumer. The broader concept of the consumer citizen, derived from the political sciences, will also be featured in a discussion on political consumerism where choice across all sectors of the market becomes a channel for the exercise of responsibility based on political and/or ethical considerations in consumer citizenship practice. This agency potential in consumer citizenship practice will also be shown to extend beyond such political and ethical responsibilities to include an economic responsibility that features in the Commissions' 2007 consumer policy strategy (Commission, 2007d), a strategy that recognises the relevance of empowered consumers as the 'motor of economic change'.

Normative influences and the measuring of market functioning

The figure of the consumer citizen, as the empowered agent of political, ethical and economic change, will be argued in Chapter 3 to have theoretical validity through a legitimate conflation of the conceptually distinct notions of the consumer and the citizen. Yet many individual and structural barriers have been shown to limit the influence of this notional market actor. The aspirational focus of consumer policy will be shown to be better rewarded with the concept of a consumer citizenship practice in which individuals' behavioural changes are 'motivated by the internalisation of particular normative orientations' (Barry, 1996, p. 122).

This book draws together a four-level hierarchical model that helps to explain the relationships between the different normative orientations in consumer citizenship practice. It is a model that identifies the primary drivers for effective consumer empowerment that is central to the Commission's consumer policy strategy. It is a model that highlights the features and enablers for consumer citizenship practice; it also highlights the individual and structural barriers that limit the degree to which practical consumer agency can influence market shaping. The application of this normative hierarchy of consumer citizenship practice provides a functional framework for formulating policy or for evaluating market functioning and consumer agency. As a case in point, the case study of the energy sector illustrates the challenges facing policy- and law-makers who seek to promote consumer empowerment. The complex relationships between the four generic normative orientations of the model – consumer protection, consumer information, consumer capability and consumer motivation – are shown to be further influenced by the consumer segmentation utilised in marketing models that, in particular, emphasise sector-specific issues of consumer capability and motivation. My arguments suggest that effective consumer empowerment, and an increased application of consumer citizenship practice, requires policy initiatives that provide a balance of normative orientations in which the relational consequences of initiatives provided for at any particular level of the hierarchy are understood in the context of the other levels.

2

From Cog to Cognisance: Evolution of the Consumer Citizen

Introduction

This chapter provides a critical review of the conceptual development of the consumer in EU law and policy. It analyses the taxonomy used by both the Court and the legislature where the term consumer describes the final, individual, purchaser of goods and services. Sometimes, as will be shown, the various descriptions applied to the final purchaser appear interchangeable, with no specific legal meaning attached to the word used; at other times, it is clear that a much tighter legal meaning is intended. Such descriptions as 'consumer', 'customer', 'citizen' and 'individual' appear throughout the broader consumer law *acquis* and, even in those instances where an attempt at a tighter legal definition is applied to any particular description, such definition may vary between different legislative instruments or judgments of the Court (Ebers, 2008).

The development of neo-liberal economic theory over the final quarter of the twentieth century brought with it the term *consumer citizen*, or its reversed or hyphenated forms, as yet another description of consumer behaviour: a term that has most frequently appeared in, or has even been the focus of, academic political science literature (for example, Trentmann, 2006a; Clarke and others, 2007). In reviewing this and other descriptions applied to the final purchaser in EU law it becomes clear that, over time, there has been, on the one hand a growing certainty over the meanings attached to the basic descriptions, or at least a transparent debate over the differences, and on the other hand an expansion of sub-categories that qualify the description of the consumer and, in the context of *rights and duties*, highlights a harmony between notions of citizenship and the citizen.

This chapter follows the development of these sub-categories and will show the origin and progress of a practical connotation of the consumer citizen: its purpose, to demonstrate that the consumer in EU law has come from obscurity to gain recognition, and some legal definition, as a market agent. A role that has become essential to the economic performance of the internal market and deserving of protection as a key player in the Community's policy objectives of open borders and regulated competition. The *consumer* is seen to develop from a position as a mere cog in the economic machinery of the internal market into an influential market actor, cognisant of a role that demands a broader contribution to European society than the mere final purchase of a good or service. This chapter will argue, in support of this assertion, that the development of both capable and vulnerable sub-categories of the consumer help to define generic descriptions for the capabilities and behaviours of the consumer, individually or collectively, when acting within a particular commercial transaction. The conclusion is that amongst the capable consumer behaviours there are traits more normally associated with those of the citizen: that at a practical level there is evidence to support the notion of the *consumer citizen*, politically, economically, legally, socially, civically and constitutionally active in the European Union. The citizen, in this context, is that individual capable of performative 'definition' in the rights afforded to him or her through the Court and the legislature: a notion of the citizen that exists, in a sense, in 'as many kinds as there are roles in the complex [of modern] civil societies' (Balibar, 2004, p, 195).

As these descriptions and categories are exposed, so also are the significant barriers that limit the exercise of consumer citizenship practice. Whilst the consumer citizen can readily be identified by social scientists and can find a theoretical role in neo-classical and neo-liberal economic models, reference to behavioural economics suggests that normative fallacies of consumer behaviour, together with structural flaws in the market, *limit the exercise of consumer choice*. The institutions of the EU have nevertheless encouraged the development of consumer citizenship practice through an evolutionary policy approach and consequential legislation. They have sought to counter the asymmetrical power differential in the market between producers or providers on the one hand and the consumer on the other, but this encouragement is founded on the narrow definition of the *rational consumer* who

always reaches the decision that is objectively, or substantively, best in terms of the utility function [not the] rational person of cognitive

psychology [who] goes about making his or her decisions in a way
that is procedurally reasonable in the light of the available knowledge and means of computation. (Simon, 1986, p. S211)

This chapter concludes that it is a combination of the consumer's behaviour, *and* his or her motives that identifies a *consumer citizenship* event
within the context of the consumer transaction and that the relevance
of the consumer citizen, as a category, has come about by the evolutionary development in law and policy of the role of the consumer in the
internal market (Figure 2.1). In Chapter 3 the idea of consumer citizenship practice is considered in terms of post-transactional and extra-
transactional events but here the focus is on the evolution of consumer
descriptions at the transactional level. It is an evolution of consumer
descriptions that, in the internal market, has seen a benchmarked
average consumer complemented by various characterisations of both
vulnerable and capable consumers.

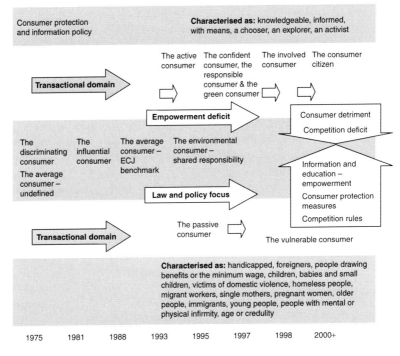

Figure 2.1   Evolution of the European consumer citizen in law and policy

Through an introduction to the notion of consumer detriment it becomes clear that such categories apply not to the consumer as an individual *per se* but rather to the role adopted by an individual in a given consumer transaction. This chapter explores the development and encouragement of consumer empowerment (through information and education) and of consumer activism (through competition and environmental policy) in EU policy and law. When this analysis is balanced alongside recent research concerning *consumer detriment* (Harker and others, 2008) – that is those characteristics of both the market and of individual consumers that are likely to militate against consumer empowerment or consumer activism such that '*any* consumer can be vulnerable in certain circumstances' (Europe Economics, 2007) – a question is raised over the need for a new, additional, focus in market policy. The categories are seen to define the nature of a transactional domain, one that the consumer will shape, dependant on their personal capacity, and/or inclination, and that may be influenced by market barriers or policy deficit.

Foundations of consumer policy: the birth of the average consumer

Prior to the 1970s there was little recognition of the consumer at the EU level and consumer protection measures were left to develop separately within the Member States. This began to change following the Paris Summit in 1972 where the Heads of State and Government emphasised, under the development of the social policy, that they attached much importance to strengthening and co-ordinating measures of consumer protection (EC Bulletin, 1972). In 1975, the Commission introduced the preliminary programme for a consumer protection and information policy.[1] Commentary following this initiative warned that in taking the 'two paths', one of consumer protection and the other of open borders with competition rules, Europe had failed to create the institutions necessary for achieving these objectives harmoniously (Bourgoignie and Trubek, 1987, pp. 4 and 25).

Conflicts emanating from this approach were highlighted by the case law associated with the consumer protection Directives. In seeking to meet the twin aims of consumer protection and effective competition these Directives challenged the traditions of the Member States in contract,[2] tort[3] and administrative law,[4] and began a development away from unitary national measures, first to quasi-federalist measures of minimum harmonisation and subsequently to debates associated with maximum harmonisation (see, for example, the judgment and opinion in *Antropos and Others,* Case C-84/06).

Running parallel with the development of a consumer protection *acquis,* welfare economics underpinned the Community's development of competition law. The economic goal of competition law was the protection and promotion of effective competition, not 'only because of the benefits that it delivers to European consumers' (Bishop and Walker, 2002, p. 16) but because the traditional competition policy approach focussed more on the outcomes produced by effective regulation rather than the process of competition management itself. As a consequence, the European consumer of the early 1970s held little formal status as an economic agent.

Economic cogs and transposable definitions: early policy development

Explicit recognition that the status of the consumer was about to change came in the 1975 preliminary programme for a consumer protection and information policy. This marked a modest but significant start. The consumer was no longer to be the stereotypical utility maximising model of microeconomic theory (see Drakopoulos, 1992, p. 318). No longer to be seen merely as a purchaser and user of goods and services for personal, family or group purposes, the consumer was, according to the text of the preliminary programme, to be recognised 'as a person concerned with the various facets of society which may affect him either directly or indirectly as a consumer' who, as a consequence of the globalisation of markets had now become 'merely a unit in a mass market, the target of advertising campaigns and of pressure by strongly organized production and distribution groups'. The consumer had lost power in a changing market environment and was to be protected at the Community level by positive harmonisation and the introduction of five basic rights:

1. the right to protection of health and safety,
2. the right to protection of economic interests,
3. the right of redress,
4. the right to information and education, and
5. the right of representation (the right to be heard).

This marked a recognition that consumer protection should become a policy focus in the Community built on a set of rights with the potential to check the power of capital and restore market efficiency. It was, however, made clear that these rights were to be addressed through 'action under specific Community policies such as the economic, common agricultural, social, environment, transport and energy policies as well as by the approximation of laws' (Weatherill, 1999). Progress was slow with positive harmonising measures restricted by the necessity for Council unanimity[5] and a resulting legislative hiatus that was to last through to 1986.[6]

The Court suffered no such restriction and significantly influenced the development of consumer policy during this period, particularly following its seminal judgment in *Cassis de Dijon* (Case 120/78). The case concerned the regulation of alcoholic beverages and introduced the principle of *mutual recognition*, whereby, effect is granted 'to foreign legal rules or acts occurring in the territory of another State' (Ortino, 2007): a development described as 'a move away from highly technical, complex and maximum standard sectoral legislation' (Szyszczak and Cygan, 2008, p. 9).

This period, between the late 1970s and mid-1980s, saw the Court active in a number of other cases involving alcohol that serve to illustrate the development of the internal market and the expansion of consumer choice. Excise taxation imposed on alcoholic beverages by national governments had led to market distortion with national governments providing preferential treatment for domestic products. With complex motives driving selective and protectionist national policy, at a time when European economic integration was deepening and broadening (Lubkin, 1996, para. 7.2), the Commission brought actions against Denmark, France, Italy and the United Kingdom (Cases 171/78, 168/78, 169/78, and 170/78). These were cases that concerned a consequential limitation in consumer choice that the Court was not prepared to tolerate. The response was to develop principles of non-discriminatory taxation treatment, relevant to individual instances: principles that were then to be extended by the Court in another series of cases concerning VAT (Cases 319/81, 278/83, and 230/89).

The Economic and Social Committee and the development of consumer descriptions

In 1985 legislative proposals for the harmonisation of excise tax appeared in the Commission's White Paper on Completing the Internal Market (Commission, 1985). This White Paper was criticised for its rigid approach by the European Economic and Social Committee (EESC) and subsequently revised with an acknowledgement, from the Commission, 'that complete rate harmonisation was not necessary for the completion of the Internal Market' (Lubkin, 1996, section 8.2.1). This time, in response to the Commission's amended proposals (Commission, 1989), the EESC criticised the proposals for the excessive flexibility 'that ... could defeat the purpose of the whole exercise, which is to standardize excise duties so as to ensure that they have a neutral effect on the movement of goods' (EESC, 1990, p. 2).

In its capacity to influence legislative proposals the EESC, as a constituency of the Union, included consumers who, together with the other members representing economic and social activity, enjoyed a legal relationship with the Union on the basis of Article 257 EC (repealed by the Treaty of Lisbon 2009 but replaced, in substance, by Article 300 TFEU) and whose Opinions are forwarded to both the Council and the Commission. Although now diminished in status *vis à vis* the European Parliament, its recommendations at the time of the alcohol taxation cases, carried more weight with the Union's executive bodies than those of the European Parliament and it constituted a

> forum of debate and a sounding-board for the sections of the community most directly affected by the decisions of the executives, and contributes to the formation of a European consciousness among the leaders of the most influential interest groups. (Zellentin, 1962, p. 27)

Even the structure of the EESC, from as early as the beginning of the 1960s, was likened by Zellentin 'to a parliament in its division into "parties"' with interest 'parties' representing employers, the employed and a third group that included the consumer representatives. This structure continues to exist in the present EESC and is replicated in the Treaty of Lisbon 2009 under Article 300(2) TFEU. Article 300(2) TFEU provides for the EESC to consist of 'representatives of organisations of employers, of the employed, and of other parties representative of civil society, notably in socioeconomic, civic, professional and cultural areas'. Whilst the individual consumer may have lost power in a market that was changing from local to global, there was, and continues to be, at least some representative consumer influence on the regional stage that is capable of influencing policy and legislation.

In the year following the Commission's White Paper on Completing the Internal Market, the Single European Act 1986 significantly altered the relationship between consumer policy and the process of approximation of laws as it affected the functioning of the internal market. In particular, the addition of Article 114 TFEU (Article 95 EC) required the institutions to 'take as a base a high level of protection' in proposals concerning 'health, safety...and consumer protection' and procedurally introduced qualified majority voting for adoption in Council. Legislative development of the consumer *acquis* was soon to follow, and with it the evolution of consumer descriptions.

From an existing policy perspective, the consumer protection *acquis* is marked by an inconsistent and complex approach to informational obligations with only the package travel, and timeshare Directives offering any targeted, sector-specific, consumer protection (Bradgate, Twigg-Flesner and Nordhausen, 2005). Policy direction in consumer protection is under pressure to develop a more horizontal approach with vertical sector-specific action limited to that 'where necessary' (Commission, 2006e, p. 8): a policy approach that is unlikely to address the issues of informational needs in complex transactions, nor one that could provide a response to the irrationality of consumer behaviour. As noted in the Department for Business, Enterprise and Regulatory Reform (BERR) consumer empowerment report,

> [t]o the extent that consumer empowerment is outcome driven, the regime ought to be capable of identifying features of the market which impede the realisation of consumer benefits or cause consumer detriment, and have the necessary tools to deal with such problems. (Harker and others, 2008, p. 1)

In 1989 the Council, composed of Ministers for Health, adopted its first Directive on the labelling of tobacco products, on the legal base of the then new Article 95 EC (now Article 114 TFEU) (Directive (EEC) 89/622). A Directive that marked the beginning of a sequence of legislation and litigation that highlighted the interchangeable nature of the descriptions applied to the final purchaser, the individual whom the health and safety measures were intended to protect. This first Directive required tobacco products to carry specific warnings yet it carried no mention of the consumer, but identified in its preamble 'the objective of contributing to an improvement of the health and quality of life of citizens within the Community'. In contrast, the second 'tobacco' Directive that followed in 1998 and sought to ban all forms of advertising and sponsorship of tobacco products emphasised the health protection of individuals, without mention of citizens or consumers (Directive (EC) 98/43). This second Directive, however, sparked litigation in two cases that challenged its legal basis and subsequently led to its annulment (Cases C-376/98 and C-74/99). During this litigation, the Court made reference to the consumer, but merely as the recipient or target of promotional advertising, whilst highlighting the use of the term individual in the Directive, as the recipient of the guarantee of health protection.

The Community institutions responded to the annulment within months, adopting a new Directive on the manufacture, presentation and sale of tobacco products (Directive (EC) 2001/37). This time the rhetoric in the Directive was couched in terms of the consumer, both in terms of the protection and information offered to the final purchaser, and in terms of consumer acceptance of a safer product. Whilst the term citizen gets no mention in this Directive concern is expressed over the level of protection given to the 'health of individuals' (Recital 3) and the 'health of the consumer' (Recital 23).

Although challenged in *British American Tobacco* (Case C-491/01) the Court held this Directive valid. The language of the Court is, however, interesting in the context in which it places the terms consumer, citizen and individual. In both the judgment, and the Opinion of Advocate General Geelhoed, the term consumer is repeatedly used in a product-specific sense. It is used either in the context of the need to provide the final purchaser with objective product-related information:

> Article 7 of the Directive has the purpose therefore of ensuring that *consumers* are given objective information concerning the toxicity of tobacco products. (Case C-491/01 para. 135, emphasis added)

Or, in the context of behavioural changes that may be effected in the final purchaser by the efficacy of such information:

> saying on the tobacco products' packaging...that the amounts of noxious substances inhaled depend also on the user's smoking behaviour would have ensured that *consumers* received objective information. (Case C-491/01 para. 140, emphasis added)

The action of the consumer is, in this context, the agency role played by the final purchaser at the end of a supply chain, influenced perhaps in the pursuit of self-interest by the provision of objective information, but merely located in a private law economic relationship (see Clarke and others, 2007, p. 2–4). The use of the terms citizen and individual appear essentially interchangeable. The objective of the protection of health and of quality of life, attributed as the first of the rights attaching to consumers in the preliminary programme for a consumer protection and information policy, is addressed towards Community citizens in both the judgment

> the prohibition of exports is intended only to prevent illegal re-imports of cigarettes into the Community in order to protect the health of Community *citizens*. (Case C-491/01 para. 51, emphasis added)

and, in the Opinion:

> The programme of action came into being...with the objective of contributing to an improvement of the health and quality of life of Community *citizens*...(Case C-491/01, AG Opinion, para. 71, emphasis added)

but also towards the individual later in the Opinion:

> In the absence of exhaustive harmonisation, it is for the Member States to decide on the extent to which they wish to safeguard the protection of the health and life of *individuals*. (Case C-491/01, AG Opinion, para. 226, emphasis added)

The last of the rights attributed to the consumer in the preliminary programme for a consumer protection and information policy, the public law right of representation (the right to be heard), is addressed solely in the context of the individual in both the judgment and in the Opinion. In response to arguments presented by both the French government and the Commission over the timing of the creation of rights 'for individuals which the national courts must protect' the Court held:

> [t]he opportunity open to individuals to plead the invalidity of a Community act of general application before national courts is not conditional upon that act's actually having been the subject of implementing measures. (Case C-491/01, para. 40)

Whilst this sequence of litigation marked a lack of certainty, and inter-changeability, of the description applied to the individual final purchaser, consumer policy was continuing to develop its scope. In its second programme for a consumer protection and information policy the Council proposed a series of directives for the protection of the economic interests of consumers that would lead to the introduction of new *categories* of consumer (Council, 1981).

Protection of the economic interests of consumers and consumer categorisation

The principles that had been identified in the preliminary programme for a consumer protection and information policy identified six priority areas in which the Council sought proposals from the Commission for harmonisation of consumer protection measures. These included research to identify improvements that could be made to the range and quality of services provided for consumers and the promotion of the more general economic interests of consumers. The objective of this research was predicated on better satisfying the individual and collective needs of consumers through, it suggested, obtaining better value for money and waste prevention. The remaining priority areas in the preliminary programme focussed on the private law areas of product liability, consumer credit and hire purchase, unfair commercial practices and false or misleading advertising.

Confirmation to pursue these priorities came with the second programme for a consumer protection and information policy and marked the beginning of an expansion in consumer protection measures of minimum harmonisation.[7] It was a period marked by an inevitable process of change in the Communities legal order in which 'the European Court ... played a major role in moving the Community along a continuum from Market towards State' on the basis that the 'executive force of Community law cannot vary from one State to another in deference to subsequent domestic laws, without jeopardising the attainment of the objectives of the Treaty ...' and explained by the Court as early as 1964 in *Costa* (Case 6/64) (Micklitz, Roethe and Weatherill, 1994, pp. 14 and 12). The Court recognised in this second programme the assumption that improved consumer choice would be delivered as an element of the policy and, as a consequence, in a succession of cases from 1978, promoted market integration through the elimination of barriers to trade (negative harmonisation).[8]

In 1985 the Council adopted the Directive on contracts negotiated away from business premises (Directive (EEC) 85/577). This required Member States to ensure that consumers had the right to cancel a contract of sale concluded at home such that they would have protection from unfair commercial doorstep selling practices. Article 8, however, allowed the State to 'adopt or maintain more favourable provisions to protect consumers' and the final recital, expressly recognised that 'Member States might introduce or maintain a total or partial prohibition on the conclusion of contracts away from business premises'. This flexibility in the legislation became the focus of litigation in *R Buet and*

EBS SARL v Ministère public (Case 382/87) where the Court found the French prohibition on doorstep canvassing in relation to the sale of educational material compatible with Article 34 TFEU (Article 28 EC). Whilst the notion of an *influential consumer* had been suggested in a written question to the Commission in 1985 (Pitt, 1985), this was the first case to raise the issue of *different categories of consumer*. It recognised that where persons are 'behind with their education... [it] makes them particularly *vulnerable* when faced with salesmen of educational material' (Case 382/87, ground 16).

Advertising had also presented a number of problems and, as a consequence, administrative controls to protect the consumer from unscrupulous marketing devices first appeared in the form of the 1984 Directive on *misleading advertising* (Directive (EEC) 84/450). The minimalist nature of this harmonising Directive provided a general notion of misleading advertising, leaving Member States to 'ensure that adequate and effective means exist for the control of misleading advertising'.[9] The case law that followed was initially concerned with preliminary rulings on cross-border issues but was to lead to the Court's benchmarking of the *average consumer*. In *GB-INNO-BM* (Case C-362/88, para. 8) the Court established that consumers, particularly in frontier areas, who were 'resident in one Member State may travel freely to the territory of another Member State to shop under the same conditions as the local population' and that such a freedom would be compromised if such consumers were to be deprived of advertising available in the country where the purchases were to be made. In *GB-INNO-BM*, as well as in *Pall*, and *Clinique* (Cases C-238/89 and C-315/92), the Court determined that such trade restrictive rules could not be justified and that the provision of information to a consumer was considered one of the principle requirements, necessary to enable him, the notional average consumer, to make his choice in full knowledge of the facts (for example, *GB-INNO-BM*, Case C-362/88, paras 17 and 18).

The notion of the average consumer, but without any definition of the category, had appeared as early as 1976 in a Commission Decision relating to competition and trademarks (Decision (EEC) 77/129). It also marks the starting point for the chart of the evolution of the consumer citizen given in Figure 2.1. It was January 1988 when the average consumer first appeared in the Court's jurisprudence, given explicit recognition by Advocate General Mancini in the video cassette copyright se *Warner Brothers* (Case 158/86, AG Opinion, para. 2). The development of the definitional test for this notional average consumer was later catalogued by the Court in *Gut Springenheide*. *Gut Springenheide* concerned a printed statement that was provided inside pre-packed egg cartons and stated the beneficial effects on the quality of the eggs from the particular cereal grain mix the hens had been fed on. According to the German authorities responsible for the supervision of foodstuffs in the Rural District of Steinfurt this misled the consumers and, in the subsequent reference for a preliminary ruling, the Court, in a review of the test it had applied in its earlier case law to purchasers who may have been misled, held:

> [i]n those cases, in order to determine whether the description, trade mark or promotional description or statement in question was liable to mislead the purchaser, the Court took into account the presumed expectations of an *average consumer who is reasonably well-informed and reasonably observant and circumspec.* (Case C-210/96, para. 31, emphasis added)[10]

This notion of the average consumer who is reasonably well-informed and reasonably observant and circumspect has now become established in the Court's jurisprudence. It appears, as a complete phrase, in some 57 separate judgments of the Court or the General Court and in 27 opinions of the Advocate General that have come to the Court since *Gut Springenheide.*[11] The ambiguous notion of the average consumer, as an interpretive criterion, was not, however, without its critics and the EESC expressed the concern that 'consumer protection policy [would lose] its protective nature and...fail...to protect less well-informed or less well-educated consumers' (Commission, 2004b).

The EESC had been prompted to make this observation as a response to the Commission's proposal for the Unfair Commercial Practices Directive (Commission, 2003c) but the Commission disagreed, emphasising that

> [t]he 'average consumer test' has been devised by the ECJ. The proposal aims at ensuring that this test is adopted throughout the EU to minimise the risks of divergent interpretations by the national courts, while ensuring that there are appropriate protections to prevent particularly vulnerable groups from being targeted and exploited. (Commission, 2004b)

The subsequent appearance of the Unfair Commercial Practices Directive (Directive (EC) 2005/29), introduced to harmonise the consumer protection measures of the Member States from unfair commercial

practices harmful to consumers' economic interests, gave the ambiguous average consumer 'statutory authority, standing and permanence'
(Incardona and Poncibò, 2007, p. 26). It also established the concept
of the vulnerable consumer as a 'clearly identifiable group...because of
their mental or physical infirmity, age or credulity in a way which the
trader could reasonably be expected to foresee', as assessed from the
perspective of the average member of that group.

Weatherill had already provided an analysis of the Court's case
law where it balances the interests of consumer groups with particular vulnerabilities against the reasonably circumspect consumer. He
had identified that 'the majority of the Court's rulings have found
national laws to be unjustified by an interest of sufficient weight to
override the free movement of goods or services', concluding that
there has been a 'generalised consumer protection...(itself) vulnerable
to the Court's perception that most consumers are sufficiently robust
and well-informed to take care of themselves in the market place'
(Weatherill, 1999, pp. 700–701). In his consideration of the Court's
presumed expectations of the reasonably well-informed and reasonably observant and circumspect average consumer, Advocate General
Geelhoed concluded that, in assessing whether product information
was misleading or not,

> before acquiring a given product (for the first time), a consumer will
> always take note of the information on the label and...assess the
> value of that information. It seems to me that a consumer is suffi-
> ciently protected if he is safeguarded from misleading information on
> products and that he does not need to be shielded from information
> whose usefulness with regard to the acquisition and use of a product
> he can himself appraise. (Case C-239/02, AG Opinion, para. 54)

Such presumptions led Stuyck to pose two questions developed
from the proposition that *some categories* of consumer may need to be
protected:[12] 'but what is the point of "protecting" those who should
take care of their own interests and, who can rely...on the general principles of (private) law'. The first question he suggests is then 'whether
citizens in general, in their capacity as consumers, should be protected
by specific measures...' that depart from the fundamental principles of
(in particular) private law. The second question broadens the proposition, beyond the scope of this book, to consider whether measures of
consumer protection should be extended to professionals in positions
of inferiority *vis-à-vis* their suppliers (Stuyck, 2000).

Shared responsibility: a citizen's role for the individual consumer?

A common theme running through all of the above presumptions is that the category of consumer attaches to the individual such that he or she is the *average consumer* or the *vulnerable consumer* or even an *influential consumer*, that once allocated to a category the only outstanding question is to what degree, if any, should the individual be protected by specific measures. The efficacy of identifying the individual with a particular category of consumer is discussed below, but at this point, the focus remains on the evolving consumer descriptions. One of the policy objectives being developed in parallel with the Court's average consumer benchmark was that of the influential consumer in the role of a concerned and active economic agent. The ongoing programme for a consumer protection and information society acknowledged that, in part, the consumer's situation is improved 'by giving him a voice in decisions which involve him' (Council, 1981, para. 1). More significantly, consumer policy was specifically seeking to develop a positive approach in which the consumer would become 'a participant in the preparation and implementation of important economic decisions' (Council, 1981, para. 4). Consumer education was to be the mechanism such that

> [f]acilities should be made available to children as well as to young people and adults to educate them to act as *discriminating consumers*, capable of making an informed choice of goods and services and conscious of their rights and responsibilities. To this end, consumers should, in particular, benefit from basic information on the principle of modern economics. (Council, 1981, para. 44, emphasis added)

Greater involvement of the consumer as an active market agent was not to be confined to the purely economic aspects of the internal market for long. In 1993, as concerns grew over environmental matters, the consumer was to be found in a new role with the objective of changing European society's patterns of behaviour. In a new strategy for the environment and sustainable development the Council sought 'the optimum involvement of all sectors of society in a spirit of shared responsibility, including public administration, public and private enterprise, and the general public *as both individual citizens and consumers*' (Council, 1993, emphasis added).

Previous environmental action programmes had relied almost exclusively on legislative measures but this new initiative from the Council sought to bring about substantial changes that would involve all sectors of society in a full sharing of responsibility. Under a broad mix of instruments designed to effect this change the Council proposed *inter alia* to introduce

> [m]arket-based instruments, designed to sensitize...consumers towards responsible use of natural resources, avoidance of pollution and waste by internalizing of external environmental costs (through the application of economic and fiscal incentives and disincentives, civil liability, etc.) and geared towards 'getting the prices right' so that environmentally-friendly goods and services are not at a market disadvantage vis-à-vis polluting or wasteful competitors. (Council, 1993, Executive Summary, para. 31)

The *environmental consumer* was to take a share of the responsibility for environmental protection and sustainability but, as with the notion of the reasonably well-informed, observant and circumspect average consumer, the proposals relied on the '*use of information* for promotion of better consumer choice and for improvement of public confidence in industrial activity and controls and in the quality of products' (Council, 1993, Executive Summary, para. 20, emphasis added). Such reliance was, however, to rest on the premise that had been raised before: that 'a consumer will always take note of the information on the label and...assess the value of that information' (Case C-239/02, AG Opinion, para. 54), a reliance that, it will be argued below, is misplaced.

The programme itself acknowledged that it was a turning point for the Community in which the reconciliation of environment and development was one of the principal challenges facing it, and the world at large. The Council made explicit recognition that the programme was not 'for the Commission alone, nor one geared towards environmentalists alone' (Council, 1993, para. 39), but rather that it provided

> a framework for a new approach to the environment and to economic and social activity and development, and requires positive will at all levels of the political and corporate spectrums, and the involvement of all members of the public active as *citizens and consumers* in order to make it work. (Council, 1993, para. 39, emphasis added)

This framework marked a shift away from a purely legislative and regulatory approach to environmental issues and introduced a concept of shared responsibility that gave individuals an active involvement alongside other economic actors. The objective was to develop a balance between the short-term benefits attainable by individuals, companies and administrations and the longer-term benefits attainable for society as a whole, and to apply the principle of subsidiarity to the concept of shared responsibility. The 'general public' was identified as having three crucial roles:

> as an individual who may be concerned about the quality of the general environment, personal health and the quality of life of succeeding generations, and as a responsible citizen having the possibility of influencing policies and decisions; as a direct producer of pollution and waste within the home, as an employer or employee, as a commuter and in the pursuit of leisure interests, and finally as a consumer of goods and services, since the causes of and solutions to environmental problems are often a function of consumer choice. (Council, 1993, part 1 chapter 3(3))

The resolution acknowledged that before the individual could play his or her full potential, good knowledge and information provided through awareness campaigns would be essential for them to be able to relate their own activities to environmental pollution or protection. The active involvement of the consumer was to be encouraged through overcoming practical problems, such as a lack of, or higher priced, more ecologically friendly products where the consumer would normally do their shopping, and the provision of well-founded environmental claims regarding the characteristics of products. The general process of awareness-building was also recognised to rest on the 'active involvement and participation of non-governmental organisations (NGOs), both environment and consumer oriented, as well as trades unions and professional associations,' and was felt to be crucial to the 'motivation and engagement of the members of the general public themselves' (Council, 1993, part 1 chapter 3(3)).

Of importance to this narrative, the key element of the Council's Resolution was that the consumer had become a stakeholder of society, a stakeholder that shared responsibility with government and enterprise and represented an *essential economic agent* whose decisions could either benefit or adversely impact upon the environment (Council, 1993, part 1 chapter 7(2)). For the individual to be able to effectively fulfil this role the policy approach is one of information provision,[13] a policy approach that caters to the reasonably well informed and reasonably observant and circumspect average consumer. It is unquestionable that information is essential to enable the individual consumer to make choices but there are barriers to optimising such decisions. Optimal decisions are dependent on such information being appropriate, sufficient and clear; on the capability of the individual to understand the information, and/or be sufficiently motivated to act on it; and on the elimination of any structural barriers that exist in the market.

Recognition of these dependencies has led to a twin track development of consumer characterisation that sits on either side of the notional average consumer. On the one side, with a developing taxonomy, are the transactional domains populated by the active and capable consumer whilst on the other side there is the vulnerable consumer, a vulnerable consumer who has emerged in the literature as an individual belonging to defined stereotype, and therefore somewhat in conflict with the idea that has already been suggested: that any consumer can be vulnerable in certain circumstances.

Vulnerable consumers and limits of empowerment: none of us is average!

The role of the average consumer as an economic agent capable of influencing the development of the internal market had been noted by Weatherill who identified that 'the well-informed consumer serves as a lever to prise open markets sheltered by national regulation' (Weatherill, 1999). However, in their review of the case law Incardona and Poncibò identified that

> [i]t is not easy to reach a balance of understanding that makes the average consumer standard a predictable one, capable of determination in the courts. The case law depicts the average consumer as informed, observant and circumspect, but it also recognises that he or she may have an imperfect understanding of a product purchase and may not even pay attention to some features of the product. (Incardona and Poncibò, 2007, p. 26)

This is a point that they associate with Weatherill's observation that consumers do not fall into a consistent unvarying category 'precisely because consumers themselves do not form a homogenous group' (Weatherill, 2007, p. 1). Not all consumers are able, or interested, in taking note of information, whether provided with the product or sought out by themselves, nor are they always able, or interested, in acting rationally on such information. In this section of the book, we begin to examine the barriers and limitations to effective consumer influence in the market.

Vulnerable consumers: evolution of a species definition

In its proposal for the Unfair Commercial Practices Directive in 2003 the Commission acknowledged that the test for the average consumer, 'reasonably well informed, observant and circumspect' had been established by the Court (Commission, 2003c, p. 5). It also observed that 'several Member States do not apply this test and instead examine the effect of commercial practices on, *inter alia*, vulnerable consumers' (Commission, 2003c, p. 5). As a response to the legal uncertainty and complexity of not knowing what level of consumer protection was provided in other Member States, the proposal made clear that the Directive would establish the Court's average consumer as the benchmark consumer. It made clear that the test, as an expression of proportionality, is 'modulated when a commercial practice is specifically targeted at a particular group (e.g., children), when the average of that group will be considered'(Commission, 2003c, p. 8).

The Commission Staff Working Paper, accompanying the proposal, further highlights that not all consumers are average consumers and that there was a balance to be stuck between the 'need to protect the most vulnerable consumers and the freedom of business to assume a certain level of understanding of their commercial practices' (Commission, 2003d, para. 7.3). The notion of vulnerable consumer groups had originally been recognised in the Common Position adopted by the Council in March 1996 (Council, 1996, para. 20) during the process that led to the adoption of the misleading and comparative advertising directive (Directive (EC) 97/55). Concern over the exploitation of those consumers who were seeking out the new products and services of the information society was also reflected in a 1999 Council Resolution that called for 'non-discrimination in the access to products and services and consideration of the needs of *vulnerable consumers*' (Council, 1999a, emphasis added).

Recognition of the existence of groups of vulnerable consumers and the need to provide them with protection through the addition of new provisions to the existing consumer protection legislation also featured in the Council's 1999 Resolution on the Consumer policy action plan 1999–2001 (Council, 1999b). It was in the EESC's response to this Resolution that we find the first identification of which groups could be considered vulnerable consumers and some reasoning as to why (EESC, 1999). The EESC was critical of the fact that whilst the consumer policy action plan was 'striking' it also dealt only briefly with the position of vulnerable consumers. It emphasised the importance of the need 'to realise that by no means everybody has the necessary self-assurance and assertiveness to make his or her own choices and to come to sensible decisions'. The reasons, suggested in the Opinion, may be 'economic deprivation, lack of knowledge or social and/or cultural backwardness' and that groups of vulnerable consumers would include '*the handicapped, foreigners, people drawing benefits or the minimum wage and children.*' These, the EESC suggested should be subject to a specific policy tailored to their needs (EESC, 1999, para. 5.4, emphasis added).

The EESC was more positive in its Opinion on the General Product Safety Directive (EESC, 2000) and noted that that the Commission had included education for vulnerable consumers in its budget allocation for 2000. Recognition, in far broader terms, of the need for a policy document on poverty and social inclusion came with the Draft Joint Report on Social Inclusion. The purpose of the document was to promote the Union's strategic goal of greater social cohesion by using the open method of co-ordination that had been agreed at the Lisbon Summit in March 2000. Within this broad approach it identified a commonly agreed objective to help the most vulnerable and weak consumers, in particular those consumers on the housing market: an objective that, at the Nice Summit of December 2000, led to the Member States committing themselves to overcoming the deficiencies in the national housing markets. Amongst the policy approaches employed for improving access and addressing 'the growing precariousness at the bottom end of their housing markets' a variety of Member States' measures were identified that added *low-income groups; young people; women and children who are victims of domestic violence and single mothers* to the categories of the vulnerable consumer (Commission, 2001c, paras 38 and 67).

The key principles identified for delivering the social inclusion policies brought a focus to developing the individual capability of vulnerable people. Amongst the principles, the doctrine of subsidiarity is identified as being vital in reaching particularly vulnerable people whilst a holistic approach to the delivery of services according to individual needs is encouraged. These principles also embrace 'inclusive policies and services [that] tend to be developed and promoted in ways which enhance solidarity and cohesion within society and promote partnership and co-responsibility between all actors ... with the participation of those affected by poverty and social exclusion'. Participation of such vulnerable groups was to be encouraged by empowerment and personal development delivered through inclusive policies and services aimed at reducing dependence and supporting the empowerment, autonomy and self-reliance of people (Commission, 2001c, paras 63 and 64).

In 2003 the EESC considered that adult consumer education and ongoing training were of sufficient importance that they should be extended to 'types of consumers who have no contact with school or academic life'. It felt that consumer associations and other social organisations could offer the most effective channels for distributing specifically devised training materials and tools to address everyday problems. It also felt that account needed to be taken to reach the most vulnerable consumer groups and should target, in particular, '*immigrants*, so that they are fully aware of their rights and duties as citizens and ... as consumers throughout the European Union [and] ... *young people* who are not in higher education and who can best be reached via youth associations in the various Member States' (EESC, 2003, para. 3.4.3, emphasis added).

Discussion of the relationship between the average consumer and the vulnerable consumer became prominent in the development of the common position of the Council on the adoption of the Unfair Commercial Practices Directive (Directive (EC) 2005/29). Following the European Parliament's first reading of the draft Directive, and the Commission's position on the Opinion of the Parliament, the Council contended that the common position represented a balance of the concerns. The Directive was to retain the average consumer benchmark established by the Court but would include explicit provisions for the protection of the vulnerable consumer (Council, 2005). It contained 'provisions aimed at preventing the exploitation of consumers whose characteristics make them particularly vulnerable to unfair commercial practices' (Directive (EC) 2005/29, Recital 18). Firstly, using 'children' as a definable group of consumers it identified that the average consumer test was not a statistical test but one where, if the commercial practice was specifically aimed at a particular group of consumers, its impact should be assessed from the perspective of the average consumer of that group. The national courts and authorities would have to exercise their own judgement, having regard to the case-law of the Court, to determine the typical reaction of the average consumer in a given case. The Directive also added to the list of demographic descriptions used to identify the vulnerable consumer by suggesting that 'certain characteristics such as *age, physical or mental infirmity or credulity* make consumers particularly susceptible to a commercial practice' (Directive (EC) 2005/29, Recital 19 and Article 5(3), emphasis added).

Empowerment through information and education?

The notion of empowering consumers has become both enduring and central to the Union's consumer policy strategy. In its 2007
Communication, the Commission acknowledged that

> [t]he 493 million EU consumers are central to the three main chal-
> lenges facing the EU: growth, jobs and the need to re-connect
> with our citizens. They are the lifeblood of the economy ... [c]onfi-
> dent, informed and empowered consumers are the motor of eco-
> nomic change as their choices drive innovation and efficiency.
> (Commission, 2007a)

The objective of this strategy is to equip the consumer 'with the
skills and tools to fulfil *their role* in the modern economy'. This, the
Commission acknowledged was a change of focus in consumer policy,
but a necessary consequence of a 'new economic, social, environmental
and political context' that places consumer policy at the heart of the
next phase of the internal market. A next phase that has the objective
of shifting the focus of regulation 'towards citizen-focussed outcomes',
a policy that, the Commission asserts,

> can provide the market tools to empower citizens, as consumers, to
> make sustainable environmental choices. It can also play a part in
> guaranteeing core European values of fairness, openness, solidarity,
> sustainability and transparency and exporting them internationally.
> (Commission, 2007a, p. 3)

The approach is both welcomed and criticised by the EESC who highlight a mismatch between the ambition of the strategy and the resources
allocated to its implementation. The EESC, for their part, assert that for
the consumer, together with the retailer and service provider, education
'is a key component to the observation and knowledge of legislation but
also crucial for responsible and sustainable consumption and production'. They endorse the observation that the 'retail and services market
is growing in a manner that greater empowerment has been devolved
to the consumer' but express concern that the gap between those consumers with knowledge and means and those belonging to vulnerable
consumer groups will grow (EESC, 2008a, paras 1.4 and 2.1); a problem
recognised by the Commission, in its 2007 communication on a internal market for twenty-first-century Europe, in the context of consumer
rights and redress. Here, it identified that a central goal of the consumer

policy strategy was to empower consumers 'including more vulnerable consumers with special needs or disabilities' (Commission, 2007d).

The strategy of empowering consumers through information and education has also been recognised as having the dual objective of both providing consumers with the means to protect themselves and the consequential drive towards quality improvement and competition for goods and services in the market. As such, consumer empowerment has been explicitly linked to a healthier economy such that 'the rationale for consumer protection becomes in part the health of the economy' (Howells, 2005, p. 350). It is in this vein that, in the United Kingdom, the Department of Trade and Industry (DTI) has suggested that

> [e]mpowering consumers benefits not only the individuals concerned, but consumers and markets as a whole. Competitive markets are driven by empowered consumers because people who vote with their feet prompt businesses to improve, and to offer even better deals to their customers. Empowering consumers is therefore central to our strategy for improving Britain's consumer regime. (DTI, 2005, para. 5.2)

One of the desired outcomes of such a policy approach is to bring about change in the in the manner in which individuals act when engaged as consumers. In seeking to empower consumers through education and information, such a policy extends the role of the consumer to one more akin to that of a citizen. In the case of the United Kingdom, through the auspices of the DTI, there is an express desire 'to see consumers who understand that they have responsibilities as well as rights' (DTI, 2005, para. 5.3). British consumer law does not, however, stand alone; it is strongly influenced by EU consumer policy and its preference for providing information rather than interventionist norms (Howells, 2005, p. 351). As Howells identifies, this approach is epitomised in a Commission Communication that includes an action point for the development of better informed and educated consumers whereby

> consumers, through better information, are able to make informed, environmentally and socially responsible choices on food, the most advantageous products and services, and those that correspond most to their lifestyle objectives thus building up trust and confidence. (Commission, 2005b, section 4.2.4)

This action was reflected, in the context of its focus, in the DTI publication some two months later introducing a new Government service, 'Environment Direct',

> which will provide consumers with information and advice on how to reduce the environmental impact of the goods and services they buy and use. This will raise awareness of the collective effects of individual consumption decisions, but will also help empower consumers to take personal responsibility through more informed choices. (DTI, 2005, para. 5.6)

and, in the context of its scope, by the DTI's objective that did

> not only want to empower consumers shopping in Britain, we also want consumers to have the confidence to shop across national borders. The Government may have a role to play in helping consumers get advice or redress in cross-border cases as it may be hard for them to do so on their own. We will push for our vision of the empowered and responsible consumer, with appropriate protection for vulnerable consumers, to become the norm in the EU consumer regime. (DTI, 2005, para. 5.7)

This chapter has, so far, sought to outline the development of the notion of the consumer in European law and policy. It has charted the development of the average consumer and the recognition of particularly vulnerable groups and recognised the value attributed to the consumer as a key market actor and environmental activist. The focus for empowerment has been found in the consumer information and education policy, whereby, as Howells and Weatherill assert, 'the notion that the consumer, duly informed and thereby protected, is able to participate fairly and effectively in the market has assumed the status of a guiding principle of policy' (Howells and Weatherill, 2005, pp. 63–64). Such a paternalistic policy approach fails to take account of negative behavioural biases in the individual and in structural failures of the market or regulatory regimes. Information can only be empowering for the consumer when it can be understood and where, if understood, the individual is motivated and able to act on the information.

Limits of empowerment: unmanageable consumers and consumer detriment

The policy requirement for information provision is a response to the information asymmetry that exists between traders and service providers on the one hand and consumers on the other, and with the perceived necessity for active consumer participation in the economy (Howells, 2005, p. 354): a participation that is to take place in 'increasingly complex, dynamic and ever-changing knowledge based economies' (Brennan and Coppack, 2008) with a rapid growth in both the diversity and availability of products and services. As an example of the scale of consumer choice, and an indication of the development of the breadth of market sectors subjected to consumer choice, *Which?* Magazine's policy report on product choice suggested that

> Choice is everywhere. A typical supermarket carries 26,000 product lines and there are around 40,000 financial products on the market... 41 per cent of people feel overwhelmed by the choices available to them. Against this background, a huge debate is under way about extending 'choice' as a means of meeting core public policy objectives. The Government is introducing new choices into the National Health Service (NHS) and wants to enhance the role of choice in education, nutrition and pensions. (Which?, 2005)

Such choice exists in an increasingly global consumer society that, Howells suggests, is 'characterised by affluence and a seemingly ever increasing diversity of goods and services and options relating to them, information is indeed necessary for consumers to participate successfully in the economy' (Howells, 2005, p. 354). Information requirements underpin the growth in autonomy of the consumer who can then make informed choices of products or services. Information as a tool to empower consumers so that they are able to protect themselves and to influence quality and competition in the market is central to EU consumer policy, and to the process of enabling consumers to make informed choices.[14] It must therefore be appropriate to ask to what degree and in what way, if any, are vulnerable consumers empowered and other, perhaps more invincible, consumers influenced by the information rules?

In a catalogue of the limitations of information as a tool for consumer empowerment Howells suggests that effort made to inform consumers is wasted on many. Citing existing empirical studies he identifies that busy lives and the frequent need to seek out information result in few consumers taking any notice of the information provided, although some do, and some of those may have more reason to than others. Those that do, form a 'margin of active information seeking consumers [that] can have a healthy impact on the market... [and] are likely to be the more affluent, well-educated middle-class consumers' (Howells, 2005, p. 357). This is a margin that consumer credit disclosure rules confirm is populated by the 'better off' consumer (Whitford, 1973, cited in Howells, 2005): a margin that can use information to push up standards for all, but that will not help the poorer consumers in segmented markets. The poor, Howells suggests, 'may rationally decide not to make use of information, if they feel no alternatives will be available to them' whilst choice for all may merely be illusory with some product offerings as a consequence of increasing standardisation (Howells, 2005, p. 358).

The very notion of consumer empowerment has, however, been described as a 'slippery concept', a term that '[m]ost of us would claim to have an intuitive grasp of…yet, hitherto, it has lacked both formal definition and the specification of theoretically-informed parameters' (Harker and others, 2008). The analysis of contemporary consumption by Gabriel and Lang suggests that any simplistic notion of the consumer is misplaced and choice, a reality for most consumers, also has important limitations. Whilst acknowledging the essential nature of information as a precursor to real choice their writing identifies 'the vital unpredictability which characterizes some of our actions and experiences as consumers, both singly and collectively'. They identify that as consumers, individuals can be just as irrational, incoherent and inconsistent as they can be rational, planned and organised; we may act in an individualistic way or follow social norms and expectations; we may seek out risk and excitement or look for comfort and security; and that we may, or may not, be fettered by moral considerations. In the context of a succession of portraits of the consumer seen as a chooser, a communicator, an explorer, an identity-seeker, a hedonist or artist, a victim, a rebel, an activist and a citizen, they discuss the fragmentations and contradictions of consumer definition and behaviour that they suggest 'should be recognised as core features of contemporary consumption…[and] the pertinence of the idea of the *unmanageable consumer*' (Gabriel and Lang, 1995, p. 4).

This fragmentary and contradictory nature of the unmanageable consumer resonates with the insights into the possibility of consumer detriment arising from biases in consumer behaviour highlighted by studies in behavioural economics. The term consumer detriment lacks any universally accepted definition although it has been suggested that any definition would fall into two broad categories. Personal detriment, as the first category, can be seen as comprising *ex post* negative outcomes for individual consumers that may be either a financial or non-financial detriment. It may also include loss of time and psychological detriment 'that should be assessed against a counter-factual of "reasonable expectations"' (Europe Economics, 2007, paras 16 and 17).

Structural detriment comprises the second category and is, by way of contrast, based on the *ex ante* reduction of consumer surplus resulting from market or regulatory failure. Within the context of consumer detriment the Europe Economics report suggests that the most significant sources of such failure are market power and problems with information. Market power arising, for example, through barriers to entry or high concentration can result in consumer detriment through raised prices, above the competitive level, that deters marginal consumers from making a purchase and leads to a transfer of welfare from the remaining consumers to the producer. Prices may also rise above the competitive level as a result of imperfect pricing information or imperfect information on quality that may prevent consumers from making optimal choices.

Behavioural economics provides two categories of model that provide insight into the reasons why such consumer detriment may arise from biases in the consumers' behaviour. The first embraces '*preference-based theories* in which consumers have preferences different from those assumed in mainstream economics', whilst the second is based on *cognitive-based theories*. The authors of the report suggest that it is this second category, 'in which consumers make cognitive errors in taking their decisions...[and] fail to maximise their well-being given their underlying preferences' that leads to the majority of transactions which result in a consumer detriment. Together, it is these two models of consumer behaviour that identify, in certain circumstances, that *any consumer can be vulnerable*: that consumer detriment is not only evidenced in those stereotypical groups identified as having a particular vulnerability (Europe Economics, 2007, paras 26 and 27).

Whilst the effect of consumer detriment may not yet be as well understood as exploitation of market power, or barriers to market entry, Graham identifies that in the United Kingdom the Office of Fair Trading (OFT) has been working to clarify its nature and extent. In his paper he suggests that 'the corresponding deadweight loss from consumer detriment is probably just as significant as that from market power' and cites an OFT estimate for the consumer deficit of UK economy as a whole as a cost to consumers of £8.3 billion per annum. His paper acknowledges a lack of powers available to the OFT to counter consumer detriment but also identifies some structural aspects of the market that are most likely to lead to its increase. He suggests consumer detriment is most likely to arise when

> there is price dispersion; there is focal point competition, that is suppliers promoting particular characteristics while ignoring others; there is bundling, that is, the packaging of a number of services together; there are payments of commission to intermediaries; goods and services are complex; goods and services are purchased infrequently [and where] there is significant sunk consumer cost, so that the consumer cannot reverse out of the transaction costlessly. (Graham, 2000)

Competition, modernisation and the consumer enforcement deficit

One specific aspect of structural consumer detriment in the market is associated with the enforcement deficit in competition law. On 2 April 2008 the Commission published its White Paper on Damages Actions for Breach of the EC Antitrust Rules, a policy document that marked the latest stage in the debate over the modernisation of European competition law. As things stand, private damages actions are not precluded by existing law but legal and procedural rules in most of the Union's Member States present a barrier to private anti-trust litigation. The White Paper proposes changes that are intended to overcome some of these barriers through the application of three guiding principles: first, that the primary goal of private enforcement should be attained through *full compensation*, with the acknowledgement that this contains an inherent deterrent element; second, that the legal framework for improving the effectiveness of private anti-trust damages actions should be based on *a genuinely European approach*; and finally, that such private actions should *complement* the strong public enforcement of Articles 101 and 102 TFEU (Articles 81 and 82 EC) (Commission, 2008c).

A long-standing background debate over the right to private damages claims was accelerated by the Court in *Courage* (Case C-453/99), and later in *Manfredi* (Cases C-295–298/04), and broadened by the Commission in its 2005 Green Paper (Commission, 2005c). In the seminal case of *Courage*, the Court, in considering the role of private damages actions, held that

> [t]he full effectiveness of Article [101 TFEU (81 EC)] of the Treaty ... would be put at risk if it were not open to *any individual* to claim damages for loss caused to him by a contract or by conduct

liable to restrict or distort competition. Indeed, the existence of such a right strengthens the working of the Community competition rules and discourages agreements or practices, which are frequently covert, which are liable to restrict or distort competition. From that point of view, actions for damages before the national courts can make a significant contribution to the maintenance of effective competition in the Community. (Case C-453/99 paras 26 and 27, emphasis added)

Following the *Courage* case Neelie Kroes, as European Commissioner for Competition, provided a succinct précis of some of the objectives of this debate, in the context of European competition law, when she said:

The more European citizens and undertakings stand up for their right to damages, the more the potential perpetrators of illegal actions will think twice. Public enforcement alone is not enough. *Full respect of the competition rules will only be a realistic goal if victims of antitrust infringements know they are able to fight and win their case in court.* Even without a prior finding of an infringement by a competition authority. Victims need appropriate procedural tools to put them in a position to pursue and prove cases in their own right. (Kroes, 2006, emphasis added)

The evidential burden is such that the cost of proving a breach of the competition rules in a private action is usually prohibitive. In its 2005 Green Paper, the Commission sought to highlight the obstacles to private redress in the national procedural rules and encouraged debate to identify a more efficient system for private anti-trust damage claims. It proposed a range of options for change that, in line with the Court's ruling in *Courage* (Case C-453/99), bring the individual consumer closer to the competition rules with an active enforcement role. Amongst the options was the proposal to enlarge the range of infringements for which competition law could be enforced and to increase the level of enforcement generally. This, the Commission proposed, would 'arise in particular from litigation which is *not* brought on the back of decisions adopted by public authorities' (Commission, 2005e). The rhetoric of this ambition for private enforcement was then, in the Green Paper, focussed *both* on follow-on actions, where the private action is brought following a public competition authority inquiry where an infringement has been proved, and on stand-alone actions instigated without any public precursor.

With regard to damages, the White Paper welcomed the Court's decision in *Manfredi* (Cases C-295–298/04) where it held that victims must, as a minimum, receive *full compensation* of the real value of the loss suffered: that is, the actual loss due to the anti-competitive price increase, the resulting loss of profit stemming from any reduction in sales and any interest due. The White Paper proposed a minimum level of disclosure rights that, subject to specific conditions, would enable national courts to order disclosure of precise categories of relevant evidence. The conditions, the White Paper suggests, should include: requirements for the claimant to have presented all the facts and means of evidence that are *reasonably available to him*; that these facts show plausible grounds *to suspect* that an infringement of the competition rules caused the claimant harm; for the claimant to satisfy the court that having pursued all other reasonable avenues he is unable to obtain the information requested; for the claimant to specify sufficiently precisely *the categories of evidence sought*, and that it is both relevant to the case and necessary and proportionate. The conditions suggest that the claimant would be required to describe the infringement and the damage in more general terms than has hitherto been required in order to effect disclosure through a court order – a significant change, in particular to national civil law systems and to a lesser extent in civil actions within the European common law traditions. In this respect, the proposals lose some of their genuinely European approach and lean towards the United States system of 'notice pleading' where the specific detail of the argument is developed through such discovery processes (Komninos, 2008, pp. 88–89).

Gaining access to such evidence, and the associated costs, is likely to remain one of the primary obstacles to private actions. Even with such procedural changes these discovery proposals appear particularly limited given the evidential difficulties that have always constituted a significant barrier to private competition enforcement. There are risks to the individual claimant, stemming from the proposed proportionality tests that national courts would apply. As the Court recently confirmed in *Promusicae*, the right to judicial protection for victims of infringements of EU law and the right to privacy of the infringer are both fundamental rights under Community law that must be balanced (Case C-275/06, paras 115 and 116).

The Commission recognises that the costs of anti-trust damages actions can be a decisive disincentive to bringing claims. The White Paper, however, makes no clear proposals for reversing this barrier; it merely invites and encourages Member States to reflect on their cost rules and court fees in order to more readily attract meritorious claims and to consider mechanisms for fostering settlements. The Commission also suggests that the requirement to prove fault, with its associated costs, and common to many but not all Member States, should no longer apply where the victim has already proved a breach of Article 101 or 102 TFEU (Article 81 or 82 EC). Whilst this may encourage follow-on type of actions there would remain a significant barrier to the private victim wishing to build a stand-alone case from the start. The White Paper prepares the way for follow-on collective actions for victims of cartel infringements and in doing this fulfils the third of its guiding principles, that private actions should complement strong public enforcement. Enforcement is, however, reliant on the active, motivated, organised and capable consumer pursuing such an action and thereby contributing 'to the maintenance of effective competition in the Community' (Kroes, 2006).

The active consumer: another step towards the consumer citizen

Whilst expressing a strong belief that education and information are thoroughly integral to consumer protection, and acknowledging that the European Consumer Centres network (ECC-Net) has been a successful initiative in providing information for consumers, the EESC has encouraged the Commission to find more innovative and creative means of communicating with the consumer in general (EESC, 2008a, para. 4.4). The EEC-Net provides an *ex post* protection initiative for consumers purchasing across borders but it fails to address issues of responsible and sustainable consumption. Consumer empowerment through information and education can clearly offer a benefit to many but the Commission are suggesting that consumer policy is

> increasingly at the crossroads of the main challenges that face our citizens, economy and societies [and that] the sophistication of retail markets is increasing the role of consumers. The greater empowerment of consumers has...led to greater responsibilities for them to manage their own affairs...Our need for confident consumers to drive our economies has never been greater however. (Commission, 2007a)

This section follows the development of those transactional domains in which confident and active consumers have become increasingly recognised as essential to the internal market and increasingly expected to show responsibility for making sustainable consumer choices. It considers whether there is a deficit in consumer law and policy, in regard to the active consumer, and questions if this is the path that leads to and legitimises the notion of the consumer citizen.

Opportunities and obstacles in the internal market

In March 1995, the EESC presented an opinion on opportunities and obstacles in the internal market in which it acknowledged that the Commission had adopted a position recognising that the internal market would 'not function properly without the active and genuine participation of consumers' (EESC, 1996, para. 2.2.1.2). The EESC was, however, concerned that, following the Maastricht Treaty of 1992 and the expansion of Article 169 TFEU (Article 153 EC) as an explicit legal base for consumer protection, only one decision, out of many initiatives, had been taken on the new basis. Instead, there had been a continuing recourse to measures of minimum harmonisation under Article 114 TFEU (Article 95 EC) that the EESC suggested 'confirmed and even highlighted difficulties in mutual recognition and shortcomings in the harmonisation process' (EESC, 1996, para. 2.2.2.1)

The principle of minimum harmonisation allows for Member States to enact consumer provisions that provide for extra protection, going beyond that agreed in EU legislation. What concerned the EESC was the 'lack of clear and precise definitions of the basic concepts and legal principles', and that the principle of subsidiarity, on which the measures were applied, had led to 'enormous differences in interpretation and practical application' (EESC, 1996, para. 2.2.1.2). The focus of the committee's concern was the potential for the principle of subsidiarity to be interpreted too narrowly with the consequence that the Commission could become 'increasingly apprehensive about, and the Council gradually less interested in, proposing and taking decisions on new Community-level action to protect and defend consumers' (EESC, 1996, paras 1.1.1 and 2.1.2). This, the EESC decided, would be detrimental to the harmonisation of binding Community legislation and noted 'the subsidiarity principle cannot merely be a token for identifying decisions or for fettering the autonomy of participants' (EESC, 1996, para. 2.1.2.1).

The interpretation of the principle of subsidiarity has not been the only inherent internal market obstacle to consumer empowerment. Issues over a lack of coherence between instruments, forming part of the EU contract law *acquis*, in their drafting and in their implementation and application have led to work on a common frame of reference. This work was intended to provide for best solutions in terms of the taxonomy and the applicable rules by giving common definition to 'fundamental concepts and abstract terms like "contract" or "damage" and of the rules that apply for example in the case of non-performance of contracts' (Commission, 2003b, Executive Summary). The Commission recognised in this work the criticism that the minimal harmonisation approach in consumer protection legislation had failed to achieve the uniformity of solutions, for similar situations, that the internal market required. The Commission acknowledged

> the difference, from one Member State to another, in cooling-off periods in the context of Doorstep Selling, Timeshare and Distance Selling Directives, financial thresholds of implementation laws of the Doorstep Selling Directive or divergent concepts in the implementation of the annex to the Unfair Contract Terms Directive. (EESC, 1996, para. 24)

The barriers presented to consumers by this lack of coherence represent disincentives to the cross-border transactions that are necessary for the efficient functioning of the internal market. In most cases, the consumers' national law will not be the law applicable to the contract but may be the law that the trader has chosen as the applicable law, under standard terms, or because it is objectively determined as the applicable law under Article 4 of the Rome Convention. The Commission also highlights that the Rome Convention, applying to contractual obligations in any situation involving a choice between the laws of different countries (Rome 1), offers no significant help to the consumer under Article 5 on certain consumer contracts 'because it does not apply in the case of an *active consumer* who wants to take advantage of the opportunities offered by the internal market' (Commission, 2003b, emphasis added).

The notion of the active consumer first appeared with the Commission's acknowledgement that the internal market would 'not function properly without the active and genuine participation of consumers' in its 1994 report on the internal market (Commission, 1995, point 319). Evidence of the potential for the active consumer to influence the functioning of the market has more recently appeared in the Commissions' 'Technical Annex' on the creation of the internal gas and electricity market (Commission, 2005d). In the energy sector, the incumbent suppliers argued that customers had achieved benefits, without switching suppliers, because their prices had been reduced through the threat of competition under the internal market rules. This was countered by arguments from smaller suppliers and new entrants, and from consumer groups. The smaller suppliers and new entrants suggested that real competition was constrained by a range of obstacles leaving established companies in a strongly advantageous position in their particular region. It was, they suggested, impossible for either new entrants or even incumbents from other areas or Member States to compete whilst the incumbent suppliers were able to segment the market between *active and passive customers.*

Some caution is necessary with the interpretation of the taxonomy applied to the energy end user in this document; 'consumer' appears over 100 times whilst 'customer' appears over 300 times. Frequently the use of the words 'consumer' and 'customer' appear interchangeable with discussion *inter alia* of both 'vulnerable customers' and 'large consumers'. The scope of the document is, however, defined by the primary communication (Commission, 2005a) that draws a distinction between 'businesses' and 'households' and identifies, with reference to the 'Technical Annex' that for the consumer

> switching supplier is not always a simple procedure and in some cases the complications (e.g. possible mis-selling, complicated contract structures or unclear network access rules) means that households will be reluctant to use their new rights. (Commission, 2005d, section 3, discussed further in Chapter 5)

The general tone is one of support for the active consumer, for the individual or household who wishes to take advantage of the internal market and switch between network service providers and/or shop across borders. The active consumer is the antithesis of the passive consumer and can be shown to display, in the context of the development of the consumer citizen, characteristics that are contrary to those of the vulnerable consumer. As Reich observed,

> EU consumer philosophy has changed substantially over time. Even in 1992, a shift from a 'consumer rights' and 'citizen' rhetoric to a more 'internal market approach' could be observed. The consumer was not seen so much as a 'weak person' needing protection against the intricacies of the market, but as an active partner who should be encouraged to use the increased possibilities of cross-border shopping. (Reich, 2006)

He suggested that the most interesting paradigm shift was to do with 'recognising the consumer as an active market subject whose opportunities for increased choice in the internal market should be protected by confidence building measures'.

Consumer confidence and responsibility

The term *confident consumer* was first introduced by Weatherill (1996, p. 423) who identified what was to be seen as a 'new and important aim of EC consumer policy to create confident cross-border consumers' (Wilhelmsson, 2004, p. 318), who would *contribute* to the strengthening of the internal market. He had identified this new Community definition of the consumer through a review of the secondary Community legislation, particularly that relating to misleading advertising, contracts negotiated away from commercial premises, package travel and package tours, consumer credit and unfair contractual terms. Introduced to the Court in *Commission v France* (Case C-184/96), this new confident consumer was no longer to be a mere passive beneficiary of freedom to trade and an incidental beneficiary of the harmonisation of legislation, he or she was to be encouraged to effect cross-border transactions, in the knowledge that he was protected in the operation of the market by a minimum network of protective measures.

This notion of the confident consumer, empowered through information, education and protection has now been recognised in the 2007–2013 Consumer Policy Strategy. It is a strategy that places consumer policy 'increasingly at the crossroads of the main challenges that face our citizens, economy and societies' (Commission, 2007a, section 2.1) It acknowledges that the sophistication of retail markets is *increasing the role of consumers* and that the greater empowerment of consumers has also led to *greater responsibilities* for them to manage their own affairs.

The consumer environment is rapidly changing and the strategy highlights that the need for 'confident consumers to drive our economies has never been greater'. Services that are increasingly being tailored to the individual will bring changes that will place greater individual responsibility on the consumer, changes that the strategy attributes to a number of developments. Firstly, the strategy cites the development and growth of services in general and, the liberalised services in particular. Secondly, the strategy identifies that the technological digital revolution and the internet will grow even faster with the rollout of broadband technology: a development that is likely to give a significant boost to e-commerce and make a yet greater range of products available that will boost price competition and develop new markets. These new e-markets, the strategy suggests, will weaken the grip of traditional advertising and retail mediums over consumer markets and challenge traditional modes of regulation and enforcement, whilst traditional consumer rights will be less and less adapted to the digital age. Finally, the strategy draws attention to the continuing globalisation of production and the challenge this brings from global e-commerce to effective market surveillance.

The first formal reference to a *responsible consumer practice* from the EU institutions had appeared a decade earlier in a 1997 Written Question to the Commission regarding the Directive on packaging and packaging waste. The question related to the labelling of packaging material to indicate the nature of the packaging material used in order *inter alia* to facilitate recycling and the voluntary nature of the provision. The questioner was concerned that the voluntary nature of the identification system suggested that it would be 'ineffective as a means of establishing an environmentally effective approach to the management of packaging waste and promoting responsible consumer practices' (Díaz, 1997). In response, the Commission suggested that the voluntary approach was a considered, reasonable and appropriate solution in a sensitive area, subject to important technological progress.

The importance attached by the Commission to encouraging responsible consumer behaviour is reflected in its project initiative to promote the introduction of consumer education into the national schools curricula. Within this project the Commission introduced the 'Young Consumer Competition' in 1993 'to encourage young people to become more aware of consumer issues and to become responsible consumers' (Commission, 2003a, p. 22). The specific targeting of young consumers remains a policy objective of the Commission which, through education, is intended to ensure that as consumers they will be able to 'make informed, *environmentally and socially responsible choices* on food, the most advantageous products and services, and those that correspond most to their lifestyle objectives thus building up trust and confidence' The Commission acknowledges, however, that to support such an educational objective considerably more research is required. There is a need to establish a knowledge base in such areas as consumer detriment, safety of services, satisfaction and confidence of consumers on the market, on services of general interest and on the information society (Commission, 2005b, para. 4.2.4, emphasis added).

The increasing level of accountability that is settling on the consumer to make socially responsible choices is at its most evident relevant to green issues. The EESC maintain that

conservation of the environment in its broadest sense is becoming, alongside the fight against world hunger, one of the two main challenges facing the human race. It is therefore essential that the European Union seek to play a leading role in processes allowing *responsible consumers* to distinguish between, and opt for products, the extraction, processing and marketing of which has complied with environmental protection standards. (EESC, 2006, emphasis added)

This concern of the EESC, for consumers to be both enabled and encouraged to make green choices with environmentally significant products and services, had already been made evident in its 1997 Opinion on renewable sources of energy: an opinion in which it argued for the Commission to give consideration to the ways in which green consumer demand for renewable energy at an affordable price could be encouraged (EESC, 1997, para. 3.4.3.5).

The development of the consumer, from a mere cog in the economic machinery of the internal market to an effective and influential market actor cognisant of his or her role in shaping environmental impact through their product choice, was recognised in the Commissions Green Paper on integrated product policy (Commission, 2001a). The Green Paper was concerned with stimulating the potential for market-driven continuous environmental improvement of products, through a *mutual education process between companies and responsible consumers* and with modifying the consumers' environmental impact during the 'use' stage.

Producing companies should, the Green Paper suggested, actively promote environmental information whilst consumers should challenge the companies to improve the environmental characteristics of their products. Through the use of eco-labels that provide a credible and transparent measure for distinguishing the more environmentally friendly products from the less environmentally friendly ones, the objective was twofold: firstly, to increase the population of consumers who would use the information on the label to make an informed and environmentally friendly choice; secondly, the Green Paper recognised that modern communication technologies, including the internet, offered the opportunity for consumers to provide feedback to producers in an 'exchange of best practice and evaluation' (Commission, 2001a, p. 14). The active consumer, at least in the environmental field, has thus attained a shared responsibility for sustainable consumption, along with other stakeholders including producers, distributors, educators and public authorities, that the EESC has recently suggested should be identified within a European charter for sustainable consumption and production (EESC, 2008b, para. 3.13).

The involved consumer and European consumer activism

Gabriel and Lang, in their historical review of consumer activism, identify that '[c]onsumer activism has always functioned within a moral context', that consumers, as activists, always have been, and continue to be, morally driven individuals cognisant of the necessity for collective organisation. They describe four 'waves' of Western consumer activism that began with the widespread Co-operative Movement, formed in Rochdale, in North West England, in 1844. Founded in a *collective* working class reaction to excessive prices and poor quality goods it has grown into a global social movement with a pragmatic retail vision embracing environmental concerns (Gabriel and Lang, 1995, pp. 152 and 156).

In contrast, the second wave of consumer activism, originating in the USA's 1930s 'information co-operatives' (Winward, 1993, cited in Gabriel and Lang, 1995) developed with the aim of informing and educating *individuals* in order that they could act effectively as consumers, exercising rights to information and redress when things went wrong. The approach of this second wave of consumer activism has subsequently been criticized for having an 'overwhelmingly middle-class orientation whilst failing to embrace longer term social and environmental issues' (Gabriel and Lang, 1995, p. 159).

Emerging in the 1960s, 'Naderism', based on the campaigning of Harvard-educated lawyer Ralph Nader, formed the third wave of consumer activism identified by Gabriel and Lang. It was a movement that saw the consumer activist's role as confronting the power of large corporations, to expose abuse of such power, 'to stand up for public rights [and] to be a citizen' (Gabriel and Lang, 1995, pp. 160–161).

The final fourth wave of consumer activism defined as 'alternative consumerism' by Gabriel and Lang, is a form of consumer activism more recently described by Heldman as

citizen action aimed at influencing corporate decisions, corporate power, or the allocation of societal goods and values. Examples of this 'new' and increasingly popular form of political participation include boycotts, buycotts (purchasing products for political reasons), socially conscious investing, a variety of politically-oriented shareholder tactics (e.g., proposing a resolution, testifying at a shareholder meeting, disrupting a shareholder meeting), protests directed at corporate or quasi-governmental organizations (e.g., chambers of commerce, the World Trade Organization, the International Monetary Fund), and protests targeting businesses directly (e.g., protests in front of stores selling animal fur, union picket lines). (Heldman, 2003)

These actions represent changes in political protest action that are evident in the transnational nature of consumer activism that has taken the opportunity presented by the internet. The interdependency between changes in protest movements and technological developments is well documented,[15] and has 'contributed to a growth in the number of both formal and informal groupings of civil society actors' (Baringhorst, 2005). New communication technologies have provided a platform for extended communication flows and resource mobilisation for social activists. Baringhorst asserts that current political consumerism in Europe 'is neither simply anti-capitalistic or anti-consumerist, nor simply based on working-class or middle-class actors'. He suggests that

> [i]ts master frame is neither solely materialistic in the sense of Marxist or anti-imperialistic ideologies, nor solely postmaterialistic... It is rather a new synthesis of both: a reframing of working-class issues like workers' rights – fair pay, humane working conditions and the right to collectively organise – in a global dimension linked in with middle-class 'lifestyle politics' of ethical consumption. Agents of change are a broad coalition of diverse working-class and middle-class based civil society organisations... Despite their different social and ideological backgrounds they all address a new prime mover of social and political change: the *citizen as ethical consumer*. (Baringhorst, 2005, p. 4)

In seeking to explain the rise of political consumerism Baringhorst suggests that this latest wave of consumer activism is characterised by 'a gap between the denationalisation of economics and the denationalisation of politics': a gap that in twenty-first century is one where 'the consumer citizen... has become a key figure in international markets.' Consumers have become able to 'use their purchasing power as a kind of vote and thus are capable of successfully scandalising corporate giants like Shell, Nike or Monsanto in collective action' (Baringhorst, 2005, pp. 5–6).

Taking Monsanto as a case in point, this international biotechnology company, met with such collective action following the introduction into the EU of its genetically modified (GM) soybean product. In 1996, the Commission authorised its storage and processing in a measure that allowed plantings to be imported into Europe without any additional testing or labelling (Decision (EC) 96/281). Within a few months, environmental protection organisations, including Greenpeace and Friends of the Earth, had sabotaged and destroyed field trials and led a vocal protest over GM products. Broader European consumer opinion of GM technologies began to steadily decline with popular resistance focussing on the need to label such products. Suspicion grew over Monsanto's argument that, as the product had been established as a 'substantial equivalent', there was no need for it to be labelled. Growing popular resistance focussed on the lack of public consultation and the issue of labelling GM foods whilst consumer advocates were arguing that if GM foods were not labelled, then the food producers must have something to hide. Werhane and others suggest that for many European citizens this was such a limitation of 'choice over what was a basic human necessity: food. [That] [t]hey revolted against GMOs in order to regain decision-making control over biotechnology'. Identifying the biotechnology food industry as secretive, members of the active German Housewives Association felt that their fears were being treated as irrational and 'argued for the right to choose regardless of GMO safety: "People in China eat water-beetles... [we are] perfectly sure they these beetles are safe to eat, but [we] don't want to eat them. GMOs are similar"' (Werhane and others, 2008, pp. 9–10).

Although there had been no breach of the EU regulatory framework Directives for the development of biotechnology (Directives (EEC) 90/219 and 90/220, now repealed), genetically modified organisms (GMOs) provided a focus for concerns about the functioning and evolution of society and the modernisation of agriculture (Bonny, 2003). Concerns that were fervently expressed in a December 2000 *Le Monde Diplomatique* leader article:

> People no longer automatically accept that scientific development is necessarily beneficial to humanity. Particularly because that progress has become inextricably tied up with money, hijacked by companies greedy for profit... It is not hard to see that the social institutions... which should have been overseeing public safety have repeatedly failed us. They have acted unwisely and negligently. In addition, our decision-makers have developed a bad habit of mortgaging our collective futures without first asking us, the people. The basis of the democratic pact has thus been altered. As a result, people have become more and more suspicious. They are increasingly unwilling to give the powers-that-be the authority to play with our collective futures by rubber-stamping scientific innovations that

are risky and insufficiently tested. A new spirit of distrust is abroad among the sorcerer's apprentices of neo-scientism…They are simply and legitimately uneasy about the way that public authorities choose to put commercial interests and corporate egos before the common good. Shouldn't we all have a say in defining what is acceptable risk, and not just leave it to the 'experts'? (Ramonet, 2000)

Whilst Directive (EEC) 90/220, on the deliberate release into the environment of GMOs, had been implemented in all Member States by 1995 no new GMO approvals were made after April 1998. With only 18 GMOs approved for commercial use the Directive failed in its primary goal of harmonisation and found itself subject to a moratorium, with no transgenic crops under cultivation in the EU from 1999 and 'hostility towards the importation of GM products' (Bonny, 2003, p. 50). European food and retailing industries were reticent to market GM food products as a result of the negative consumer reaction, recognising that 'consumer and public perception drives market forces and that a high level of health and environmental protection must be ensured in order to be able to market GM products' (Commission, 2006a, p. 4) Grass roots environmental activism and consumer demand for information and choice had fostered the emergence of biopolitics that, Morris and Adley suggest, had

> shown its effects at all political levels in the EU, whether expressed through the local banning of GM food from school dinners by local councils in the UK, the failure of national governments such as Greece or Austria to pay due regard to European law, or even the international political effects on global trade. It seems that the public perceptions of modern biotechnology are having an effect on the public policy process, which in turn is causing changes in the regulatory guidelines. The vehicle for these changes has been, and will continue to be, biopolitics. (Morris and Adley, 2000)

Led by France, Bonny identifies that, with regard to public policy at the EU level, the moratorium on the release of GMOs was to continue until the introduction of new EU labelling and traceability laws (Bonny, 2003, p. 55). Such political pressure was underpinned by continuing public concern and consumer rejection of GMO foods, as the Eurobarometer survey of December 2001 identified:

> The most commonly encountered attitude is the demand to be able to choose and the demand for information: 94.6% of Europeans

want to have the right to choose when it comes to genetically modified foods. There are no exceptions to this demand. (Eurobarometer, 2001, p. 40)

The original European GMO Release Directive of 1990 was repealed and replaced by a Directive that recognised the need for public consultation in introducing a new comprehensive and transparent legislative framework (Directive (EC) 2001/18, Recital 10). Related instruments subsequently reinforced acknowledgement of the consumers' demands for involvement in the authorisation process for GMOs (Regulation 1829/2003, Article 6(7)) and for accurate labelling 'so as to ensure that accurate information is available to operators and consumers to enable them to exercise their freedom of choice in an effective manner' (Regulation 1830/2003, Recital 4).

The European consumer citizen: behaviour within a transactional domain

In her keynote paper, delivered to the International Conference on Developing Consumer Citizenship, McGregor asserts that citizenship is to be found in consumption and that 'when transnational corporations flouted their ability to escape state regulation, they...highlighted their own responsibility for...corporate social responsibility', a phenomenon that has triggered the *politicisation of consumption*. Fundamental to this notion of politicised consumption, and in addition to corporate social responsibility, is that individuals and groups have become concerned with environmental, social justice, rights, labour and gender issues as political participants in the market place (McGregor, 2002). Scammell asserts that one effect of such political participation is that '[c]onsumer activism has forced a powerful political agenda on to the public stage to which business has been compelled to react, with a speed and innovation that makes politics seem sluggish' (Scammell 2003, p. 134). An assertion that is, to some degree, is reflected in the statement by Anita Roddick, at that time the owner of The Body Shop, who said that

> [b]usiness has overtaken politics as the primary shaping force in society, which means consumers are voting every time they flex their spending muscle, and that in turn makes the vigilante consumer into a powerful consumer, capable, as we have seen, of humbling even the likes of...Monsanto. (Roddick, cited in Scammell, 2000, p. 351)

From a European perspective, the positive effect of such interaction between consumer activism and global corporations was reflected in the Commission's 2001 integrated product policy (Green Paper) and its advocacy for a mutual education process between companies and responsible consumers (Commission, 2001a).

The literature identifies two aspects of the citizenship role as it is applied to the consumer citizen. In the first, the consumer has 'a vote in the maintenance of the market structure; each time they purchase, they cast their ballot' (McGregor, 2002, p. 5) whilst in the second, the consumer is:

> a responsible … socially-aware consumer, a consumer who thinks ahead and tempers his or her desires by social awareness, a consumer whose actions must be morally defensible and who must occasionally be prepared to sacrifice personal pleasure to communal well-being. (Gabriel and Lang, 1995, pp. 175–176, and cited in McGregor, 2002, p. 5)

The development of the active consumer in EU policy has seen both of these aspects drawn together. The Commission's Green Paper was not only concerned with stimulating a mutual education process between companies and consumers, it also acknowledged the effectiveness and influence of the consumer as a market actor with a shared responsibility, at least in the environmental field, for sustainable consumption.

Scammell argues that the act of consumption 'is increasingly suffused with citizenship characteristics and considerations', that '[c]itizenship is not dead, or dying, but found in new places, in life-politics … and in consumption'. She suggests that

> a model of citizenship, with some of the classical republican dimensions of civic duty, public-spiritedness and self education, is an increasingly apt description of consumer behaviour … [that] the day-to-day activity of increasing millions of ordinary folk whose regular conduct of leisure and consumption has an ever-stronger political edge. (Scammell, 2000, pp. 351–352)

Globalisation is changing the relationships between the individual, the state and the economy: as Scammell asserts, 'National sovereignty, and what is left of it in the era of globalization, is at the heart of modern European politics' (Scammell, 2000, p. 353). Nussbaum echoes this sentiment, suggesting that 'the power of the global market and of multinational corporations has considerably eroded the power and autonomy of nations' (Nussbaum, 2006, p. 225). This is the environment in which the Commission's 2007–2013 Consumer Policy Strategy recognises the definitions of consumer citizenship and the need to reinforce the consumer dimension of the internal market. Whilst lacking any specific explanation, it explicitly acknowledges that the 'new economic, social, environmental and political context calls for a change in focus of EU policy towards consumers' (Commission, 2007a, p. 2).

Specifically, the Commission's strategy highlights a growing role for the consumer where empowerment brings with it responsibility to manage both 'their own affairs' and 'to drive our economies'. It recognises the challenges stemming from increasingly interlinked goods and services and in particular the consequences of the liberalisation of the networked services such as electricity, gas, post and telecommunications. It also recognises the advantages and challenges brought by the internet and broadband technology, the significant boost this will bring to e-commerce, the development of new markets and the tailoring of goods and services to the individual. This final point is also discussed by Scammell who suggests that

> [t]hese possibilities of information and choice are effectively transforming the market such that it is now the consumer, not the producer, who is the hunter. Increasingly producers will have to find products for consumers, not customers for pre-designed products. (Scammell, 2003, p. 120)

Whilst information and education, supported by consumer protection and competition measures, are provided to increase confidence and consumer citizenship, capability and rationality, in consumer choice and behaviour, are limited by vulnerability and consumer detriment. Such behavioural limitations have also been acknowledged in the Commission's 2007–2013 Consumer Policy Strategy which recognises the need for additional research to develop a deeper understanding of consumer behaviour and, in particular, to understand how rational consumers are in practice, and how new technologies and marketing practices affect them (Commission, 2007a, p. 9).

This chapter has already identified that consumer vulnerability is not confined to stereotypical groups, that we can all be vulnerable and susceptible to consumer detriment; equally, not all vulnerable consumers will experience consumer detriment in every consumer transaction they undertake. The opportunity for making the choices, and exercising the behaviours that define consumer citizenship, will improve with information, education and individual capability. But, increasing the effectiveness of consumer citizenship practice will depend on the continuing development of consumer empowerment through general education and information (Commission, 2008b, para. 32); on the removal of structural elements of consumer detriment; and through a more developed understanding of the significance of personal detriment (Europe Economics, 2007, para. 27). It is in this vein that the Commission acknowledges that, in seeking to make the market more responsive to the expectations and concerns of citizens, more attention needs to be paid to final outcomes; that policies need to be more evidenced-based and outcome-orientated. It recognises that the 'ability of consumers to understand the choices available in the market affects the successful functioning of the market' and that in assessing complex products consumers may require professional advice (Commission, 2008b, paras 1 and 19).

Conclusion

This chapter has provided a review of the history of consumer descriptions in the development of the internal market and the establishment of the benchmark 'average consumer' in the Court's jurisprudence. It has also followed the development of such descriptions in the divergent aspects of the vulnerable and capable consumer. The chronology of these developments is captured in Figure 2.1, as is the empowerment deficit that results from personal and structural consumer detriment, and the specific structural detriment associated with the enforcement deficit in competition law.

The proposition argued in this chapter has been that the consumer of the EU internal market has, over time, gained status as an influential market actor and that law and policy have evolved to the point where they reflect the attributes of the consumer citizen found in the social science literature. As recognised above, there is no explicit use of the term in the legislation or case law, but there is explicit recognition of the essential nature of the attributes of the consumer citizen. EU policy now reflects the existence of the consumer citizen, and acknowledges the economic and social importance of the role in both a European and the global market context. The challenge now is to address the issues of consumer empowerment raised by the transactional nature of both effective consumer choice decisions and the incidence of consumer detriment. Whilst structural consumer deficit may be addressed in part through enforcement and redress, consumer detriment arising as a result of individual cognitive error make this a complex arena in which research and analysis is still at an early stage.

Citizenship and consumerism may not share any common historical foundation but at a practical level they appear to have come together in EU consumer policy. The Commission's 2007–2013 Consumer Policy Strategy reflects the essential nature of both the economic and social aspects of consumer citizenship practice and a new importance is attached to the monitoring of consumer outcomes. This chapter has sought to review and question the practical existence of the consumer citizen; the following chapter considers the question of the consumer citizen as a new tradition and the theoretical potential for conflating the separate concepts of the consumer and the citizen.

3
European Consumer Citizenship: A Coherent Theoretical Model?

Introduction

The previous chapter was primarily concerned with aligning the definitional rhetoric of the consumer with policy development at the European level. It was a review that revealed an evolutionary development of the adjectival descriptions that have been used to define particular attributes of consumer behaviour and that have taken us towards the use of the expression consumer citizen: an expression associated with the paradigm of a thoughtful and informed individual displaying a particular set of behavioural characteristics within the context of a consumer transaction. In this chapter I develop and build on this model in two distinct parts. Firstly, the narrative briefly examines the distinct traditions of the consumer and the citizen before concluding that it is reasonable to conflate aspects of these traditions in such a way as to accommodate the consumer citizen as a theoretical concept. The second half of this chapter then develops a model of consumer citizenship in a constitutional setting before elaborating on the organisational structures and networks that provide the functional platform for consumer citizenship practice.

It has already been established that the tradition of the consumer identifies that it is something that the law has a limited capacity to define in anything other than the stereotype of the *average consumer*: a conclusion drawn from analysis of the case law of the Court and from statutory, procedural and regulatory law. However, if a broader perspective is pursued, the political and social science literature provides some legitimacy for concepts of the consumer that have been fragmented into a number of sub-divisions identified within contemporary consumption. It provides an analysis of the consumer as the social, political and economic actor that was identified in Chapter 2, and suggests that if we draw a comparison between the consumer and the citizen we can show them as contingent universal concepts, sharing both similar boundaries and conceptual constraints.

Similarly, when the focus of the analysis in this chapter switches to the institution of citizenship it identifies that, even at a basic level, the concept of citizenship remains contested: it means different things in different contexts, although Wiener does suggest that even within these contextual tensions 'it is possible to state that citizenship is about rights, access and belonging' (Wiener, 1998, pp. 3–4). Despite such difficulties in locating a consensus on the meaning of citizenship, the combined notion of the consumer citizen has appeared in the literature reflecting the rise of the consumer culture since the 1990s; although we should recall that overtones of such a conception are clearly evident in the 'duty' aspect of Barrington's rhyme from the 1930s. In the United Kingdom, one conceptual notion of the consumer citizen emerged from the Conservative government's aim of discrediting 'the social democratic concept of universal citizenship rights ... and ... [replacing] it with a concept of citizenship rights achieved through property ownership and participation in markets' (Gamble, 1988, p. 16). It was in John Major's *Citizens Charter* of 1991, that the duty of consumer citizens, to apply pressure for improved quality, choice, standards and value on those responsible for providing public services, was proposed 'to advance the interests of the individual consumer-citizen' (Harris, 1999, p. 923). It was with the rise of such neo-liberal economic thinking that notions of individualism became associated with the consumer and were reflected in a growing importance for the citizen's role in the market (Powell, Doheny and Greener, 2006, p. 4).

Given that conceptions of both the consumer and the citizen are contentious, and whilst bringing them together may be seen as factoring in a multiplication of the controversies, my argument in this chapter is that such a synthesis can be seen to facilitate a coherent theoretical definition for the consumer citizen: a definition that complements and extends the practical model considered in Chapter 2. In the final sections of this chapter this developed model of consumer citizenship is considered from a constitutional perspective. Beginning with a discussion of whether consumers can constitute a Demos and hold constituent power, these issues are considered in the context of the developing network of new governance structures and organisations that appear to be increasingly entrenched in the process of consumer policy formulation. These are networks of structures and organisations that, together with consumer rights, provide a platform for voice and influence in consumer citizenship practice: a consumer citizenship practice that is being reinforced through EU-wide consumer citizenship education in schools and monitored through the Commission's new, metrics-based, Consumer Markets Scoreboard initiative.

Concepts of the consumer

Providing a definition for the consumer is, as has already been stated, not without its difficulties. Not only does the literature contain numerous variations on the theme but the definitions themselves have evolved over time to emerge as the various adjectival descriptions discussed in Chapter 2. This section develops the discussion of these conflicting definitions, in the context of legal concepts and those drawn from the literature of the social and political scientists before concluding, with a short reflective discussion, on the politicisation of the consumer as a consequence of globalisation.

A problem for law

The notion of the average consumer established a benchmark in case law such that, in determining whether a statement or description designed to promote sales is liable to mislead the purchaser, a 'national court must take into account the presumed expectations which it evokes in an average consumer who is reasonably well informed and reasonably observant and circumspect' (Case C-210/96, paras 30 and 31).[1] This definition has subsequently been refined such that now the average consumer can be depicted as 'informed, observant, and circumspect, but it is also recognised that he or she may have an imperfect understanding of a product purchase and may not even pay attention to some features of the product' (Incardona and Poncibò, 2007, p. 26). This, these authors suggest, is 'no more than the final step in an ECJ process which has developed a judicial portrayal of the consumer as sensible, attentive, and cautious, as well as being able to analyse, critically and discerningly, the messages behind advertising and commercial practices in general'(Incardona and Poncibò, 2007, p. 30).

The general presumption, that consumers will make intelligent choices based on an informed and enquiring approach, echoes the idealistic economic paradigm of the rational consumer in an efficient market, but it fails to reflect the unpredictable realities of individual human behaviour and capability. 'Even well-informed consumers of a high intellectual and educational level...may often base their decisions on custom and feelings rather than on an analytical approach' (Incardona and Poncibò, 2007, p. 35). Consumer detriment may typically arise where consumers make cognitive errors; however, a consequential result of the individualistic nature of modern consumer activity is highlighted by the correspondingly limited cognitive capacity of law: a limitation recognised by Everson who states that the 'law itself [has] proved to be too self-contained an instrument to allow for the coherent translation of economic and political conceptions and constructions of the consumer into a legal framework of regulation' (Everson, 2006, p. 106).

A consequence of this friction between the individualistic nature of the consumer and the limited capacity of the law is perhaps, at least in part, influential in the constant reformation and modernisation of Community consumer protection law. In its Green Paper on the Review of the Consumer *acquis* the Commission acknowledges *inter alia* that the existing consumer protection rules are fragmented such that 'many issues are regulated inconsistently between directives or have been left open' (Commission, 2006d, p. 6). Amongst these issues is the lack of a coherent definition of core terms and, the variation in the definition of consumer that can be found in the various directives of the consumer *acquis*. The Green Paper highlights that

> the Directive on Doorstep Selling defines consumer as a natural person who is acting for purposes 'which can be regarded as outside his trade or profession'. The Directive on Price Indications refers to any natural person 'who buys a product for purposes that do not fall within the sphere of his commercial or professional activity' and the Unfair Contract Terms Directive refers to 'purposes which are outside his trade, business or profession'. (Commission, 2006d, p. 15)

A full comparison of the different notions of consumer in the consumer protection Directives is provided in the Consumer Law Compendium (Schulte-Nölke, Twigg-Flesner and Ebers, 2008, p. 713 *et seq*).[2] The Compendium reaches the conclusion that, whilst the notion of consumer is defined 'using deviating terms' in the various language versions of the directives, they all, with the exception of the Package Travel Directive (Directive (EEC) 90/314) share a common core that provides that a consumer is 'a natural person who is acting for purposes which are outside *some kind* of business, commercial or trade activity'. A definition that the authors of the Compendium suggest can also be found in the European procedural law of the Brussels Convention and the European rules on contractual obligations.[3] The somewhat loose association between the individual (natural person) and *some kind* of business, commercial or trade activity, as suggested in the common core definition provided by the Compendium, fails to convey the nature of the nexus between the *individual* and the *business, commercial or trade activity* that is personalised as 'his' in all the directives with the exception of the anomalous Package Travel Directive. This personal connection is reflected in the recent Payment Services Directive that defines a consumer as 'a natural person who...is acting for purposes other than *his* trade, business or profession' (Directive (EC) 2007/64, Article 4.11). As Advocate General Mischo's opinion in *Di Pinto* states in this regard, 'the interpretation [of the term consumer] given by Mr Di Pinto and the United Kingdom unduly neglects the word 'his' (trade or profession)...It is...the possessive pronoun which is used' (Case C-361/89, AG Opinion, para. 21).

The lack of a coherent definition of consumer is further aggravated by the fact that the Member States use the minimum harmonising character of the directives to extend the vague definitions in different ways. For example, it is again highlighted in the Green Paper:

> when it comes to individuals buying a product to be used both privately and professionally...several Member States have granted natural persons acting for purposes which fall *primarily* outside their trade, business or profession the same protection as consumers. In addition some businesses, such as individual entrepreneurs or small businesses may sometimes be in a similar situation as consumers when they buy certain goods or services which raises the questions whether they should benefit to a certain extent from the same protection provided for to consumers. (Commission 2006d, p. 15, emphasis added)

In response to such observations the Green Paper offers two options for aligning the definition of consumer in the *acquis*. In the first, consumers would be defined as 'natural persons acting for purposes which are outside their trade, business or professions' whilst in the second the notion of consumer 'would be widened to include natural persons acting for purposes falling *primarily* outside...their trade, business and profession'. The conclusion of the Consumer Law Compendium analysis is that the different definitions of the term consumer, as defined in the different legal acts of the Member States, do not necessarily differ from each other in substance. Rather, that difficulty in applying consumer protection legislation arises when a Member State applies different definitions of the consumer within its own transpositions of Union law and when there is a lack of clarity as to which definition should apply (Schulte-Nölke and others, 2008, p. 720).

The Brussels Convention, case law and the economically vulnerable consumer

Article 13 of the Brussels Convention on Jurisdiction and the Enforcement of Judgments in Civil and Commercial Matters of 1968 defines a consumer as a *person* in proceedings that concern a contract concluded for a purpose which can be regarded as being *outside his trade or profession*. This procedural law definition was recently endorsed in *Gruber* (Case C-464/01, para. 30) where the Court held that the purpose of the definition was, *inter alia*, to 'protect the person who is presumed to be in a weaker position than the other party to the contract' (Case C-464/01, para. 39) This is a theme that is also evident in the opinion of Advocate General Jacobs who, in *Gruber*, refers to the Giuliano-Lagarde Report (1980, p. 23) as casting 'further light on the concept'. In the excerpt referred to by the Advocate General the definition of a consumer contract is confirmed as being that corresponding to Article 13 of the Brussels Convention and that '[i]t should be interpreted in the light of its purpose which is to protect the weaker party' (Case C-464/01, AG Opinion, para. 24).

This thematic notion of the consumer as the weaker economic party within the context of the Brussels Convention was also recognised by the Court in *Shearson Lehmann Hutton* where the rationale for the Convention provisions was identified as 'the concern to protect the consumer as the party deemed to be economically weaker and less experienced in legal matters than the other party to the contract' (Case C-89/91, para. 18). Similarly, in *Benincasa*, the Court acknowledged that 'only contracts concluded for the purpose of satisfying an individual's own needs in terms of private consumption come under the provisions designed to protect the consumer as the party deemed to be the weaker party economically' (Case C-269/95, para. 16). Hondius, however, argues to the contrary; he suggests that this notion of the consumer as a 'rather a weak person, hardly able to read a contract, and in need of information about every conceivable item' is not the conception of the consumer in the Community directives, nor that of the Court. Their conception of the consumer, he suggests, is that of 'the well-advised citizen who wishes to make full use of the internal market' (Hondius, 2006, p. 94).

The average consumer of regulatory consumer protection law would be informed, observant and circumspect or, sensible, attentive and cautious, and existing in an efficient market. In contrast, the consumer of procedural consumer law appears weak and in need of the laws' protection from the 'professional' salesman. Such definitions may provide a particular contextual rigour for contractual certainty but the individualistic nature of the consumer is perhaps better reflected in the notion that, in practice, the consumer engages with the market not necessarily in any analytical way, but more according to their individual custom and feelings.

The mapping of the evolution of the European consumer citizen in Chapter 2 adds validity to both the notions of the consumer (as vulnerable and capable) but, drawing on evidence from the social and political sciences, the consumer can be constructed as a much broader figure, still limited to the natural person, but one carrying a degree of environmental and ethical responsibility. A construction in which consumer practices are broken down such that the consumer is described *inter alia* as both chooser and citizen; as capable of both individual and collective action; as a notion contingent with that of the citizen and capable of political and economic action, at local, regional and global levels (Gabriel and Lang, 1995).

A broader conception of the consumer: introducing a social dimension

Clarke and others, identify 'different types and images of the consumer' through history (2007, p. 5). Citing Malpas (and others, 2006) they highlight that there have been times when the consumer has been an object of scorn and criticism as the perceived agent of consumption using up scarce and valuable resource. Whilst this is a criticism rooted in history, it still has a resonance in the environmental and ethical politics of contemporary consumerism. Whilst, citing Trentmann (2001), Clarke and others, identify that a collective organisation of consumer interest around bread and milk in nineteenth-and twentieth-century Britain provided a view of the consumer that 'is somewhat at odds with the current valorisation of the consumer as the highest point of individualism'; they also cite Hilton (2003 and 2006) to make the point that, more recently, collective consumer mobilisations have been identified with 'automobile safety, corporate politics, "McDonaldisation" and economic globalisation' (Clarke and others, 2007, p. 5).

Contemporary political and economic focus has more generally identified the consumer as a chooser; as a potential universal agent, and 'one of the core dynamics of corporate globalism' (Clarke and others, 2007, p. 6). Trentmann suggests, however, that 'the formation of consumers is not much of a problem since it appears as the natural consequence of the growing commodification and creation of desire in market-based capitalism' (Trentmann 2006b, p. 4). This desire underpins the meaning attached to consumerism by Clarke and others, where they suggest it identifies

> the tendency to treat the consumer as an organising figure for policies, processes and practices. As with citizenship, however, the would-be universalism of the consumer proves subject to some social (and spatial) limitations. Most obviously, access to 'one's own money' is profoundly unequally distributed. Consuming... requires money or its proxies. Consuming thus has implications for the organisation of lives such that increasing attention needs to be given to the acquisition of money or its functional substitutes. (Clarke and others, 2007, p. 6)

This definition has the consumer and citizen as contingent figures who, whilst they may also be contested and contradictory figures, are limited by a social membership, of which access to 'one's own money' is but one criteria, with a spatial, or territorial, dimension as another. Within the context of contemporary commodity consumption, Fine asserts that there is both an absence of any social stratification, 'we are all equally consumers (although some are more equal than others)' and that 'the politics of commodity consumption begins with individual as opposed to collective perspectives...[that] *consumer politics is about everyone*' (Fine, 2006, pp. 304–305). It is also at this individual level that the consumer becomes a politicised citizen, with those more predisposed to resist the confines of a role as a simple consumer-purchaser escaping 'from preoccupation with intrinsically constructing their own identity and extrinsically [engaging] with the more distant determinants of consumption'(Fine, 2006, pp. 304–305): a first hint at the influential post-transactional and extra-transactional dimensions of consumer citizenship behaviour that we begin to examine later in this chapter.

Everson and Joerges draw attention to the European consumer as a market actor with economic interests, as confirmed by the unfair business-to-consumer commercial practices directive (Directive 2005/29) and the 'recent judgments of the ECJ [that] point in the same neo-neo-liberal direction' (Everson and Joerges, 2006, citing Case C-481/99, *Heininger* (unfair contract terms) and Case C-402/03, *Skov* (product liability law). They highlight a tension in the argument for an expanding role in consumer citizenship practice in the field of health and safety, highlighted by the reduced opportunity for consumer citizenship practice as a consequence of the technocratic intervention of the European Food Safety Agency: an agency whose role is

> to ensure that consumer confidence...is secured through the open and transparent development of food law and through *public authorities* taking the appropriate steps to inform the public where there are reasonable grounds to suspect that a food may present a risk to health. (Regulation (EC) 178/2002, Recital 22, emphasis added)

They rightly present this as a limited sectoral challenge to consumer citizenship that is argued by them to stem from the impact of globalisation, and to have manifested itself in the dispute, now settled, between the EU and the United States of America, Canada and Argentina on the legitimate use, or otherwise, of genetically modified organisms (GMOs) in foodstuffs (WTO, 2006). This was a limitation to consumer citizenship practice that arose from a specific market dependency on transnational regimes of global free trade in complex and potentially hazardous products and the reliance, in safeguarding the health of consumers, on restrictions requiring an *objective basis in science*. In their conclusion, however, Everson and Joerges identify that any limitation of the role of the consumer citizen is restricted by the constitutional framework in which

> [t]he turn to sound science and expert management in the realm of health and safety is embedded in European-wide communicative networks amongst politically accountable actors *and an ever more active civil society*. The transformation of the European consumer into a citizen is still underway. (Everson and Joerges, 2006, emphasis added)

Globalisation and the rise of the politicised consumer

As with notions of community citizenship that can be traced back beyond the formal introduction of the concept in the Treaty of Maastricht 1991, the consumer, or notions of the consumer and consumerism, have a genesis pre-dating the formal legal recognition of the Union consumer in 1975 (Council, 1975, p. 1). The notion of the consumer can be traced back to the tensions in classical economics of the nineteenth century that held 'production not as a means but an end and consumption not as the ultimate purpose of production but, instead, a threat to it' (Donohue, 2003, p. 2). This American analysis was, however, to be challenged by the paradox of poverty amid plenty, a paradox equally relevant to Europe at that time such that

> [d]espite municipal and social reforms and advances in medical science, life expectancy decreased and social inequalities in life expectancy increased until the latter part of the 19th century. These trends reflected the growth of widespread poverty alongside greater wealth. (Howden-Chapman and Kawachi, 2006)

The Victorian puritanical devotion to hard work, and contempt for indulgence, reinforced the disapproval of consumption as a waste of valuable capital marked a moralistic perspective that was to change. By the first decade of the twentieth century '[e]conomists were giving the same attention to consumption that they had once reserved for production' (Donohue, 2003, p. 115). The linking of poverty with the economics of a past deficit economy had opened the way for consideration of consumption within the new surplus economy of the age. Amongst the protagonists of such change, Simon Patten, political economist and social philosopher, was to offer an early perception of the benefits of transnational consumption, and its contribution to wealth:

> As the people become more prosperous their wants become more varied; and, through the greater variety in their wants, they will seek not only in their own country but also in foreign countries for those commodities which will satisfy their new wants. And, if other nations adhere to a sound national policy, their increased prosperity will lead them also to broaden their consumption, and thus create a demand for the commodities of the first nation. Whatever broadens consumption, therefore, has as a result an increase of foreign trade, through which both parties to the exchange add to their prosperity. (Patten, 2003, p. 14, originally published in 1890)

Such economic perceptions lead to consideration of the notion of globalisation and 'the ongoing process of greater interdependence among countries and their citizens'. Although the term *globalisation* only began to appear from the late 1980s, and ideas of *anti-globalisation* did not appear before 1999 (Fischer, 2003, p. 4), the period between 1870 and 1913 witnessed an earlier period of liberal economic integration. Low tariff barriers, technological development in long-distance transportation, the adoption of appropriate legal institutions, the workings of the gold standard and the spread of industrialisation all supported a momentum in economic convergence. This process of convergence was, however, brought to a sudden end by the two world wars, the socialist revolution and the prevalence of statist ideology that introduced a hiatus lasting through to the present period of globalisation (see Bairoch and Kozul-Wright, 1996).

The beginning of the present period of globalisation coincided with the beginnings of the EU, both emerging from the aftermath of the Second World War. The second half of the twentieth century was to witness a coincident limitation of national sovereignty, general economic growth, a return to a developing global interdependence and a technological revolution. Social researchers seeking to define the character and progress of liberal democracy, particularly in Britain and the USA, were able to draw explicit connections between a perceived weakening of the structures of national representative democracy and growth in the sphere of leisure and private sector consumption. Such research provides an understanding of the intimate, and frequently mutually dependant, nature of this connection between the citizen subjects of democratic politics and the subjects of a commercially driven consumer culture (Mort, 2006, pp. 226 and 241).

Concepts of citizenship

When we turn to consider citizenship we find that it too has always been a contested concept with its meanings dependent on context; we find that whilst it continues to provide a normative basis for the defence of the welfare state, changes in the organisation of global systems have rendered some aspects of the concept of citizenship redundant and obsolete. The reason, Turner suggests, is identified by two contradictory social processes: on the one hand, there are powerful pressures towards regional autonomy and localism whilst, on the other hand, there is a stronger notion of globalism and global political responsibilities. The concept of citizenship is still in a process of change and development and as yet 'we do not possess the conceptual apparatus to express the idea of global membership[:] ... in this context a specifically national identity appears anachronistic' (Turner, 1990, p. 212).

Turner's observations serve well to provide a link between the last section as well as providing a succinct introduction to the issues discussed in this one. It reminds us of the globalisation debate whilst identifying citizenship as a fluid and changing concept. This section starts with a discussion of the rights-based notion of EU citizenship before going on to examine the contestations and complexities of Union citizenship and the additional dimensions brought to the citizenship debate by the European Charter of Fundamental Rights (the Charter).[4] This section concludes by drawing together notions of the individual and belonging, of individual membership, capability and participation. It argues a case for a consumer citizenship practice that can be defined by the relationship between the individual, with his or her constituent *market* power, and the European polity.

Citizenship Rights: the Treaty base and judicial development

It has been suggested that it was in response to concerns about the EU's lack of political legitimacy that the status of 'Citizenship of the Union' was introduced by the Treaty of Masstricht in 1991 as a measure to codify the *economic* rights associated with freedom of movement and to add certain new rights. The new rights encompassed the right for citizens residing in a Member State of which they are not a national to vote in local and European elections on the same basis as nationals, the right to petition the European Ombudsman or Parliament on Union matters, and the right to the same diplomatic protection as nationals from all Member States when outside the EU. However, in their paper advocating a model of European citizenship that entailed multiple identities and loyalties, Bellamy and Warleigh, assert that there is little in the Treaty that 'facilitates the involvement of citizens with the actual process of European decision-making'(2009, p. 3). Based on data from 1998 (Eurobarometer, 1998), they argue that the Union's ability to offer a common economic and regulative framework is reliant on the need to build 'some sense of participating in a collective European enterprise', that there is need for

> a plausible way for the European peoples to be citizens of Europe, having a joint responsibility for developing and implementing collective policies, without assuming they must share a deep identity as European citizens. (Bellamy and Warleigh, 2009, p. 4)

The nature of a rights-based citizenship rests, they argue, on the universal rights of all individuals: that, in this context, individuals are more important than communities or groups and that democracy plays an instrumental, but subsidiary, role as an aid to the protection of these individual rights.

European citizens already enjoyed a wide range of civil, political and market rights such that if Union *citizenship* rights were to be distinguished from the rights conferred on *citizens* of the Union by Article 20(2) TFEU then '[a]s citizenship goes, Union Citizenship has an anemic content' (Follesdal, 2001, p. 314). The formalisation of Union citizenship was not, with the exception of the new rights mentioned above, a new policy innovation. It was merely the beginning of a new stage in the development of the status of the individual under Union law within an ongoing process of the constitutionalisation of free movement and the right to non-discrimination on the ground of nationality (Shaw 1997b, p. 556). Analysis of this development takes place with the recognition that although there is a focus on citizenship, its meaning remains vague. The Treaty highlighted the contrast between the individual and his or her relationship with, on the one hand, the Union and on the other hand, his or her Member State. Across this divide, citizenship embraces a psychological dimension that, together with a legal dimension, is parasitic on its political and economic dimension (Barber, 2002). Nationalist perspectives combine with political realities to ensure citizenship at the Union level remains contentious. Even then, the conceptual difficulties of citizenship do not embrace all of the issues, the notion of citizenship itself is exclusionary and yet its psychological, legal, economic and political dimensions also have a relevance to those legally resident third country nationals who fall outside it.

The introduction of the formal citizenship provisions in the Treaty prompted a significant amount of debate as to its substance and, amongst these commentators, Warleigh outlined the main areas of this debate in a table offering both 'thick' and 'thin' conceptions of Union citizenship (Warleigh, 2001, p. 24). Warleigh's 'thin' conception of citizenship also suggests that the Treaty provisions of Articles 20 to 25 TFEU (Articles 17 to 22 EC) added little to the value of the citizenship *acquis* existing at the time, arguably, one that had been developing with a significant input from the Court since the mid-1950s. Alternatively, the elements comprising his 'thick' conception provided a more optimistic model against which a developed concept of citizenship can be assessed.

To a large degree many of the substantive aspects of Union citizenship, particularly with regard to the free movement of persons, had already been developed by the time the formal Treaty provisions came into force. Development of the concept of citizenship did not, however, stop with the Treaty of Maastricht 1991 but continues through to the present. These developments, as with the developing concepts of the consumer appear evolutionary, marking a gradual change from the promotion of non-discrimination on the ground of nationality and freedom of movement rights for the economically active, to the recognition of free movement as a fundamental right for all citizens and the realisation of political rights for the individual at the European level. While citizenship case law, in the context of the formal Treaty provisions, is limited to Articles 20, 21 and 22 TFEU (Articles 17, 18 and 19 EC) it provides support for the notion that even 'thick' conceptions of citizenship are constructs of their time and require regular refining and updating.

After the Treaty of Maastricht 1991 the Court began to shift its policy approach, at least in some sectors of the market, from the removal of obstacles to free trade to one of positive integration more closely linked to the notion of *political citizenship*. Community provisions were established, with regard to access to public welfare that national governments could be obliged to comply with; the right to welfare benefit was recognised by the Court to rest solely on the basis of Union citizenship and the nexus between the non-discrimination provisions of Article 18 TFEU (Article 12 EC) and those citizenship rights confirmed by Articles 20 to 23 TFEU (Articles 17 to 20 EC). From non-discrimination the Court moved on to establish the principle of proportionality in its interventions between Member States and their own nationals, its judgments reflecting the wider debate over the replacement of the nationality criterion for welfare benefits by residency requirements.

Principles of equal treatment and objectivity have appeared in the case law now emerging in actions that have focussed on the explicit political provisions of Article 22 TFEU (Article 19 EC), whilst much of the Court's earlier developments have been codified in the new 'Citizenship Directive' (Directive (EC) 2004/38). Increased population mobility and an expanding Union membership, together with the Court's development of a policy approach to citizenship along a series of principles suggest an ongoing role for the Court. History also suggests that the Court will lead in addressing the complex rights issues relevant to residency and the focus that it will bring to the status of legally resident third country nationals.

Citizenship: a contested and complex concept

The Court has continued to develop and define the substantive nature of individual EU citizenship rights but the notion of citizenship remains both a contested and complex concept (Maas, 2007, p. 2). Historically, there has been some general scholastic agreement, a common understanding, that citizenship was linked, in one way or another, to the state or nation state: a common understanding that was 'dramatically challenged' with the formal establishment of Union citizenship when the Treaty of Maastricht 1993 came into force.

It has already been suggested that a notion of European citizenship, albeit in 'an incipient form', had been present in the Treaties stretching back to the European Coal and Steel Community of 1951 (Olsen, 2006, p. 1). As a contested concept however, citizenship has generated a vast literature and 'means different things in different contexts' (Wiener, 1998, p. 3). Aron found no difficulty in stating explicitly that 'there are no such animals as 'European citizens'...[t]here are only French, German or Italian citizens' (Aron, 1974, cited in Olsen, 2006). Lecca (1990) also emphasised the connection between nationality and citizenship but with the link derived from sociological and ideological, rather than logical, reasoning. Meehan (1993, p. 4) highlights that Heater (1990) had recognised both Lecca's socially contextual concept and a broader contestable notion of citizenship proposed by Van Gunsteren that identified

> from very early in its history the term [citizenship] already contained a cluster of meanings...[that] may also lead us to question the modern assumption that the status [of citizenship] necessarily adheres to the sovereign nation state. [It] can be associated with any geographical unit from a small town to the whole globe itself. (Van Gunsteren, 1978, p. 163)

Wiener has also acknowledged the contestable nature of citizenship that varies from the basic notion of citizenship, as an aspect of membership of a community, to more complex notions of citizenship that comprise 'an understanding of intersubjectively shared practices that contribute to democratic changes of and within a community' (Wiener, 1998, p. 4).

There is then a complexity to the concept of citizenship that Wiener asserted was, on the basis of conceptual and historical approaches to citizenship, about civil, political and social rights, access to political participation and belonging in the context of rootedness in a community. The challenge to the notion that citizenship was to be linked, *in one way or another*, to the nation state was not, however, solely based on the desire for ever closer integration in the EU. The development of a new era of globalisation, particularly since the mid-1970s, has provided a new challenge to the cultural and economic notions of the citizen–state relationship. Meehan, in considering liberal ideas of human relations, acknowledged that 'the more that cultural and economic transactions take place on a global scale, the more states and competition between them become redundant'. She cites Turner's structural reference to the *globalisation of citizenship* and draws on his arguments to provide an analysis identifying that,

> on the one hand, international economic trends have diminished the capacities of nation-states to respond to the demands of their citizens. On the other hand, modern global communications facilitate widespread knowledge of what is possible elsewhere, thereby informing domestic conceptions of the rights of citizenship, raising demands or dampening them according to knowledge of successes and failures in other systems. (Meehan, 1993, p. 8)

At the same time, a set of rights was developing at the Community level attaching a legal status to a conception of the *economic citizen*. Firstly, under the Community's economic policy objectives promoting free movement, national restrictions on the factors of production and their deployment were reformulated as economic *rights* rather than economic instruments. Secondly, the Court was able to expand and develop these rights and to challenge discriminatory national legislation. From as early as the 1960s the Court was enforcing the principle of non-discrimination in relation to the right to freedom of movement for individuals in their role as 'workers' (for example, Case 6/66, *Labots*) and by the 1980s was explicitly recognising the notion of Community citizenship in relation to free movement rights. The concept of the European economic citizen was developing such that in *Heinrich Wolf* the Court held

> [t]he provisions of the Treaty relating to the free movement of persons are thus intended to facilitate the pursuit by *Community citizens* of occupational activities of all kinds throughout the Community, and *preclude national legislation* which might place Community citizens at a disadvantage when they wish to extend their activities beyond the territory of a single Member State. (Joined Cases, 154 and 155/87, para. 13, emphasis added)

The Court was not limiting itself merely to the rhetoric of citizenship. As Downes suggests, the substantive nature of the rights developed by the Court were much more like the kinds of rights that we associate with the status of citizenship. Freedom of movement rights for individuals, even if they were not engaged in true market activity, did not arise out of any identified status of citizenship, in origin they were economic or market-related (Downes, 2001, p. 94). These are developments that can be placed both within the experience of modern forms of neo-liberalism and nineteenth-century economic orthodoxy. On the one hand there is an explicit commitment to the internal market and recognition of the benefits of competition associated with the idea of consumer sovereignty, and on the other the recognition that the benefits of competition extend to an understanding that 'competition can only serve the consumer interest when it is [subject to] a feasible and stable regime [and] when it is not vitiated by consumer ignorance' (Winch, 2006, p. 31). The fundamental character of the free movement provisions are exposed by the Court in *Receveur des Douanes* where any actions by the Community that infringed the free movement rules would be a form of

> prejudice to what the community has achieved in relation to the unity of the market [that] moreover risks opening the way to mechanisms which would lead to disintegration contrary to the objectives of progressive approximation of the economic policies of the Member States set out in Article 2 of the Treaty. (Joined Cases 80 and 81/77, para. 36)[5]

Beginning in the 1970s, the vision of a politically integrated Europe began to emerge 'capable of transcending economic integration and addressing the social rights deficit' (Kenner, 2003, p. 6). This 'political imagination' incorporated a formative notion of citizenship based on the recognition and protection of rights, including economic and social rights (Ward, 2001, cited in Kenner, 2003). The economic base of Community citizenship rights developed coincident with the burgeoning notions of the active consumer and the consumer citizen, 'a creative, confident and rational being articulating personal identity and serving the public interest' (Trentmann, 2006b, p. 2). The evolving concept of an individualistic economic citizenship that was, from the beginning of the second half of the twentieth century, to appear 'everywhere from rational choice economics to environmental discourse and from public policy to marketing and cultural studies' (Trentmann, 2006, p. 2). A developing concept that, as Balibar identified, placed us

> in the middle of a historical crossroads, only partially and reluctantly acknowledged ... [T]he fact [is] that these issues typically illustrate a

global-local problem...The contradictory and evolutionary pattern of 'European'...statutory, ascriptive citizenship in a sense is a *reaction* to real and imaginary effects of globalisation. (Balibar, 2004, pp. 123–124)

European citizenship: individuality and capability

The Charter of Fundamental Rights of the European Union provides for extensive social rights, in particular in the areas of equality and solidarity.[6] In its Preamble, the Charter provides that the Union 'places the *individual* at the heart of its activities, by establishing the citizenship of the Union and by creating an area of freedom of, security and justice' (emphasis added). In its French version Salais highlights that the Charter speaks of "the person" rather than '"the individual" but emphasises that 'the person' is more in France and in English, than a pure atomistic individual. The notion incorporates the fact that a person lives in society and is in complex interaction with others, which shapes her identity' (Salais, 2005).

The appearance of the Charter in 2000 followed a decade of overlapping conferences at the intergovernmental level (IGCs) and semi-annual European Council sessions. These almost continuous meetings resulted, on the one hand, in the meta-constitutional authorisation of extended Union competence to areas such as health, education and protection against discrimination and, on the other hand, in quasi-constitutional operational innovations for new governance mechanisms such as the Open Method of Coordination (OMC) (Cohen and Sabel, 2003, p. 349). Introduced subsequent to this intensive period of integrational debate the Charter finally gained the 'same legal value as the Treaties' with the entry into force of the Treaty of Lisbon in 2009.

The individualistic nature of the Charter is emphasised in its provision on human dignity (Article 1), based on the 1948 Universal Declaration of Human Rights, and the recognition of dignity of the human person as the real basis of human rights. The economic freedom to choose an occupation and engage in work is extended to *everyone* by Article 15(1) and rests on the case law of the Court developed *inter alia* in *Nold* (Case 4/73, paras 12 to 14), *Hauer* (Case 44/79) and *Keller* (Case 234/85, para. 8). This freedom is not unfettered and a distinction is drawn between Article 15(2), which provides that 'the freedom to seek employment, to work, to exercise the right of establishment and to provide services in any Member State' is extended only to Union citizens[7] and Article 15(3), which provides that '[n]ationals of third countries who are authorised to work in the territories of the Member States are entitled to working conditions equivalent to those of citizens of the Union'. This is a distinction that raises a question over the exclusive nature of citizenship, and in particular that of economic citizenship: where Article 15(2) defines a membership boundary for access to its rights provisions, that citizenship boundary is weakened, or 'thinned out' by the equivalence requirement of Article 15(3) and the broad application of Article 15(1) (see Ferrera, 2005a, p. 16).

Significantly, the Charter provides for an equal constitutional recognition of social rights, with civil, political and economic rights, that Deakin and Browne recognise as 'following a practice which can be traced back to the case law of the...Court' (2003, p. 27). They cite *inter alia*, *Defrenne* v *Sabena* (Case 43/74) regarding equal pay and *United Kingdom* v *Council (Working Time)* (Case C-84/94) regarding health and safety, noting that 'the Court has consistently emphasised that the social goals of the EC Treaty do not have to yield to the economic objective of an integrated internal market', rather that 'the European market order can be said to incorporate a set of core social rights' (Deakin and Browne, 2003, p. 27).

The thrust of their argument is that the welfare state and the market function well together, that traditional interpretations of the meanings of the term 'social rights', as developed in T H Marshall's classic threefold distinction between civil, political and social rights (1950), and Hayek's critical analysis of social legislation (1980), fail to account for the 'market constituting' or 'market-creating' role of social rights. The basis of this argument is that social rights underpin the redistributive and protective rules of labour law and welfare that are essential preconditions for the market to work. Without these social rights, extremes of inequality would exclude certain groups from the market and deprive them from access to goods; unable to take part in the system of exchange, the rest of society suffers as resources which could have been mobilised for its benefit remain unutilised (Deakin and Browne, 2003, p. 33).

Where social rights manifest themselves as immediate claims on resources they can be seen as 'the equivalent of commodities which individuals can convert into potential or actual functionings' (Deakin, 2005, p. 22): functionings that, in this context equate to the concept of individual capability, and that the Supiot Report (1999) argued (in the context of labour market participation) would help to provide a basis for a real freedom of choice. The concept of 'capability', developed by Amartya Sen,[8] provides a 'broad normative framework for the evaluation and assessment of individual well-being and social arrangements, the design of policies and proposals about social change in society' (Robeyns, 2005). It is a tool within which such phenomena as poverty, inequality or well-being can be conceptualised and evaluated through a 'focus on what people are effectively able to do and to be' (Robeyns, 2005). At its core the capability approach provides a focus on individual capabilities, on what people are able to do and able to be, it

> offers a response, based on the market-creating function of the rules of social law. In order to participate effectively in a market order, individuals require more than formal access to the institutions of property and contract. They need to be provided with the economic means to realise their potential. (Deakin, 2005, pp. 6 and 7)

The capability concept also recognises *inter alia* that economic resources alone are not sufficient for the individual to be able to exercise their ability to achieve a particular set of functionings. Effective participation in the market, in the context of consumer citizenship practice, can be improved with a relevant knowledge of consumer rights and individual consumer responsibilities. The foundations of this knowledge are being established through formal consumer education, and specifically consumer education of the young that, as a policy objective of the Commission, has become a social norm, entrenched within the school curriculum, in all Member States.

Taking stock: accommodating the European consumer citizen

The discussions of the consumer and the citizen above have touched on aspects of both theory and law; they have examined the challenges and contestations of both concepts as they have developed over time. The question now addressed is whether aspects of these two distinct traditions can be conflated in order to derive a coherent legal concept of consumer citizenship.

It is clear that both traditions have social and political dimensions and share many characteristics that have developed in the face of a changing economic, technological and political landscape. Both traditions in the European dimension share conceptions that are varied or vague and have a complexity that the law finds difficult to define. Both share an economic rights-based core but both are also subject to a wider rights regime embracing social and political rights and both are conceptually and practically challenged by aspects of globalisation.

Taken separately, they are traditions that lack coherent definitions but taken together they appear as contingent concepts confined by the same social and spatial limitations.

The parallels are significant, although individually the traditions lack a conceptual coherence that the hypothesis underpinning the question demands. Conflated into the narrower concept of consumer citizenship my argument is that the two traditions are able to assume a legitimacy that has come about through a convergence of ideology and perception of the market from both the political left and right.

The left has sought to shift the paradigm of the consumer towards that of the citizen, it has

> sought to enlarge the consumer into a responsible consumer, a socially-aware consumer, a consumer who thinks ahead and tempers his or her desires by social awareness, a consumer whose actions must be morally defensible and who must occasionally be prepared to sacrifice personal pleasure to communal well-being. (Gabriel and Lang, 1995, pp. 175–176)

In contrast, the right is argued to have sought to shift the paradigm of the citizen towards that of the consumer, where consumers vote in the marketplace, such that,

> the marketplace becomes surrogate for political discourse ... [t]he citizen is being redefined as a purchaser whose 'ballots ... help create and maintain the trading areas' ... [b]uying becomes tantamount to voting, market surveys the nearest we have to a collective will. (Gabriel and Lang, 1995, p. 176, citing Dickinson and Hollander, 1991, p. 12 and Ewen, 1992, p. 23)

The approach to these movements may be marked by political contrast and opposing perceptions but the resulting models of consumer citizenship and of the political-market-space which consumer citizenship occupies provide further reference points for exploring the coherence of the consumer citizenship concept. In the following sections of this chapter the hypothesis for a coherent model of consumer citizenship is tested by exploring the role of the European consumer beyond the transactional domain; into the domain of post-transactional and extra-transactional empowerment. It considers whether individuals, acting as consumers, can constitute a Demos through a post-modern form of collective citizenship and discusses what, if any, constitutional attribution can be associated with the evolution of the consumer citizen described above. Emergent structures of new governance are identified that can be associated with the concept of constituent consumer citizenship and its constitutional entrenchment: an entrenchment identified in the organisational architecture of consumer policy formulation and the educational focus given to consumer empowerment.

Constitutionalising European consumer citizenship

In his consideration of European constitutionalism in 1997, Weiler reviewed the constitutional thesis that claimed that in critical aspects; the Community had evolved, behaving as if its founding instrument were not a 'normal' treaty of international law but a constitutional charter governed by a form of constitutional law. He asserted that constitutionalism was both 'inevitable and profound', with economic, social and political programmes 'written in' and 'written for' a constitutional setting and suggested that 'the single most important [narrative]…in the process that transformed the EC treaties from a set of legal arrangements binding only upon sovereign states, was the rendering of individuals…subjects of the law' (Weiler, 1997, p. 98).

Weiler identified constitutionalism as 'but a prism through which one can observe a landscape in a certain way…an intellectual construct' (Weiler, 1997, p. 99), where the success of the construct 'would depend not only, or even primarily, on the utterances of the European Court but on their acceptance by national actors, mainly courts, and principally national constitutional courts' (Weiler, 1997, p.101). The discourse in this book has, so far, concentrated on the evolving role of individuals acting as consumers, both alone and collectively, in the internal market: an evolution that has been evidenced through developments in policy, legislation and judgments of the Court. These are developments that have extended European law through positive administrative measures that, according to Majone's notion of a European 'regulatory state' (1994),

> focus on risk-regulation in matters…where expert knowledge is paramount and where accountability is served by administrative law measures aimed at transparency and enhanced participation in decision-making by interested and knowledgeable parties rather than the volatile preferences of broad representative institutions. (Walker, 2007, p. 253)

The consumer as Demos? Consumer citizenship and the constitutional actor

In practice, the scope of EU citizenship has developed from an original 'market citizenship' (Everson, 1995, p. 73) to embrace an as yet under-developed social citizenship and an emerging political citizenship associated with the free movement rules (Maduro, 2000, p. 352). Maduro associates this 'evolving notion of citizenship' with an expression taken from Peebles of a 'community of economic circulation' (Peebles, 1997) and Everson's 'market citizen'. This is an evolving notion of citizenship in which the specific of the Demos is identified by those 'rights granted to individuals as participants and beneficiaries of economic integration' (Maduro, 2000, p. 359). This section argues that for the consumer, as the grantee of rights and a participating beneficiary of economic integration, consumer citizenship can be explained in terms of opportunity and power, of the capacity to influence and change law and policy through, on the one hand, representative and expert network structures of new governance and, on the other hand, the market through direct action in the form of complaints, enforcement of consumer rights, redress, switching and ethical buying.

Walker has identified that '[p]olitically, the conditions do not exist for making of a transnational demos' (2007, p. 259), yet he is able to identify additional ways in which constituent power may be invoked by 'the people' as *subjects*, as *legislators*, as *editors* and as *reflexive interpreters* (Walker, 2007, p. 263). This leaves open to revision the image of what constitutes the European citizen through, as suggested by Haltern, the 'coming to terms with the market citizen' (2002, p. 2) and, at the same time, to align Walker's references for constituent power with the empowered behaviours of consumer citizenship practice. Walker's reference to the people as *subjects* is premised on the acknowledgement of people as members of the political community that 'helps to engage their ongoing or even retrospective claim as putative authors and as beneficiaries of a democratically responsive system of government' (Walker, 2007, p. 263). There is, however, a major obstacle that needs to be overcome in pursuing this aspect of constituent power, and that lies in the *complete indifference* of European citizens to the European Union (Haltern, 2002, p. 20).

Haltern suggests that the Union's attempts to overcome the alienation of its citizens are best understood from the perspective of consumer aesthetics: consumer aesthetics that, according to Haltern, lack any substance, but provide a cultural disguise or camouflage to protect citizens from seeing themselves as consumers or belonging to a consumerist culture, they 'shore up our sense of selfhood and individuality, which have been deeply compromised by the conditions of urban society'. The mechanism for such delusion, he suggests, lies in the marketing of individuality and rebelliousness through advertising strategies adopted on the principles of 'cuteness, zaniness, coolness and idyllic quaint-ness' in popular culture. Such consumer aesthetics provide, however, something of a bleak and one dimensional description of post-modern consumer culture that appears at odds with the notions of the active, responsible and involved consumer discussed above; consumption is both a broader and deeper activity than mere high street shopping and its aesthetic veneer of 'ineffectual strategies of rebellion' (Haltern, 2002, pp. 22–23).

It is broader in the sense that a post-modern consumer-centred model of market choice has developed beyond the high street, it is as equally applicable to services of general interest, the public sector and even the social welfare sectors of the market. It is deeper, and this appears to be implicitly and partially acknowledged by Haltern, in that there has been a transformation of the citizen into the consumer that has been accompanied by a shifting mode of governance 'that involves the simultaneous remaking of subjects (citizens to consumers), sites (from state institutions to plural and competing agencies) and practices (from bureau-professionally structured delivery to choice) (Clarke and others, 2007, p.148). Haltern cites Bauman (1992), 'it is the consumer activity which makes me into the individual' before concluding that

> European citizenship cannot be defined through essentialist human rights, or exclusive demands on loyalty. It is very much the question whether or not it makes sense to craft social rights on to a laissez-faire economic framework that is indifferent, perhaps even hostile to T.H. Marshall's concept of social citizenship... There are signs that the two domains are increasingly being conflated, with 'consumers' and 'citizens' becoming essentially one and the same thing. (Haltern, 2002, p. 33)

Walker's reference to people as legislators and as editors rests on 'popu-lar involvement in parliamentary and other mechanisms of the law-making process' and 'participating in the process of continual revision' (Walker, 2007, p. 263). Such participation takes place through civil dia-logue as a mechanism of participatory democracy in a political net-work of consumer advocacy NGOs at Member State level and a sectoral platform of representative and advisory consumer organisations at the

European level. For European consumers this is a network that has increasingly become entrenched within the European consumer policy process and that, for the consumer citizen, acting as the reflexive interpreter, provides the potential for a developing framework of continuous self-governance.

Governance, consumer power and constitutionalisation

The Commission recognises 'governance' as a versatile term originating in the contemporary social sciences, especially economics, in the context of corporate governance, and in political science, in the context of state governance. As an overall concept, the term 'governance' takes from these diverse meanings and is applied to the exercise of power not covered by the traditional notion of 'government'. 'Governance' corresponds, the Commission suggests, to 'the so-called post-modern form of economic and political organisation' (Commission, 2011b).

Della Sala associates these economic and political structures of governance, and in particular the displacement of national governance by supranational governance, with that of globalisation. Both, he suggests, contribute to processes that challenge traditional structures of political monopoly and include *inter alia* 'other levels of formal government [and] parts of civil society (especially markets)'. Many governance arguments, he suggests, 'including those that look at the European Union, fail to deal with fundamental questions about power and its legitimate use'. Erosion of power and of national autonomy, as a consequence of globalisation, has already been raised in the context of the Commission's current strategy to change the focus of EU policy towards that of the consumer, as has the rise of the politicised consumer. Where globalisation has displaced political authority, away from the nation state, a new modern manner of governance is emerging in which the boundaries between public and private authority has become blurred (Della Sala, 2001, p. 2).

Traditional structures of economic, social and political power, as mechanisms for solving problems of governance, are being replaced in what has been described as 'a "post-political" search for regulation and accountability' (Della Sala, 2001, p. 3, citing Hirst, 2000). Governance arguments, Della Sala suggests,

> challenge the notion that the *demos* is a permanent community defined by territory…The relevant political community changes constantly, and individuals are not constrained by an exclusive membership…They promote the idea of the individual belonging to many different *demos*. (Della Sala, 2001, pp. 3–4)

The emphasis in such ideas of governance is concerned with relationships, processes networks and organisation of collective action; it is about multi-level regimes with many centres of competing authority that have emerged, or are emerging, as a consequence of ending the monopoly of traditional power mechanisms. Such new ways of organisation are divorced from territorial or exclusive political belonging and are founded on individual choice of authority, a choice that results from a pluralism of forces of new associations in civil society (Della Sala, 2001, p. 6, citing Hirst, 1997). If such choice is not to lead to an unlimited downward pressure on regulatory competition the argument for governance, through associative democracy, rests on 'a level of openness and participation that is determined largely by who is affected by decisions... [and where,] [w]hat creates a sense of cohesion is a shared interest amongst the various stakeholders' (Della Sala, 2001, p. 8).

Della Sala provides a critique of such participatory and inclusive governance arguments and draws attention *inter alia* to their participatory limitations, although he suggests that 'the debate about citizenship in multi-level governance is perhaps most advanced in the EU' (Della Sala, 2001, p. 9). In the EU it is the Commission alone that makes legislative and policy proposals,[9] limiting access to decision-making at policy level through structural and systematic constraints. Yet, in its White Paper on European Governance the Commission undertook to help reinforce a culture of consultation and dialogue in the Community (Commission, 2001b). This may not provide a complete basis for a new style democratic legitimacy but in the context of consumer citizenship this appears to be drawing individuals, as representatives of consumer associations, into the locus of the political community. It provides the constitutional platform for elements of citizenship practice that were identified by Wiener (1998) and who, with Della Sala, concluded that

> citizens have begun to engage with their political elites in a process that seeks to define their rights, access to them and who they are as citizens... [in] a process that may enshrine the constitutive elements of citizenship practice. The result is a democratic surplus as citizens seek ways to be part of the constitution-building process. (Wiener and Della Sala, 1997, p. 611)

Initially, the Commission's White Paper was criticised by the EESC, as the 'institutionalised representative of organised civil society', for omitting to mention *inter alia* consumer protection (EESC, 2002). This specific omission has, more recently, been addressed through the Commission's Decision to set up a *stakeholder dialogue group* in the areas of public health and consumer protection (Decision (EC) 2007/602). This initiative can be seen as part of the practical response from the Commission to develop the wide and inclusive participation in policy development that it identified as one of the principles of good governance in the White Paper. For the stakeholder dialogue group its role is limited to merely advising on how to improve the stakeholder consultation process, it has no remit to discuss policy initiatives. This is, however, in the area of consumer policy, another step in a process by which complex governance structures that embrace civil society already exist and provide a platform for consumer citizenship practice.

Entrenching the consumer policy process and new governance

In October 2003 the Commission issued its decision to establish the European Consumer Consultative Group (ECCG) as a body representative of non-governmental, non-profit making and independent national consumer organisations. Article 169 TFEU (Article 153 EC) was identified as the legal base within the framework of consumer protection for the Commission 'to consult consumers on problems concerning the protection of their interests at Community level' (Decision (EC) 2003/709, Recital 1). The Decision acknowledged that, with the accession of new Member States and a lack of conformity in the definitions of consumer organisations in the legislation, the political and legal framework was in an evolutionary state. A key objective of the decision was an explicit requirement to increase the transparency and efficiency of the ECCG and to set out the rules and definitions for participatory membership (Decision (EC) 2003/709, Recital 4).

The Decision has all the hallmarks of the 'new governance' structures of policy process that 'tend to be grouped under the label of the open method of co-ordination' (de Búrca, 2003, p. 815). These are governance structures in which de Búrca succinctly identifies the paradoxical constitutional character revealed by the tension between on the one hand, the reality of such reflexive and pragmatic 'new governance' structures, with a profound degree of variety in the sharing of competence between levels and sites of decision-making, that sit alongside the formal structures of government, and, on the other hand, the powerful political attachments to traditional 'high' forms of constitutionalism focussed on limited EU powers and the shaping of an effective and visible EU government (de Búrca, 2003, p. 814).

The structures of this pragmatic 'new governance' method, de Búrca suggests, can be identified in the practices of the network of permanent committees and informal or temporary bodies that service the Commission and Council in their legislative capacity. There are, however, difficulties in attempting to understand such *infranational* structures in conventional constitutional terms. These difficulties, in which the emergence of *infranationalism* 'as a central figure of Community governance [in which] increasingly large sectors of Community norm creation are done at a meso-level of governance', are discussed by Weiler (1999, p. 98). He suggests that infranationalism is neither constitutional nor unconstitutional, it is simply outside of the constitution and 'characterised by the relative unimportance of the national element in decision making ... [that] [t]echnical expertise, economic and social interests, and administrative turf battles shape the process and outcome rather than "national interest"' (Weiler, 1999, p. 272).

Infranational governance structures may be, as Weiler suggests, extra-constitutional but, in the area of consumer policy, two of the formal organs of European government, the European Parliament and the Council have established a programme of funding that has effectively entrenched such a network of committees, associations and representative organisations in the policy process. First appearing in 2004, a general framework for financing Community actions in support of consumer policy was introduced with the strategic objective of supporting 'a new and economic social agenda ... and ensuring a better quality of life for Europe's citizens' (Decision (EC) 2004/20, Recital 1). The explicit purpose of the framework was to 'support and build the capacity of organisations and bodies which work to promote consumer interests at Community, national or regional level' (Decision (EC) 2004/20, Recital 6). In addition, the Commission was to ensure that consumer organisations and other relevant NGOs could contribute to the development and implementation of consumer policy, and other Community policies affecting consumer interests, through their involvement in the work of the ECCG (Decision (EC) 2004/20, Recital 7 and Article 3(c)).

The general framework was replaced at the end of 2006 by a programme of Community action, running through to 2013. The new Decision ensures a continuation of funding and provides that such support should not be subject to the principle of gradual decrease of the extent of Community support (Decision (EC) 2006/1926, specifically Recital 5). The objectives of the first Decision are reflected in its successor with both Decisions intending to achieve better consultation and representation of consumers' interests through the collection, exchange, and analysis of data and information. This is data and information that is to be sourced from *inter alia* surveys of consumers, collection and analysis of consumer complaints and collection and analysis of data on cross-border business-to-consumer trade and markets. Actions of individual consumer citizenship are thus extended, from the transactional domain of the active, ethical and responsible purchaser of consumer goods and services discussed in Chapter 2. They now extend into empowered post-transactional or extra-transactional activities and the exercising of consumer rights: of complaining and switching; of pursuing enforcement actions; of engaging with consumer market surveys and of joining and lobbying consumer organisations at the national level.

Theory and practice: initiatives for the development of consumer citizenship

Having considered the development of the notion of consumer citizenship, and discussed its theoretical and constitutional basis, the discourse of this book is now developed to consider the post-transactional, and extra-transactional, roles that have been developed for the consumer citizen. It is a role that has been provided with an organisational framework for influencing policy in which the exercise of the *relationship* between the individual and the polity/community completes the constitutive elements of citizenship (Wiener, 1998, p. 22). It is relationship nurtured by a consumer education policy that is focussed in particular on young consumers and one in which the consumer dimension is increasingly being integrated into the machinery of market monitoring.

Networks and structures of European consumer policy governance

Empowerment and enforcement provide the two channels that underpin European consumer policy and the institutional environment that it has created. The two channels are interlinked and interdependent; they are established on a framework of EU and national Member State legislation, on consumer policy and on a network of institutions, but they also rely on the actions of empowered consumers for

> the smooth functioning of markets as they reward suppliers that operate fairly and best respond to consumers' needs. Empowered consumers have the capacities to understand and process the information available to them. They know their rights and they exercise these rights. They are willing to pro-actively seek information, to

complain when faced by a problem and to seek redress when their rights are violated. They also know the institutions and organisations available to help them or know how to find the information they need. (Commission, 2009c, Part 3, p. 1)

The definition has clear resonance with the concept of consumer citizenship discussed in this book. The institutions and organisations of European policy governance are continuing to develop to accommodate the increasingly citizenship-like role of the consumer and to meet the challenges of the changing political and market environments. These are challenges that, the Commission suggests, flow from the increasing sophistication of retail markets; the growth in services and liberalised services in particular; the increasingly interlinked nature of goods and services; the internet, digitalisation and growth in e-commerce; and globalisation of production (Commission, 2007a, pp. 3–4).

The Commission asserts that EU Consumer policy is central to addressing these challenges, that it can address the problems that individuals lack the capacity to tackle and create the environment in which consumers can make rational choices and take on *responsibility* to promote their own interests. The developing model of consumer policy governance reflects this growing individual and collective consumer responsibility, as well as the primary objectives of the Consumer Policy Strategy that seek to

> empower EU consumers. [Because] [p]utting consumers in the driving seat benefits citizens but also boosts competition significantly... To enhance EU consumers' welfare [because] [c]onsumer welfare is at the heart of well-functioning markets. [And] [t]o protect consumers effectively from the serious risks and threats that they cannot tackle as individuals. (Commission, 2007a, pp. 5–6)

The Commission's implementation of consumer policy involves the development of legislative and other actions that actively support consumer organisations, enhance the role of consumer representation in decision-making and complement the development of consumer policy at Member State level. Figure 3.1 is intended to provide a generic overview of the governance networks and structures of consumer policy: an attempt to graphically represent the framework that is becoming embedded within the European internal market and in which the consumer citizen is able to influence policy through empowerment and enforcement actions.

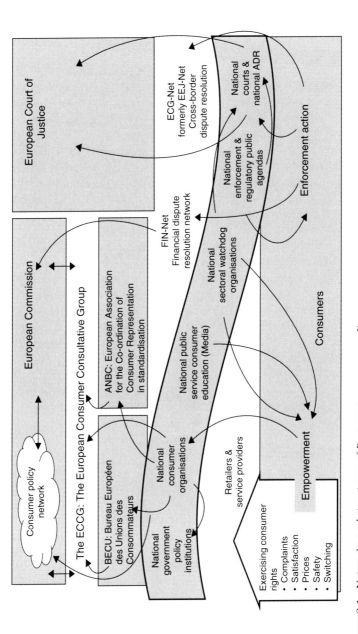

Figure 3.1 Networks and structures of European consumer policy governance

In 2003 the European Consumer Consultative Group (ECCG) was created as the Commission's main forum of consultation with national and European consumer organisations (Decision (EC) 2003/709). It constitutes a forum for general discussions on consumer-related problems; provides opinion on the protection of consumer interests; advises and guides the Commission on policy and activity having an effect on consumers and informs the Commission on Member State consumer policy developments. It provides *inter alia* a representative voice for one national consumer organisation per country and for each of the European consumer organisations, Bureau Européen des Unions des Consommateurs (BEUC) and European Association for the Coordination of Consumer Representation in Standardisation (ANEC). The convergence of hitherto discrete policy areas is reflected in the make-up of the ECCG forum that is attended by Commission representatives from the Directorates-General responsible for Health and Consumers, Information Society, Internal Market, Employment, and Competition.

Of the two European consumer organisations the BEUC comprises a membership of well-respected, independent national consumer organisations from some thirty European countries: a representation that extends to European Economic Area (EEA) and applicant countries as well as existing Member States. Its members act independently of the national consumer organisations to defend and promote the interests of European consumers as purchasers or users of goods and services in the EU policy process.

The second European level consumer organisation is the European Association for the Coordination of Consumer Representation in Standardisation (ANEC), a European consumer voice for standardisation, representing and defending consumer interests in the process of standardisation, conformity assessment and related legislation. It is comprised of national representatives (one from each of the EU and EFTA (European Free Trade Association) Member States) chosen by the national consumer organisations that are recognised by the European Commission and EFTA and have the task of representing all the consumer organisations of their country, the same nomination procedure as for the ECCG. Figure 3.1 attempts to position these and the other European level organisations for consumer policy formulation with the national and individual consumer dimensions of the policy process architecture. The organisational structure depicted at the national level can only be generic in form as detail varies between, and even within, the Member States.[10] Equally, the lines of communication indicated by the arrows are themselves merely indicative of the complex interrelationships between the different organisations and the organisations at different levels.

Two further European networks with national points of contact have been specifically established to assist consumers with cross-border issues. Of these, the European Consumer Centres Network (ECC-Net) provides a free of charge information service on cross-border shopping to consumers, advises on consumer rights and gives support in the event of a complaint or an agreement via an out-of-court dispute resolution mechanism (Alternative Dispute Resolution or ADR). It provides a policy input to the Commission and has a presence in all 27 EU Member States plus Iceland and Norway. These national 'Consumer Centres' are located in host organisations (for the UK this is the Trading Standards Institute) that are public or a non-profit-making bodies designated by the Member State, or the competent authority concerned, and agreed by the European Commission. Operating in a similar vein, but primarily through ombudsman schemes at national level, FIN-Net provides a financial dispute resolution network of national out-of-court complaint schemes across all EEA countries. It is responsible for handling disputes between consumers and financial services providers; however, the structure, nature and competence of different FIN-Net members vary and even schemes within a single country may take different forms in different sectors.

The Consumer Policy Network has also been established by the Commission to facilitate the exchange of information and good practice between consumer policymakers in the Member States. It comes together as an informal and temporary body providing an exchange of views and expertise to the Commission when it is drafting new measures and before the Commission submits the draft measures to a comitology committee (Commission, 2007a, p. 8).

The national framework for consumer empowerment and enforcement, represented in Figure 3.1 by a range of generic institutional typologies, is intended to convey the breadth of the consumer policy infrastructure in the Member States. The reality is that, across the EU, the consumer movement at national level varies substantially in terms of strength, structure and capacity. The Commission acknowledges that a strong consumer movement at national level is essential both to a strong EU consumer movement and to well-functioning national markets. In order to improve the normative effectiveness of these national fora, the Commission has adopted a policy approach to provide multilateral training in the core skills areas of management, lobbying, and consumer law in those Member States where consumer policy delivery, in terms of empowerment and enforcement, is at its weakest (Commission, 2007a, p.10). In spite of the disparity between the national structures, the Regulation on consumer protection cooperation ensures designated national institutions exchange information on market surveillance and enforcement activities and act generally in a spirit of mutual assistance (Regulation (EC) 2006/2004).

The black and white arrows in Figure 3.1 indicate the channels through which, respectively, enforcement and empowerment take effect. The black arrows depict the more formal channels for enforcement of consumer rights through litigation or third party ADR mechanisms and provide for the Court's involvement, typically in the context of a reference for a preliminary ruling concerning the interpretation of European legislation.[11] Similarly, the white arrows provide a representation of the channels connecting the different levels and agencies that form the network of consumer policy governance. They show, on the one hand, the channels through which consumer information and/or advocacy may be disseminated from the national consumer organisations to the individual consumer and, on the other hand, the channels through which individual consumers can exercise their consumer rights and/or communicate with the national consumer organisations.

The notion of consumer citizenship developed in this book is identified by transactional, post-transactional or extra-transactional consumer behaviour that involves individuals interacting with retailers and service providers as well as consumer organisations and enforcement agents. Figure 3.1 accommodates such direct consumer interaction with retailers and service providers as a channel through which individuals directly exercise their consumer rights. At the transactional level, consumer empowerment is supported by product information that, as Howells identifies, '[t]he European Court of Justice...shows a preference for...as a way of achieving protection [that is]...less of a threat to integration' (Howells, 2005, p. 352). Empowerment through such information is nevertheless a contrivance of limited effect for the consumer: it is unable to provide the education and awareness necessary for individuals to develop an understanding of the spectrum of behaviours that define consumer citizenship practice. We can, however, identify at least two policy approaches that extend the idea of consumer empowerment through information beyond the limitations of product labelling and the small print of service contracts. The first, provides for a broader, more comprehensive and established approach to developing consumer empowerment through an EU-wide programme of consumer education that is provided through the school curriculum to young consumers.

The second, and more recent policy approach, consists of market monitoring through statistical analysis of consumer outcomes at the EU level and through market performance in targeted sectors. It is an analytical policy approach that provides for a more direct awareness of the veracity of market functioning for the consumer, that feeds directly into the EU's policy development process, and that may provoke strategic investigations of market sectors that appear to be failing consumers.

Young consumers and generational preparation

The 2007–2013 Consumer Policy Strategy recognises that the greater empowerment of consumers brings greater responsibilities for them to manage their own affairs. Such responsibilities leave the most vulnerable, less well-equipped to engage with the market as consumer citizens, yet the 'need for confident consumers to drive our economies has never been greater' (Commission, 2007a, p. 3). The 1975 preliminary programme of the European Economic Community for a consumer protection and information policy established the principles that provide the rationale for the Community's approach to consumer information and education. It identified that sufficient information should be made available to the purchaser of goods or services to enable them to

> assess the basic features of the goods and services offered such as the nature, quality, quantity and price; make a rational choice between competing products and services; use these products and services safely and to his satisfaction; claim redress for any injury or damage resulting from the product supplied or service received. (Council, 1975, para. 34)

The notion of empowering consumers through information and education was introduced in Chapter 2. Here, a broader notion of consumer education, targeted at young consumers through their school's curriculum, is discussed. It suggests that consumer education was to be made available to children and young people, as well as to adults, in order that they would be able 'to act as discriminating consumers, capable of making an informed choice of goods and services and conscious of their rights and responsibilities... [They were to] benefit from basic information on the principles of modern economics' (Council, 1975, para. 42). The preliminary programme charged the Commission with undertaking studies with the Member States and consumer organisations to determine the methods and materials necessary for encouraging consumer education in 'schools, universities and other educational establishments' (Council, 1975, para. 43).

By June 1986 the Council and Ministers for Education of the Member States adopted a resolution to 'promote, within the bounds of what is constitutionally possible and in the framework of national legislation and regulations, consumer education in school curricula, at primary and secondary level, as appropriate, so that consumer education is provided during the period of compulsory education' (Council, 1986). The resolution suggested that consumer education in schools should be illustrated by practical and specific examples, with suggested objectives for consumer behaviour, and be set in the context of teaching 'those aspects of contemporary society which affect the *rights and responsibilities* of consumers'. The 'aspects of contemporary society' it identified as

> the operation of market forces, the role of consumers in the economy, an awareness of environmental questions, attitudes to advertising, attitudes to the mass media [and] the use of leisure time. (Council, 1986, emphasis added)

Consumer education *per se* became a *right* for European consumers with the introduction of Article 169 TFEU (Article 153 EC) by the Treaty of Amsterdam 1997, a joint objective to be fulfilled by the European Community and the Member States. One of the aspects of contemporary society is that this right to consumer education has developed an importance for this knowledge to be acquired at compulsory school age. In this context, the Swedish Consumer Agency has drawn attention to the fact that the market has undergone major changes in recent decades, changes that have made it more difficult to obtain an overview of the market, due to increased globalisation of trade. The increasingly concentrated integration of production, distribution and retail trade, and an increased range of products are reflected in the sophistication of intensified marketing which has brought an ever-increasing flow of information and advertising increasing demands on consumers who need to be able to evaluate and take a position on information and claims made for products, including environmental and ethical aspects.

These changes, the Swedish Consumer Agency has suggested, are presenting challenges that are stimulating the argument for strengthening the ability of children and young people to develop their analytical ability and critical awareness as consumers, to manage their personal finances and to relate to economic developments in the wider society, and to choose lifestyles that are in harmony with the requirements for sustainable consumption and a sustainable development in general. The overall objectives of Swedish consumer policy are for consumers to have the power and possibility to make active choices, to be 'aware and secure consumers' (Swedish Consumer Agency, 2011).

Consideration of the delivery of consumer education and the development of consumer citizenship through the school curriculum has been the subject of a project sponsored by the European Commission's 'Socrates' scheme. It has, as its main objective to further co-operation between Member States in the field of consumer education, in the context of citizenship development, through compulsory graduate and initial teacher training (Commission, 2011b). The project sits within the EU's strategic objective of becoming the most competitive and dynamic knowledge-based economy in the world, capable of sustainable economic growth with more and better jobs and greater social cohesion. It is intended to pave the way for coherent co-operative education and training policies between the Member States through the open method of co-ordination and is a field in which the concept of consumer citizenship has gained increasing attention: attention that lends itself to a definition of consumer citizenship that reflects the paradigm of individual responsibility within a collective context that was developed for the active consumer in Chapter 2:

> [c]onsumer citizenship is when the individual, in his/her role as a consumer, actively participates in developing and improving society by considering ethical issues, diversity of perspectives, global processes and future conditions. It involves taking responsibility on a global as well as regional, national, local and family scale when securing one's own personal needs and well-being. (Thoresen, 2003, p. 12)

Rinaldi draws attention to the importance of consumer education in schools to promote awareness and social involvement in the young, as well as the cultural differences, in terms of values, norms and pedagogical approaches, which characterize the Member States. She identifies that although the national schemes took different approaches, the new millennium saw the notion of consumer citizenship widely introduced into consumer education programmes. These are programmes aimed at promoting 'an active participation in developing and improving society by considering ethical issues, diversity of perspectives, global processes and future conditions' (Rinaldi, 2005, p. 139).

The educational focus is now adding responsibility in global, regional, national and local contexts to the traditional consumer education topics of consumer rights and obligations, food quality and nutrition, advertising and commercial pressure. Rinaldi highlights that 'consumer educators are slowly trying to promote, among young people, a deeper awareness of their role as active citizens and not only consumers' (Rinaldi, 2005). For its part, the Commission has, since 1993, organised the 'European Young Consumer Competition' with the aim of encouraging young people to become more aware as consumers, by getting them to work on consumer-linked themes in teams under school guidance (Commission, 2011c).

Consumer-focussed market monitoring: the Consumer Markets Scoreboard

The Commission's Consumer Markets Scoreboard is a new consumer-focussed approach to market analysis that should be complementary to competition policy and action on supply side issues. The objectives of the new approach were outlined in the first Scoreboard published at the end of January 2008 and indicated a shift in policymaking towards an approach founded on consumer outcomes (Commission, 2008b). It marked a new metrics-led approach for policymakers that places an increased focus on empowered consumers making informed choices and rewarding efficient market operators; on consumers making use of both advocacy and complaints processes with the national consumer organisations and, for some, engaging directly with annual Scoreboard data collection. Scoreboard data acts passively as a tool of soft governance 'where the emphasis is upon the Member States' implementation of EU legislation already adopted' (Szyszczak, 2006, p. 498). It is designed as a normative tool through which market malfunctioning may be identified in the context of economic efficiency and the safeguarding of certain social standards that include concern for human health, the environment and safety (Commission, 2008b, p. 2).

The 2007 Single Market Review, that had been designed to set out a new approach to the market, recognised a need to deliver more benefits for consumers and to renew efforts to stimulate market integration and greater efficiency (Commission, 2007d). These then became an objective of the Commission's consumer policy strategy for 2007–2013. The agency role of the consumer in promoting market efficiency then became a key driver for 'competitiveness and citizens' welfare' in the first Scoreboard which identified that the market needed 'empowered consumers able to make informed choices and quickly reward efficient operators' (Commission, 2008b, p. 3).

The Commission's approach to the Scoreboard has been to develop indicators for identifying potentially failing consumer markets. These indicators provide for a first screening phase that is followed by a detailed analysis phase comprising market studies of sectors that are identified as malfunctioning. The screening stage looks at the broad performance of consumer markets across the economy from the perspective of consumer outcomes and is accompanied by two other primary data sets. These monitor the level of integration of the retail internal market, in the context of cross-border trade, and provide a comparative analysis of the consumer environment in the 27 national markets (Commission, 2009c).

Of the three approaches to monitoring consumer markets in the screening phase the first and last are both measures of consumer empowerment *and of aspects of consumer citizenship behaviour.* The five major indicators, designed to capture the main characteristics of consumer markets, in the first approach to screen consumer markets, comprise complaints, prices, satisfaction, switching and safety. Of these indicators, complaints, satisfaction and switching data are specifically dependant on consumer behaviours.

Complaints need to be interpreted together with other indicators as 'the willingness to complain varies between countries and sectors depending on traditions in consumer protection and perceptions of the likelihood of success' (Commission, 2008b, p. 5). Complaints are also indicators of post-transaction consumer citizenship behaviour and are reflections of the 'responsibility on a...local and family scale when securing one's own personal needs and well-being' included in Thoresen's definition of consumer citizenship relevant to consumer education in schools (Thoresen, 2003, p. 12).

Consumer satisfaction is influenced by quality, choice, transparency and after-sales service, as aspects of market function and the Scoreboard draws on well-established consumer satisfaction measuring techniques. Consumer satisfaction is a key issue for all organisations operating in the internal market and has promoted research to develop accurate ways of assessing consumer satisfaction at both macro and micro levels. One consequence of such research has been the European Performance Satisfaction Indicator (EPSI): an economic indicator system based on customer evaluations of the quality of goods and services that are purchased in Europe and produced by companies that have a substantial European market share. It delivers macro-economic indicators and statistical results concerning customer-perceived satisfaction that gives, on the one hand, a voice to the European customers and, on the other hand, analysis instruments for companies, industries and government.[12]

The third of the screening measures dependant on consumer behaviour monitors supplier switching, specifically in relation to the services sector. Switching data provide an important indicator of consumer choice and of the consumer's ability to exercise that choice: measures that the Scoreboard acknowledges 'is crucial to the success of liberalisation of network services' (Commission, 2008b, p. 6). Switching behaviour is complex and while a supplier company's failures may weaken the customer–supplier relationship and predispose the consumer to switch other variables relating to the consumer or the purchase situation may 'either mitigate or precipitate the decision to switch' (Anton, Camarero and Carrero, 2007, p. 150).

The decision to switch may be dependent on three determinants: consumer involvement and their knowledge of alternative supplier products, switching costs and alternative attractiveness, all of which will vary according to the 'motive behind the consumers' dissatisfaction and switching intention' (Anton, Camarero and Carrero, 2007, p. 151). Consumers who are able and willing to switch supplier, when they can find and understand other offers in the market that give them a better deal than their current one, disclose the traits of the consumer citizen. They do a lot to improve the outcomes for all the consumers in the market: '[t]heir actions send a clear signal to companies that they should improve their service or risk alienating consumers... [They] set an example, enabling other consumers to capture similar benefits' (Commission, 2009c, Part 1, p. 45).

The third part of the Scoreboard comprises benchmarking data for the consumer environment in the Member States, providing basic horizontal data focussed on enforcement, safety and consumer empowerment. Of these, the basic indicators of consumer empowerment are provided by data sets of consumer complaints, redress, switching, enforcement of consumer rights, and trust in national consumer organisations to protect individual rights information. Such data, however, provides little understanding of how the different national markets work, or of where 'best practice' may exist. Acknowledging this, the Scoreboard identifies that little comparative EU-wide consumer empowerment data exists on the levels of 'consumer education, information, understanding, consumer literacy/skills, awareness and assertiveness' (Commission, 2008b, p. 7).

Despite its shortcomings, this approach to measuring the consumer market has, in its first two years, identified areas of market failure and highlighted areas requiring a greater focus in the analysis phase.[13] In January 2009, the Commission published the results of its 2nd Annual Consumer Scoreboard which identified that, within the services sector, public transport, banking and energy were all underperforming for consumers, but it is the energy sector that is drawing most of the attention (Commission, 2009a). The retail electricity market in particular is to be targeted by the Commission and subjected to an analysis of consumer problems that will focus on comparability of offers, unfair commercial practices and billing. In a case study of the actual and potential effectiveness of consumer citizenship practice, this book returns to the problems of this sector in Chapter 5.

Conclusion

This chapter started with a description of a transactional model of consumer citizenship practice that had evolved in European law and policy over the past quarter of a century. Following the analysis of the two distinct traditions of the consumer and the citizen, and the recognition of the significant parallels between them, the narrower but conflated concept of consumer citizenship was argued to have a legitimacy rooted in the convergence of political ideology from both the left and the right. The coherency of the concept was then demonstrated through a consideration of its constitutional credentials and a description of the structures and initiatives that have entrenched a process of policy- and law-making responsive to consumer citizenship practice.

The breadth of consumer citizenship practice is, however, not confined specifically to the consumer transaction; it extends to post-transactional and extra-transactional behaviours that embrace the pursuit of consumer rights, redress, empowerment and representation. The platform for this consumer citizenship practice, albeit to a degree developmental at the Member State level, is being created and nurtured by the Commission and funded by the European Parliament and the Council. It is from this platform that the individual consumer has the opportunity to engage in consumer citizenship behaviours according to his or her inclinations but limited by his or her capabilities.

For the individual, these are capabilities that extend beyond economic limitation and can be improved with a relevant knowledge of consumer rights and responsibilities. The degree to which consumer citizenship practice will exploit the platform that has been provided for it, and therefore the degree to which consumer citizenship practice can influence the direction and development of consumer policy and law, has a dependency on the degree to which this relevant knowledge can be disseminated within the population. To that end, and adding another prop to the coherence of the consumer citizenship concept, the Commission, with the support of the Member States, has instilled an extensive programme of schools-based consumer citizenship education. The consumer collective may not constitute the conventional notion of a Demos but the consumer citizen, both individually and collectively, has voice, rights and expertise that can be exercised through national and EU level organisational networks in a form of constituent power.

There was a suggestion, in the discussion of the relationship between the Charter of Fundamental Rights and the nature of economic citizenship, of a membership boundary for access to the Charter's rights provisions and of a synergy between these social rights and the redistributive welfare rules and the market. Where this chapter has argued that the concept of consumer citizenship has both validity and coherence the following chapter expands on this suggestion and explores the spatial and membership dimensions of European consumer citizenship. It develops a segmented model of the internal market and identifies the boundaries in which consumer citizenship practice has a tangible presence.

4
Boundaries of European Consumer Citizenship

Introduction

Building on the validity and coherence of the concept of consumer citizenship this chapter addresses issues of the spatial and membership dimensions of EU consumer citizenship and develops a brief analysis of the sectoral existence of consumer citizenship practice. The starting point for this chapter focuses on the increasing recognition that European citizenship is 'a multiple rather than a singular feeling and status' (Heater, 1999, p. 3): a concept that involves issues of individuality and of collectivity, of civil and political status and that embraces a social dimension. Adding to the citizenship discussion, Olsen argues that citizenship 'is not conjured up *ex nihilo*, but is rather a phenomenon which emerges, evolves and changes in conjunction with concrete practices of a political system': that it is a *status* of individuals in relation to a *political unit* that, in the EU context, has been differentiated into the dimensions of *membership, identity, rights* and *participation* (Olsen, 2006).

This chapter begins therefore with a discussion that frames the *duty* and *responsibility* components identified with consumer citizenship practice within the participation dimension of Olsen's model. This is a discussion that addresses those behaviours inherent in the voluntary pursuit of consumer rights; the use that consumers make of the channels that have the potential to give them voice and influence, and the exercise of ethical and responsible consumerism linked to the conscious awareness of issues of solidarity and sustainability.

The membership dimension is connected to the notion of inclusion and exclusion: that through membership the concept of citizenship '"ties" the individual to some collective organisation presupposing some self-understanding of the choosing community' (Olsen, 2006, p. 3). My argument here is that as a practical conception of citizenship, the *criteria* by which members and non-members of the consumer citizenship *space* are differentiated may be defined by two dimensions of the internal market: the 'membership' dimension and the 'territorial' dimension. This is a model, depicted in Figure 4.1, in which the 'membership' dimension is defined by broad market sectors in which individual access rights merge with individual choice rights that are shaped by the entry requirements of the sector and the porosity of the boundaries between sectors. In the territorial dimension, the boundaries of national and sub-national spaces, EU space and extra-EU space provide barriers between the territorial spaces that also provide for identity: an identity in citizenship that, as Maas has commented 'reflects the fact that Europe is no longer simply a community of states but has become a community of individuals with a common status' (2007, p. 4).

With regard to rights, Olsen suggests that they can be defined as entitlements that derive from the status of citizenship and that 'investigating the location of rights within a specific discourse can thus provide further clues as to the conception of citizenship within a political unit' (Olsen, 2006, p. 3). For the model of consumer citizenship practice proposed in this book it has already been suggested that these rights comprise the free movement rights of the internal market, those emanating from competition law and the rights accruing specifically through the consumer protection legislation. The right to these rights, in the context of consumer citizenship, being determined by the membership and identity criteria associated with the sectoral divisions of the market.

This is the EU internal market that has undergone significant change in the past 30 years with all sectors experiencing developments in privatisation, marketisation, competition and de-centralisation. These changes are discussed, sector by sector, to reveal a general shift towards individualism and a new focus on choice, on quality and on consumerisation that has manifested itself in increasingly assertive and confident consumer behaviours. These are consumer behaviours supported by a developing array of individual entitlements and consumer rights that challenge traditional notions of citizenship.

In the final substantive section of this chapter the discussion returns to the duty issue in consumer citizenship practice, this time in the context of a general (public) interest responsibility, a responsibility linked to choice and citizen participation. It discusses the ethical, environmental, cultural and political motivations that influence the exercise of choice decisions and add a broader substance to the model of consumer citizenship practice. A model that has its conceptual roots in the research and literature of political science but that, more recently, has also been argued to be developing a legal foundation in the new area of law that is forming in the regulatory amalgam of public and private law doctrines associated with the universal and public service obligations of the major network industries.

An open model for consumer citizenship practice?

The problematic 'duty' components of consumer citizenship practice

In what has been described as a 'pathbreaking historical sketch of this institution' of citizenship (Ferrera, 2005a, p. 13), Marshall suggested that 'social rights imply an absolute right to a certain standard of civilisation which is conditional only on the discharge of the *general duties* of citizenship', and that citizenship is 'a status bestowed on those who are full members of a community' (Ferrera, 2005a, p. 18, citing Marshall, 1950, emphasis added). In the EU, the landscape of citizenship has developed and grown with the formal, if limited, constitutionalised *political* and *civil* rights bestowed on those persons 'holding the nationality of a Member State' (Article 20(1) TFEU) added to an ever increasing number of *social* rights associated with the internal market, freedom of movement and aspects of solidarity. Identification of the duties associated with social rights is, however, neither certain nor uncontroversial but, as Shaw suggests, the closeness of the link between, for example, the right to social security with the right to work, highlights a reality in which:

> [t]he duty problem is not a separate issue from the questions of ... citizenship practice ... [s]ince many rights and duties are so closely linked ... the two sets of problems are soluble at the EU level, if at all, together rather than separately. (Shaw, 1997a, Section IV (C))

Perhaps a clearer expression of citizenship duty, in the context of consumer citizenship practice, is to be found in the behaviour of the dissatisfied consumer. As Hirschman suggests, '[t]he customer who, dissatisfied with the product of one firm shifts to that of another, uses the market to defend his welfare or to improve his position' (Hirschman, 1970, p. 15). A theory of *exit, voice and loyalty* that Barry suggests has an 'unlimited range of application' (Barry, 1974, p. 82). If this is so, then citizenship duties can, I would suggest, be located within both the individualistic and communitarian choices exercised by the individual in the decisions they make to voice their opinions over quality or to enter or exit any particular market, including marketised sectors that have typically been associated with solidarity and that exist under the auspices of public sector services and social welfare provision.

The nature of the duty requirement found in exercising such choice can, however, be problematic for the individual consumer who is faced with making a value-based decision between two problematic and opposing theoretical perspectives inherent in the model of consumer citizenship practice. On the one hand, the individualistic aspects of market citizenship derived from liberal economic theory suggests that the free exercise of individual choice to access goods or services, as a duty element of consumer citizenship practice, will have a tendency to improve quality and reduce costs for those that follow. On the other hand, and more closely aligned to the model envisaged by Marshall, implicit duties are imposed on citizens to contribute to a pool of welfare insurance. These are duty-based decisions susceptible to the individual consumer's value-based choice that exposes the tension between individualism and social citizenship: a tension that in the context of health care rights and market citizenship is clearly exposed in the *Watts* case (Case C-372/04), discussed below (see also Newdick, 2008, p. 102 *et seq*).

The notion of a 'duty' continuum between these opposing theoretical perspectives is argued to be evidenced by the plurality of duty responsibilities that have already been identified in the preceding chapters of this book. Chapter 1 introduced the notion of a pragmatic solidarity and the duties inherent with gaining citizen input into the political decision-making process: of a civic duty and public spiritedness implicitly encouraged through the self-education of consumer rights and responsible consumption. The duty content discussed in Chapter 2 advanced the notion of civic duty, public spiritedness and self-education and introduced the concept of shared responsibility for the preparation and implementation of important economic decisions, particularly with regard to those duties relevant to ethical and sustainable consumption, that can be identified with environmental solidarity. Chapter 3 began with an introduction to the duties of market participation associated with individualism and went on to discuss influential post-transactional and extra-transactional behaviours of consumer citizenship. These are *choice* behaviours that are construed as the duty element of consumer citizenship practice exercised through the pursuit of consumer complaints, enforcement of consumer rights, pursuit of redress, the switching of suppliers as a consequence of dissatisfaction, ethical buying and the positive participation in consumer market surveys and interaction with representative consumer organisations.

The involvement of the individual in making value-based judgements that may change their way of life through choosing to change their patterns of consumption is central to the notion of a consumer citizenship practice. Such value judgements, in the context of ideas of sustainability, have long been at the heart of green political thought. Here, citizenship

> is understood as a mediating practice which connects the individual and the institutional levels of society, as well as a common identity which links otherwise disparate individuals together as a collectivity with common interests. (Barry, 1996, p. 123)

Issues stemming from the challenges of globalised markets, and from the threat of global warming, are raising the profile of sustainability initiatives to the degree that, Barry suggests, will not only 'require major institutional restructuring of contemporary western liberal democracies both internally and externally in their relationship to the rest of the world' (Barry, 1996, p. 123), but also supplementary micro-level changes by individual citizens. A role, argued here, analogous to that of the responsible consumer citizen and to that of the ecological citizen consumer identified by Hilson.

Hilson provides an interrogation of the link between European citizenship and environmental solidarity in which environmental rights can be seen in similar terms to the welfare rights typically associated with the solidarity aspects of market-based societies. 'Instead of social inter-dependence based on the division of labour, one has environmental inter-dependence based on the cross-border, global nature of many environmental threats'. The EU dimension to the individualised nature of the duties 'owed in relation to the environment' is reflected in the preamble to the Charter of Fundamental Rights of the European Union which states that '[e]njoyment of these rights entails responsibilities and duties with regard to other persons, to the human community and to future generations'. More specifically, with regard to the individual's solidaristic duties, the EU's 5th Environmental Action Programme 'spoke eloquently of the "shared responsibility" we all have for the environment – in other words, not just business and government, but also individual citizens'. The consumer citizen identified by Hilson is capable of altruistic acts, of 'acting solidaristically because she is acting not through self-interest, but of concern for weaker or excluded others, in the form of current human victims of pollution and also future generations' (Hilson, 2008, pp. 7–12).

Market segmentation and community spaces

If the identification of the duties of European consumer citizenship practice can be located within the behaviours of individuals interacting with the market, the boundaries and membership component of that consumer citizenship is more difficult to define. Whilst the *content* of EU consumer citizenship has thickened with the process of European integration, it has been matched by a 'thinning out of the container of citizenship'. As Ferrera suggests,

> [n]ot only has the Union introduced a distinct EU citizenship superimposed on national ones, but it has also – and especially – promoted a creeping, but constant decoupling of rights from national territories. The europeanisation of options through the 'four freedoms' and accompanying measures has entailed a gradual opening up of the distinct citizenship spaces of the Member States. (Ferrera, 2005a, p. 16)

At the same time as the process of European integration was 'thinning out the container' the economic and technological forces of globalisation were resulting in an acceleration of the commodification of public services. National governments' deferential attitude towards these forces heralded the conversion of these previously non-market spheres into profitable fields for investment that saw the reconfiguration of services into commodities, the creation of demand for those commodities, the conversion of public servants into profit-oriented employees and the underwriting of risk (Leys, 2003, p. 214). Privatisation and de-regulation of what were once public sector services has brought new wholesale and retail markets to what are now identified as services of general economic interest. Remaining public sector services, in particular in the areas of health and education, have seen the 'empowerment' of patients and students and 'consumerisation' of service provision: a development that has seen the emergence of *individual–provider* relationships that stretch beyond the Member State. As identified in the context of health law,

> [o]nce the matter of health care is conceptualised as concerning consumers, and the regulation of providers acting within a market...it

becomes much easier to see that there may be a clear point of contact with EU law. (Hervey and McHale, 2004, p. 19)

Even the boundaries of national social welfare provision have been challenged by European integration such that in reflecting on the reduction of Member State sovereignty in the field of education, and the case law established in *Gravier* (Case 293/83), O'Leary holds that EU law 'cuts across Member State social welfare competence, with the result that even matters that do not fall within the scope of application of [EU] law must not interfere with the fundamental freedoms' (O'Leary, 2005, p. 59).

Ferrera presents a diagrammatic representation of 'the new spatial architecture of *social* citizenship in the EU' in which he seeks to configure the boundaries for social sharing (Ferrera, 2005a, p. 24, emphasis added). His mapping of the social welfare landscape identifies a contemporary EU structure for social protection that is accommodated within a spectrum ranging, at its base, from 'a new generation of non-contributory schemes and benefits' to supplementary schemes of social insurance that, at the top, are 'essentially based on individual choice and market criteria' (Ferrera, 2005a, p. 25). In Figure 4.1 the social welfare map described by Ferrera is replicated (shaded area) showing both the territorial and membership dimensions of his social citizenship model. The social welfare benefits that occupy the membership dimension in this figure are, in this chapter, extrapolated to accommodate the other significant consumerist market sectors. In this developed model, as each sector takes its place on the membership dimension they show an increasing porosity between the national and EU territorial boundary as, broadly, choice rights replace access rights in the definition of the content.

In the explanation of his model of social citizenship Ferrera identifies that '[s]ince the early 1970s the process of European integration has worked to thin out gradually the national boundaries of citizenship', a process that has seen social rights and their corresponding obligations 'decoupled from national citizenship within the EU and linked merely to work or residence status' (Ferrera, 2005a, p. 22). In this contemporary model the *degree* of territorial and membership closure, and therefore the definition of who has access in terms of geographical mobility to engage with the market as a legal resident in a national territory, is dependent upon the space they, as individuals, are occupying at the time of the particular market transaction that they are engaged with. Ferrera provides a detailed explanation of his

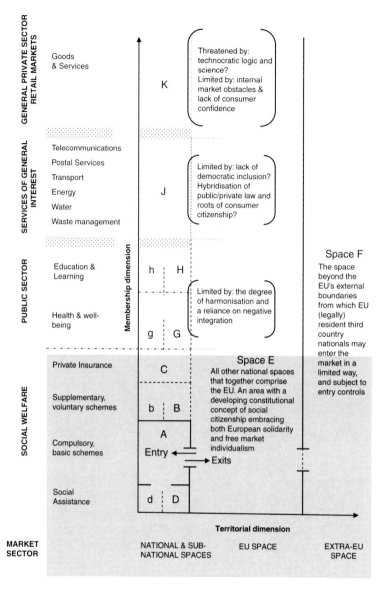

Figure 4.1   Boundaries and spaces of EU consumer citizenship

configuration of boundaries for social sharing where they are identified as occupying the social welfare sector at the base of a consumer market defined by a spectrum of membership criteria that extends from access rights and obligations to choice rights and obligations. Here, a brief overview is provided of Ferrera's explanation of these spaces of social citizenship.

Within the social welfare sector, space 'A' is occupied by the core components of national welfare systems in which the access rights to social protection benefits, either through obligatory cover or an insurance obligation and including the right to enter and exit the space through its two 'gateways', are now provided for by the EU's coordinating Regulation on the coordination of social security systems (Regulation (EC) 883/2004): a Regulation that reflects the 'principle of compulsory affiliation and public monopoly as a prerequisite for social solidarity' and that has been upheld by the Court in 'a long series of social insurance cases' (Ferrera, 2005a, p. 28). The material scope of the Regulation is wide, applying to all social security laws and regulations that apply to the whole range of social protection benefits, whilst in personal or individual scope the Regulation applies

> to nationals of a Member State, stateless persons and refugees resident in the territory of a Member State who are or have been subject to the social security legislation of one or more Member States, as well as to the members of their families and to their survivors. (Regulation (EC) 883/2004, Recital 7)

Spaces 'D and d' represent the national and sub-national regional spaces occupied by needs-based, means-tested, non-contributory and tax-funded social products that establish 'a safety net of last resort for the whole of citizenry, below which nobody would be allowed to fall' (Ferrera, 2005a, p. 25). The 'gate' from space 'A' provides access for legally resident EU citizens and, since May 2003, to legally resident third country nationals to these means-tested benefits where they meet the access criteria applying to national citizens of the host state (Regulation (EC) 859/2003). Whilst not available in all the Member States, the supplementary social insurance products that offer additional benefits and coverage to selected occupational categories, occupy spaces 'B and b' as voluntary or subsidised options in many countries. The membership dimension shows the distinct 'cap' on the compulsory basic schemes at the top of space 'A', where space 'B and b' extends 'beyond the reach of obligatory affiliation and public monopoly on provision', and where, as Ferrera also notes with regard to these supplementary second-pillar pensions:

> The Luxembourg judges found that the predominance of funding as a system of financing and the delicate nature of investment decisions (on the side of both the insured and fund managers) bring this... provision closer to the market. (Ferrera, 2005a, pp. 27 and 29)

From this point, marked by the boundary between the national and EU spaces on the territorial dimension of the consumer citizenship model and beyond the top of space 'A', the membership boundary becomes increasingly more porous.

Even within the shaded area of social sharing that replicates Ferrera's model, fundamental market freedoms mark the distinction between social welfare consumption by individuals who find themselves in a position where it is necessary for them to exercise legitimate *access rights* (spaces A and D/d) and those who are able to exercise their individual *choice rights* based on market criteria as consumers of private insurance (third-pillar pension) products (space C). Space B/b can then be seen as something of an area of transition where 'group insurance principles and categorical agreements... allowing for many of the redistributive and solidaristic effects typically linked to compulsory social insurance' categorise products protected by the market-building principles that are supported by the Court and include the freedom to provide services (Ferrera, 2005a, p. 25).[1]

Beyond space C on the membership dimension the extended model is partitioned to identify the 'Public Sector' and 'Services of General Interest' sectors of the market that are labelled with some examples of sector-specific service content that are merely intended to indicate something of the nature of the services typically provided within the sector. Both of these sectors are defined by a public interest, although the nature of that interest is different in each sector.

In the public sector, the public service provision of healthcare and education is provided within the ambit of national social policy and explains the porous horizontal boundary between the public sector and social welfare boundaries within the national and sub-national spaces. Whilst European countries differ in their approach to sourcing finance for different aspects of public service provision, from general taxation to insurance-based schemes, both of these areas have been subject to partial integration at the European level. Health services were recognised by the Court as *economic services* within the scope of the freedom of movement provisions in *Luisi and Carbone* (Joined Cases 286/82 and 26/83, para. 16) such that by the early 1980s the principle of non-discrimination became applicable to the free movement of services and was later to be confirmed in *Grogan* (Case C-159/90, para. 18). In 1998 the Court extended these rights of non-discrimination in the judgments of *Kohll* and *Decker*. In *Kohll*, the Court found that 'the special nature of certain services does not remove them from the ambit of the fundamental principle of freedom of movement' as they apply to services under the provisions of Article 56 TFEU (Article 49 EC) *et seq* (Case C-158/96, para. 20). In *Decker*, the Court recalled

> that measures adopted by Member States in social security matters which may affect the marketing of medical products and indirectly influence the possibilities of importing those products are subject to the Treaty rules on the free movement of goods...Consequently, the fact that the national rules at issue in the main proceedings fall within the sphere of social security cannot exclude the application of Article [28 EC] of the Treaty. (Case C-120/95, paras 24 and 25)

Although the porosity of the boundary on the territorial dimension between spaces g/G and E and between spaces h/H and E is shown to be similar in Figure 4.1, there is a different basis to the *choice rights* for the consumer accessing these public sector services. Where the Court had recognised the economic nature of health service provision in *Luisi and Carbone*, it found no such economic base in the provision of education services in *Humbel* (Case 236/86, paras 15–20). Instead, individual rights in education were developed on the principle of non-discrimination in a line of cases that began with *Gravier* (Case 293/83) but that were extended in *Grzelczyk* (Case C-184/99) to give non-economic actors such a choice right to social benefits that Van der Mei suggested

> that the scope of Union citizens' right to equal treatment in other Member States is, in principle, unlimited, which for students indeed seems to imply that they now enjoy in the host State equality of treatment in relation to maintenance grants. (Van der Mei, 2005, p. 226)

The broader horizontal boundaries on the membership dimension between spaces h/H and J and between spaces J and K represent their transitional nature. For example, at the lower of the two boundaries, whilst dominated by large multinational companies the location of waste management services can be seen to reach into both the private and public sectors with a complex structure spanning municipal and multinational organisations (Hall, 2007). Around this lower boundary the nature and scope of a service (of general interest) is essentially a public authority responsibility, but one that can be entrusted, albeit with inherent tensions, 'to other entities, which can be public or private, and can act either for-profit or not for-profit' (Commission, 2007e, p. 4). At the upper boundary, telecommunications terminal equipment is firmly established in the private sector retail market whilst telecommunication network services more generally attract the scrutiny of market reviews under the EU regulatory framework as a service of general economic interest (Commission, 2006b).

The economic freedom of movement rights associated with the intentions to complete the internal market provide the substance of citizenship provisions across the territorial dimension boundaries between spaces J and E and spaces K and E. Whilst virtually no market access boundary should remain between the K and E spaces business and consumer behaviour is restrained both by internal market obstacles and a lack of confidence in cross-border shopping, it remains largely fragmented along national lines leaving 27 mini-markets instead (Commission, 2007a, p. 2). Finally, the somewhat thicker boundary between spaces J and E reflects the individuals' access restrictions to the range of network services of general economic interest. This is the sector of the market that has been subject to significant regulatory changes since the 1990s, that has brought, through liberalisation and privatisation, the entry of new firms that have stimulated competition and enhanced efficiency.

Market sector modernisation

Marketisation of social welfare and the development of entitlement rights

Ferrera's model of the social welfare sector, replicated in Figure 4.1, is derived from a citizenship and access rights perspective to redistributive services. However, from the 1980s fundamental revisions of European welfare-state arrangements marked a paradigmatic shift towards 'enabling-states' or 'social-investment states' and the introduction of changes in the 'administration and management of welfare-state arrangements' (Van Berkel and Van der Aa, 2005, p. 330). The new European fight against social exclusion saw activation policies and programmes introduced to promote the transition from welfare to work and to reintegrate individuals and families dependant on welfare benefits into the labour market (Minas, 2009, pp. 3–4). Changes in which privatisation, marketisation, competition and de-centralisation became core issues in the governance of operational social policy.[2] Entry requirements for benefit and social welfare became 'sharper' with entitlements increasingly dependent on 'individual behaviour during benefit-dependency periods' (Van Berkel and Van der Aa, 2005, p. 331). A behavioural dependency that Van Berkel and Van der Aa suggest leads *inter alia* 'to a partial privatisation of risks, and to what one might call "responsibility tests" in determining eligibility for public support' (Van Berkel and Van der Aa, 2005). This, I would suggest, is a shift towards the type of individual responsibility inherent in the paradigm of a consumer citizenship practice that has become a feature of the modernisation of activation policies in social assistance and social services. A modernisation recognised at the European level as important in promoting labour market integration of the unemployed and in which active labour market policies are combined with social and other services needed at a single point for delivery (Commission, 2006c, p. 8).

These new approaches to activation of entitlement to benefits have, in many Member States, been made conditional on active job search, availability for work or participation in training (Minas, 2009, p. 4). They are changes that have been introduced in parallel with the Court's development of a non-discriminatory approach to entitlement rights that had its roots in the internal market and the free movement of workers. As the Court established its authority within the ambit of free movement in *Hoekstra* (Case 75/63, Ground 1 of the judgment), the tangible nature of EU economic citizenship began to develop as a dynamic and reactive concept. The broad interpretation applied to the nature of the 'work' and the analysis of its economic value in *Levin* (Case 53/81) and *Kempf* (Case 139/85) reflect the approach of the Court to provide access to social benefits for migrant Member State nationals, in particular, with reference to the principle of non-discrimination on the ground of nationality. Such support for the general principles of free movement were evident in the judgment in *Lawrie-Blum* where the Court held that a restrictive interpretation of the Treaty provisions 'would reduce freedom of movement to a mere instrument of economic integration, [and] would be contrary to [the] ... broader objective of creating an area in which community citizens enjoy freedom of movement' (Case 66/85, para. 12).

Downes proposes that the approach by the Court to set a minimal threshold of market activity as a prerequisite of the right to free movement provides for 'an *individual* right at least akin to a citizenship right'.

The motive, he suggests 'appears to have been to capture the involve-ment of individuals in the development of the economic Community through an embryonic ideal of citizenship' (Downes, 2001, pp. 95 and 96). The individual nature of this right stems from the directly effective nature of the right to freedom of movement for workers identified by the Court in *Commission v France* (Case 167/73, paras 41 and 43).

In *D'Hoop* (Case C-224/98) the Court appears to take another impor-tant step: diminishing the distinction between national citizenship and citizenship of the Union, and deciding that 'EU citizenship law, most notably [Article 21 TFEU] Art. 18 EC, could regulate relations between a Member State and its own nationals' (Chalmers, 2006, p. 779). This expansion of scope provides for a 'comprehensive general clause which covers all areas where application of national law concerns the lawful presence of individuals in a Member State' (Kadelbach, 2003): a situa-tion that Kadelbach suggested could lead to the nationality criterion in social welfare law being gradually replaced by a *residency principle* for Union Citizens. Although this area of law has not developed in such a way, the situation envisaged by Kadelbach is reflected in what Chalmers sees as a tension in the opportunities and restrictions applying to indi-viduals as a consequence of the continuing development of Union Citizenship (Chalmers, 2006, p. 780).

Public sector modernisation

The model of market segmentation depicted in Figure 4.1 is more than a mere extension of Ferrera's map of the social welfare sphere; it is also an elaboration of the model described by Freedland in which a public sec-tor service was located between 'on the one hand, the state sector and, on the other hand the wholly private sector'. Freedland's model asserts that 'ideas about citizenship...are particularly significant and influen-tial, especially in the way that they inform the shape and application of public law and labour law' (Freedland, 1998, p. 2). It is a model that seeks to explain the move towards a post-welfare state that involves the

> retreat of the state from the role of primary provider of many serv-ices...[with] a corresponding expansion of the...public role of regu-lating in the public interest the provision of public services which is increasingly being entrusted to private or semi-private undertakings. (Freedland, 1998, p. 28)

These were changes to the nature of public service provision that intro-duced new elements of *choice*, *quality* and *consumerisation*. The principles of neo-liberal theory gradually gave shape to new devolved, marketised, de-centralised and privatised public service delivery mechanisms over the period starting at the beginning of the last quarter of the twentieth century. Changes that provided for yet another conception of the consumer citizen in the non-cash mediated consumption of public services: a changing notion of citizenship that embraces 'empowerment' and the decline of deference. This was a restructuring of public sector services in a neo-liberal format in which '[t]he preference for *markets* over *states*, for *private* over *public* provision and for *individualism* over *collectivism* form part of a global realignment of the public realm, and its greater subordination to private/corporate interests' (Clarke and Newman, 2006). It was a restructuring predicated on the argument that the citizen's participation and involvement on both the organisational/bureaucratic level and the communal/political level, 'may increase trust in governance and potentially in administrative agencies because they enhance the information citizens have about various processes and their identification with policies and outcomes' (Vigoda-Gadot and Mizrahi, 2007, p. 80, citing Rose, 1999).

If public sector service modernisation was about the *rhetoric* of involvement and trust at the national level, *access* to public sector services, based on the development of individual rights for the market citizen at the European level had been gaining momentum from the early 1980s. A background of growing interest in the notion of European citizenship, notably in the European Parliament, was accompanied by a revitalisation of interest in European integration led by Jacques Delors and the new Commission of 1985. With a developing sense of common purpose the Community institutions pressed ahead with the development of a social dimension to the internal market. In education, the Council, in 1987, approved the European Community Action Scheme for the Mobility of University Students (ERASMUS). Education programmes were to grow into one of the key mechanisms for 'creating a sense of European identity, thus helping to promote and entrench the shift from market rights to individual rights and citizenship' (Maas, 2007, p. 40).

Maas links the promotion of economic advancement, individual social mobility and of fostering civic engagement and a shared sense of community through education at the national level with a similar, dual, role in the process of European integration. He suggests that 'questions of citizenship must be posed in terms of process and access: individuals are not automatic citizens but rather become citizens through one or several processes of citizenship creation' (Maas, 2007, p. 109). The growth of the Community's education and training programmes had coincided with the development of a 'People's Europe' where, the Commission identified that the 'idea and practice of European Citizenship is reflected in ... the reality of ... the free movement of people, ideas and products' (Commission, 1993, p. 22). In its 1996 Green Paper, the Commission anticipated that

> [with] this increasing freedom of movement should come a growing European consciousness instilled through greater awareness of others as a result of exposure to new cultures and societies. Mobility within the Community ought to contribute to the development of solidarity between all Europeans. (Commission, 1996c, p. 1)

More recently, the Council and the Commission have acknowledged that whilst progress has been made there is 'an urgent need to strengthen the people-focussed dimension of the European Union' (Commission, 2004a, p. 11). The background to this urgency stems from the Lisbon Strategy and the need to meet the challenges of globalisation and the recognition that investment in education and training was 'a key factor of the Union's competitiveness, sustainable growth and employment' (Commission, 2004a, p. 1).

The social dimension in the development of EU market rights into citizenship rights was also evident in the health sector as social policy issues took their place alongside market policy. Even though Article 168(5) TFEU (Article 152(5) EC) provides 'Community action in the field of public health shall fully respect the responsibilities of the Member States in the organisation and delivery of health services and medical care', Member States have nothing close to autonomy. Article 168(5) TFEU (Article 152(5) EC) makes clear that 'Member States shall, in liaison with the Commission, coordinate among themselves their policies and programmes ... The Commission may, in close contact with the Member States, take any useful initiative to promote such coordination.' Policy coordination is, however, complicated by the differences that exist between the services provided by the various Member States, as distinct from or complementary to the private sector and by the differences in the extent to which access to the service is free at the point of delivery. Despite the efforts of the Member States to minimise Community intervention the Court's interpretation of the free movement provisions has seen the limited autonomy of the Member States compromised as access rights to medical treatment for migrant Community citizens has been developed in case law (Shaw, Hunt and Wallace, 2007, p. 355).

The free movement of services provisions in Article 56 TFEU (Article 49 EC) *et seq* has emerged as a significant legal base for the development of individual rights for European citizens in the field of medical care and treatment. In *Luisi and Carbone*, concerning the export of currency to pay for *private* health care, the Court confirmed that the fundamental market freedom to provide services *included* the freedom for individuals, as recipients of those services, to be able to move within the Community without national restrictions on access (Joined Cases 286/82 and 26/83, para. 16). However, the Member States' approach to the financing of health services differ between national health service schemes funded from general taxation and delivered through either centralised or de-centralised administrations *or* social insurance provisions that can be classified as reimbursement or direct provision schemes (Ferrera, 2005b, pp. 124–126). Hatzopoulos (2007) also draws attention to the conceptual difficulties that arise in qualifying healthcare as a 'service' (within the meaning of Article 56 TFEU (Article 49 EC)) and the requirement for remuneration (stemming from Article 57 TFEU (Article 50 EC)) that are further compounded by the shift towards more neo-liberal inspired economic policy from the late 1980s and the introduction, at the Member State level, of competitive 'internal market' policies: particularly where the state provided centrally funded health service, free at the point of delivery.

A fuller recognition by the Court, of the social security issues associated with access to medical care and the principles of free movement, came in *Kohll* (Case C-158/96), concerning a Luxembourg national seeking reimbursement for dental treatment provided in Germany but without having received prior authorisation from his home institution. The Court held that Articles 56 and 57 TFEU (Articles 49 and 50 EC) did apply to health services, even when they were provided in the context of a social security scheme, and that a national rule requiring prior authorisation was therefore a breach of the provisions in Article 56 TFEU (Article 49 EC) (Case C-158/96, para. 20). Subsequent cases including *Decker* (Case C-120/95), *Vanbraekel* (Case C-368/98), *Smits & Peerbooms* (Case C-157/99) and *Müller-Fauré* (Case C-385/99) have endorsed the idea that healthcare is *a priori* subject to the Treaty rules, and that remuneration can exist for insurance-based schemes: although case law has yet to address the question of remuneration in those systems based on a centrally funded national health service, and found no need to in *Watts* (Case C-372/04, para. 91).

For the purposes of this book the *facts* of the *Watts* case are of particular interest. Mrs Watts' daughter had been denied authorisation from her local UK health authority for her mother to receive treatment abroad on the ground that treatment could be provided 'without undue delay', within the context of 'the way in which the NHS treated waiting lists for the purposes of managing health care provision' (Craig and de Búrca, 2008, p. 823). Mrs Watts, however, took the position that, for her, the delay was too long and so *chose* to undergo the necessary hip replacement in France for which she paid £3,900. On her return from France Mrs Watts continued with an application for permission to apply for judicial review the health authority's refusal decision and claimed in addition reimbursement of the medical fees she had incurred in France. Through her *choosing* to travel to France for her treatment *and* through her pursuit of the judicial review, options for other UK patients have been improved. The consideration of undue delay is now decided by reference to objective (international) medical standards instead of norms and, suggests Davies, 'Watts almost establishes a right to adequate medical care ... [t]his is not a right written into many constitutions, and it is controversial whether the Community should be the source of it, but nor is it something that is easy to reject' (Davies, 2007, p. 166).

Approaches to health care, both in funding mechanisms and in service delivery, span an indistinct boundary between the space occupied by the free market and the space governed by solidarity. Hatzopoulos reminds us that 'the very aim of social and healthcare policy is, precisely, to balance the extreme inequalities produced by free markets and competition'. To that end, the Court has developed a set of criteria that help to determine those aspects that operate within the market, that are subject to the Treaty provisions and the competition rules of Article 106(2) TFEU (Article 86(2) EC), and those which fall within the sphere of solidarity and fall outside the scope of Article 56 TFEU (Article 49 EC), and that are 'altogether exempt' (Hatzopoulos, 2007, p. 4, citing *Freskot*, Case C-355/00).

For the European consumer citizen the Court has done much to liberalize the provision of health services through its application of negative integration measures and development of free movement rights. Anomalies and obstacles to free movement remain but so too does the individuals' 'normal' desire to access health services close to home. The question that then arises, suggested by Hatzopoulos, is 'whether further coordination/harmonisation (through positive measures) is necessary' (Hatzopoulos, 2007, p. 10).

Services of general economic interest

Services of general economic interest are, typically, those large network services once provided by the State but that, particularly since the 1980s, have been subject to liberalisation and privatisation. They encompass telecommunications services, postal services, rail services and the supply of energy and water services: as such, we are all both dependant on, and consumers of, these services. The Commission makes the point that the 'access of all citizens...to affordable high-quality services...is essential for the promotion of social and territorial cohesion in the European Union' (Commission, 2004c, p. 8). The provision of services of general interest exposes the relationship between the individual, the Community and the market and highlights the nexus between citizenship access rights and consumer protection. In its legislative practice the Union has mixed an internal market approach with its focus on consumer protection and the universal service approach with its guarantee of access for everyone, regardless of the individual's economic, social or geographic situation, to a service of a specified quality at an affordable price (Rott, 2007, pp. 53 and 55). It is a legislative approach supplemented by soft law communications from the Commission that position 'general interest services...at the heart of the European Model of Society' (Commission, 1996a).[3]

This mixed approach belies the tension that exists between, on the one hand, the values of efficiency and consumer choice and, on the other hand, those that underlie the application of competition law and public service values based on social and economic rights and on social solidarity. The approach of the Community institutions in managing this tension has changed over time. Prior to the Treaty of Amsterdam 1997 services of general interest were seen as a 'somewhat unwelcome impediment to the creation of a single internal market' where the focus was on trying to limit their scope. Subsequently, Prosser suggests that they have become 'a desirable, and positive, recognition of citizenship rights' with a focus on attempts to improve service delivery through the application of good concepts of governance (Prosser, 2005, pp. 543 and 549).

This change of focus has been applied to interpretations of the rules of Article 106 TFEU (Article 86 EC) that apply to public undertakings and undertakings to which Member States grant special or exclusive rights. In particular this change is evident in the application of Article 106(2) TFEU (Article 86(2) EC) and the proportionality test that enables the Treaty rules on competition to be applied to such undertakings 'insofar as the application of such rules does not obstruct the performance...of the particular tasks assigned to them'. The Member States enjoy a limited freedom to decide which undertakings constitute services of general economic interest on the basis of the specific features of the activities, however:

> in every case, for the exception provided for by Article [106(2)] to apply, the public service mission needs to be clearly defined and must be explicitly entrusted through an act of public authority...This obligation is necessary to ensure legal certainty as well as transparency vis-à-vis the citizens. (Commission, 2000, para. 22)

In *BRT II* (Case 127/73, para. 19) the Court initially adopted a market-based approach, applying a narrow application of Article 106(2) TFEU (Article 86(2) EC) as a provision that permitted, in certain circumstances, a derogation from the rules of the treaty, requiring a strict definition of those undertakings which can take advantage of it. However, in *Sacchi*, the Court held

> If certain Member States treat undertakings...as undertakings entrusted with the operation of services of general economic interest, the same prohibitions apply, as regards their behaviour within the market, by reason of [Article 106(2) TFEU], so long as it is not shown that the said prohibitions are incompatible with the performance of their tasks. (Case 155/73, para. 15)

This initial development reflected the prevailing liberalisation focus of the Commission such that its restrictive approach was developed on the understanding that '[m]arket forces produce a better allocation of resources and a greater effectiveness in the supply of services, the principal beneficiary being the consumer, who gets better quality at a lower price' (Commission, 1996b, para.15). An approach that was also apparent in the Court's ruling in *RTT* where it held

> The exclusion or the restriction of competition on the market in telephone equipment cannot be regarded as justified by a task of a public service of general economic interest within the meaning of [Article 106(2)] of the Treaty. The production and sale...in particular of telephones, is an activity that should be open to any undertaking. (Case C-18/88, para. 22)

Even as late as 1997, in *Air Inter*, the rhetoric of the Court was still identifying Article 106(2) TFEU (Article 86(2) EC) as 'a provision which thus permits, in certain circumstances, derogation from the rules of the

Treaty, [as such] it must be strictly interpreted ... and its application is not left to the discretion of the Member State' (Case T-260/94, para. 135). The end of the 1990s saw a change to this approach. The Commission acknowledged a number of changes that included the recognition that *consumers were becoming increasingly assertive* in exercising their rights and in demanding more, in terms of choice, quality and price; that worldwide competition was forcing companies that relied on services to seek out better price deals; that private funding for maintaining and developing infrastructure networks was easier to raise than public resources; and that new technologies were changing the economic profile of sectors traditionally operated by monopolies and were opening up opportunities for new services. This acknowledgment of change by the Commission was accompanied by a declaration that

> [t]he Community is also helping the modernisation of general inter-
> est services to ensure that essential needs continue to be met and
> to improve performance. This dynamism is the life blood of the
> European model of society, without which European citizenship will
> never become a reality. (Commission, 1996b, para. 14)

A broader interpretation of Article 106(2) TFEU (Article 86(2) EC), allowing Member States to have a greater autonomy in taking decisions aimed at providing for a greater balance between the provision of services of general interest and the competition rules had already surfaced in the 1993 'breakthrough case' of *Corbeau* (Case C-320/91). In its judgment, the Court considered the extent to which a restriction on competition, or even the exclusion of all competition, was necessary in order to allow the undertaking to perform its task of general interest and in particular to have the benefit of economically acceptable conditions. The concern was that if other undertakings were authorised to compete with the holder of the exclusive rights they would be able to concentrate on the economically profitable operations and offer more advantageous tariffs than those adopted by the holders of the exclusive rights, they were not bound to offset losses in the unprofitable sectors against profits in the more profitable sectors. In this case the Court held that the undertaking holding the exclusive rights, in delivering its services of general interest, should be able to offset less profitable sectors against the profitable sectors and as such it justified a restriction of competition from other undertakings where the economically profitable sectors were concerned (Commission, 1996b, paras 17 and 18).

Prosser identifies that 'this left many questions unanswered and emphasised the strictness of the conditions in which restrictions on competition would be acceptable' (Prosser, 2005, p. 552). He suggests that there is a strong case to be made that the real change from the market-centred approach followed the adoption of the then new Article 14 TFEU (Article 16 EC) introduced by the Amsterdam Treaty. Article 14 TFEU provides that

> given the place occupied by services of general economic interest in the shared values of the Union as well as their role in promoting social and territorial cohesion, the Community and the Member States … shall take care that such services operate on the basis of principles and conditions which enable them to fulfil their missions.

A measure that Prosser identifies as potentially having

> considerable importance in providing a basis for a more positive approach to services of general interest [that] … serves to impose on both Member States and on the Community a positive duty to facilitate the achievement of public service missions, and … represents the basis for developing a European concept of citizenship rights. (Prosser, 2005, p. 553, citing Ross, 2000)

In *Ambulanz Glöckner* (Case C-475/99), the approach of the Court was to change from an analysis of whether the general interest service was viable on application of the competition rules towards a consideration of whether the quality and reliability of the service could be maintained. This more liberal approach is still new and tentative, and whilst there was scope for supporters of the public service approach to find some consolation in the Court's ruling in *Altmark* (Case C-280/00), where it held that subsidies that are regarded as compensation for services provided by undertakings discharging public service obligations, do not constitute state aid where four conditions could be met. The conditions, however, are ambiguous and, as Bovis suggests, '[t]he approach adopted by the European judiciary indicates the presence of *marchés publics, sui generis* markets where the state intervenes in pursuit of public interest' (Bovis, 2005, p. 27).

The key issue highlighted by this change of attitude to general interest services by the Community institutions is that the *value of citizenship* has a growing legitimacy in the context of general (and public) services that are themselves developing 'as essential expressions of our citizenship rights as Europeans' (Prosser, 2005, p. 563).

Retail markets and the changing role of consumers

A derivative of the economic citizen, the market citizen has been identified as distinguished but not distinct from the citizen proper, effectively 'the role of the market citizen is that which citizens proper are expected to undertake in the service of their community' (Everson, 1995, p. 85). A role that was to be 'the major part which the nationals of member states were expected to play within Europe' (Everson, 1995, p. 88) in the development of the status of the individual under Community law: an ongoing process in the constitutionalisation of free movement rights and the right to non-discrimination on the grounds of nationality (Shaw, 1997b, p. 556). Commenting on the concept of citizenship as defined in the Treaty, Downes suggests that 'the most effective of the limited bundle of rights' was 'market citizenship'. It is a provocative notion of citizenship that, whilst drawing legitimacy from the core rights associated with the fundamental freedoms of the free movement of goods, services, persons and capital, and the freedom of establishment, it is also a concept of citizenship that may be challenged. Analysis of the market citizen acting in the role of the *consumer* presents a particular challenge in that, where consumer rights are, as suggested above, predicated on *choice*, citizenship rights have more traditionally been associated with *entitlements* (Downes, 2001, p. 93).

The European consumer was, however, integral to the Community's internal market strategy and developed behavioural characteristics that were reflected in Community secondary legislation. Not only were consumers to benefit from market integration, but it was to be in the actions of the consumer 'that citizens will above all judge the success of the internal market. The Union must treat consumer concerns as a key element of the Internal Market's commitment to the citizen' (Commission, 1999, p. 10). Everson (1995, p. 87) highlights the notion that this active market citizen was first to appear in the guise of the *aggressive consumer* who was to be supported in his engagement with the internal market by the law. A law that was to provide for 'access to the widest possible range of... products available in the Community so that he can choose that which is best suited to his needs' (Directive (EEC) 92/49, Preamble para. 19).

The Court had already extended choice for the active market citizen beyond the national market, albeit only in the guise of the corporate or collective consumer in *Commission* v *Germany* (Case 205/84). The case concerned the free movement of services and the German insurance supervision law that required insurance undertakings in the EU, wishing to provide services in Germany in relation to direct insurance business, to be established and authorised in Germany. The Court upheld the Commission's contention that Germany had failed in this area to fulfil its obligations under Articles 59 and 60 EEC (now Articles 56 and 57 TFEU) and, in doing so, provided a role for the market citizen based on choice. At the least, one sector of the insurance market had been removed from restrictive national competition policy and elevated into the internal market with competition, and market building, predicated on *consumer choice*.

In exercising consumer choice within the trans-national market the active market citizen was, from a policy perspective, to be equipped with 'appropriate information and education' and given 'a voice in decisions which involve him': resources that were recognised to have

> [v]ery often...resulted in either eliminating non-tariff barriers to trade or harmonizing the rules of competition by which manufacturers and retailers must abide...and to help establish conditions for improved consultation between consumers on the one hand and manufacturers and retailers on the other. (Council, 1981, Introduction, paras 1 and 2)

Thus equipped, the confident consumer was to 'contribute to the strengthening of the internal market' (Wilhelmsson, 2004, p. 318). The Court, in *GB-INNO-BM*, endorsed this policy approach and acknowledged the relationship between the market access afforded to the consumer and the fundamental nature of free movement. This time, in the context of the free movement of goods, the Court reasserted that 'under Community law...the provision of information to the consumer is considered one of the principal requirements' (Case C-362/88, para. 18) and held that

> [f]ree movement of goods concerns not only traders but also *individuals*. It requires, particularly in frontier areas, that consumers resident in one Member State may travel freely to the territory of another Member State to shop under the same conditions as the local population. (Case C-362/88, para. 8, emphasis added)

It was the so-called 'Janus-faced' character of EC consumer law and policy that in one direction pursued the completion of the internal market and in the other the development of consumer protection measures (Reich, 1996, p. 56, cited in Wilhelmsson, 2004, p. 319). Consumer protection measures of minimum harmonisation were introduced and national regulatory measures judicially set aside as a way to 'stimulate the consumers to shop across the borders and this will in turn activate the internal market' (Wilhelmsson, 2004, p. 320): harmonising directives that explicitly relied on the consumer confidence argument, asserting

> the creation of a common set of minimum rules of consumer law, valid no matter where goods are purchased within the Community, will strengthen consumer confidence and enable consumers to make the most of the internal market. (Directive (EC) 99/44, Preamble, para. 5)

And,

> [i]n order to safeguard freedom of choice, which is an essential consumer right, a high degree of consumer protection is required in order to enhance consumer confidence in distance selling. (Directive (EC) 2002/65, Preamble, para. 3)

The efficacy of such interventions, established on the premise of consumer confidence, and, at a minimum, in relation to the promotion of cross-border shopping for consumer goods as an aspect of market building, was, however, to be significantly challenged. Wilhelmsson criticised the 'consumer confidence' argument 'on the basis of common sense, of self-evident knowledge about how consumers act in the marketplace'.[4] The basis of such criticism rests on the doubts over the consumers' awareness of their rights on a national level. Even where there is a general lack of knowledge of the contents of one's own legal system, it is a lack of knowledge that 'does not deter them from shopping in their national surroundings' (Wilhelmsson, 2004, p. 325). Optimistically perhaps, more recent empirical evidence from Eurobarometer surveys suggests there is 'an almost unanimous interest in cross-border shopping, or at least the principle of the idea... seems to be evolving' (Eurobarometer, 2004, p. 8). Notably, the exception to unanimity seems to be located in some ideologically based resistance in a few of the new accession States where

> the inhabitants may see themselves as still lagging far 'behind' economically (Baltic States, Slovenia and Poland), a distancing from the

'consumer society' and/or a certainty that the products considered are of far *better quality* in one's own country (notably fresh food produce in the 'least rich' and 'most agricultural' countries, countries of Central Europe, Baltic countries etc.). (Eurobarometer, 2004, p. 20, emphasis in the original)

In general this evidence suggests that deliberate cross-border shopping is only triggered if the expected price benefit is worth the trouble, a subjective approach, assessed on a case-by-case basis in terms of percentage for inexpensive products or absolute value for major purchases. The reality appears to be that, with the exception of border regions and those small countries that can be characterised as a border region in their entirety, cross-border consumer purchases are generally occasional and low in volume. Distance transactions based on mail order and on internet shopping still remain limited, attracting concern over the security of the financial transaction, fraud and non-delivery, and doubts over after-sales service and guarantees (Eurobarometer, 2004, p. 42).

Modern markets and choice in consumer citizenship practice

Consumer citizenship practice and the general (public) interest responsibility

The hybridisation of the public/private law divide, particularly in the heavily regulated environment of services of general economic interest, together with the amalgam of political and economic forces have been suggested to create *a new area of law* (Micklitz, 2009, p. 9). It is a new area of law in which citizenship, fundamental rights, and public services are closely interdependent concepts that are merging, increasingly, into one another and in which the formerly complementary but separate categories of the private individual and the citizen are coming together with a fusion of their rights (Picard, 1998, pp. 83 and 94). Picard has identified that, depending on circumstances, this modernisation of the public services sector has tended to make 'everyone either a user or agent of a universal enterprise managed or headed by itself, whose fundamental law is no longer the freedom to arrange one's own affairs, but the general interest'. A general interest in which the 'reference standard is no longer the individual autonomy of persons but the needs of the general public as translated into the interest of the service'. It is a *general public interest* where individual autonomy is replaced by the rights and duties of a consumer citizenship practice that, I would argue, bring a shared responsibility between individuals and the institutions and agencies of the EU and Member States, to participate in the decisions of production and management and in the distribution and equal redistribution of wealth (Picard, 1998, pp. 95 and 97).

The method of participation is through the exercise of choice, a thematic notion that has run throughout the notion of consumer citizenship practice that I have developed in this book. Lewis has argued that *choice* 'is the most satisfactory label for the bundle of primary or fundamental rights which have been almost universally adopted in the West' (Lewis, 1996, p. 4). He asserts that choice, as a freedom 'is at the heart of the human condition' where justification for markets is a human rights choice justification that obliges the State (i.e., government at the EU or Member State level) to restore choice and freedom in failing markets through regulation and competition enforcement. For Lewis, it is the task of government to maximise the conditions for individuals to exercise choice: for him, the market is a moral concept in which the exercise of choice is paramount. His model acknowledges the need for recognition of both the natural capacities of individuals *and* their ability to exert them in the policies for empowerment of individuals and the 'freeing up [of] the ability to realise chosen ends' (Lewis, 1996, p. 58).

It is in the nature of this empowered participation by the individuals concerned that we discover the behaviours that define the model consumer citizenship practice that is central to this book. They are the behaviours of the *consumer* who is, on the one hand bound by stricter requirements on the freedom to contract and their freedom to shape contractual relations (Micklitz, 2009, p. 11) and yet, on the other hand is now required to choose his or her service provider in an increasingly privatised and competitive service sector. They are also, and at the same time, the behaviours of the *citizen* contained within Hirschman's market metaphor of the three primary *choices* of exit, voice and loyalty (Hirschman, 1970), and Lewis' theory of public service predicated on the market concept of *choice*. Taken together, they are the behaviours that Harlow has classified as a distinct ideology of 'citizen participation', a

> pluralist *and* communitarian ideal [that] saw the function of law as 'to advance the cause of public participation against both the orthodox public administration approach to the public interest and the Common Law approach of the overriding importance of private property' (Harlow, 1998, p. 55, quoting McAuslan, 1981, p. 2, emphasis added)

The participatory behaviours that define consumer citizenship practice and that contribute to the general public interest can then be seen to extend from the exercise of choice, as seen in the individualistic pursuit by Mrs Watts, that resulted in the changed management of hospital waiting lists in the UK. Through her actions, and the Court's approach to the law regarding free movement of services and the free movement of persons to secure health care (Case C-372/04), the management of hospital capacity through waiting lists became subordinate to a patient-centred, needs-based, approach with waiting lists subject to *clinical* justification (Davies, 2007, pp. 160–161). At the other end of the spectrum, consumer citizenship practice is to be found in the broad range of more communitarian behavioural attributes of the active consumer; the confident, responsible and green consumer, and the involved consumer introduced in Chapter 2.

Such a consumer citizenship practice provides for an extension of Lewis' moral concept of the market in which individuals behavioural changes are 'motivated by the internalisation of particular normative orientations [which] is more effective and longer lasting than behavioural changes based on external or coercive imposition' (Barry, 1996, p. 122). This is the exercise of the *choice* to change one's lifestyle or pattern of consumption in the belief that it is the right thing to do: an act of *citizenship* 'understood as a mediating practice which connects the individual and the institutional levels of society [and provides] ... a common identity which links otherwise disparate individuals together as a collectivity with common interests' (Barry, 1996, p. 123). What makes this citizenship dimension of consumer behaviour important is that the state, as defined at any level, cannot do everything: an assertion that is particularly relevant in the context of sustainability and that can be illustrated through EU consumer policy proposals. Following, for example, from the initial success, in terms of economic growth and jobs, of the Lisbon strategy, the Commission has emphasised a need to 'move towards more sustainable patterns of consumption' (Commission, 2008d, p. 2). Amongst the prioritized actions to flow from this objective, and one that emphasises the citizenship dimension of consumer behaviour, has been the recasting of the Energy Labelling Directive (Directive (EEC) 92/75) as 'an essential building block for an integrated sustainable environmental product policy, promoting and stimulating the demand for better products *and helping consumers make better choices*' (Commission, 2008e, p. 2, emphasis added).

From citizen to consumer citizen: political consumption and the market politic

Product labelling as a mechanism for empowering consumer choice in the EU is not confined to energy consumption labelling of household appliances. The legislative base of product labelling and packaging extends to some 79 separate directives and regulations that cover both food and non-food products. These are legislative instruments designed to inform the consumer of the composition of products, in order that they may *choose* products that will be protective of their health and interests; to inform the consumer of the origin or production methods of the product, in order that they may *choose* products on ethical, environmental and cultural grounds; and to inform the consumer of aspects of the product necessary to guarantee safe use and to allow consumers to exercise real *choice.*

Product labelling significantly develops the political potential of consumption, 'it is no longer merely votes that matter; politically and ethically motivated consumer choice in the market arena matters as well' (Boström and Klintman, 2008, p. 2). Boström and Klintman identify that active consumer choice reflects citizens' political concerns that are exercised through either boycotting particular products or by 'consciously choosing environmentally and/or socially friendly products': 'buycotting' (Boström and Klintman, 2008, and discussed above in Chapter 2 in the context of 'Naderism'). Their research identifies that the literature on political consumerism indicates a positive trend with increasing numbers of individuals consciously boycotting or buycotting products for political and ethical reasons: a practice they describe as 'an example of "individualistic collective action"' that offers a more flexible, spontaneous and everyday channel to express engagement and responsibility over various issues (Boström and Klintman, 2008, p. 10).

Even though scientific analysis of consumer boycotts indicates significant barriers to their effectiveness (Delacote, 2009), Stolle and others, confirm the rise in political consumption through reference to recent empirical research and historical examples which identifies both 'that a growing number of citizens are turning to the market to express their political and moral concerns' and that 'political consumer activism can be an effective way of changing both corporate and governmental policy and behaviour' (Stolle, Hooghe and Micheletti, 2005, p. 248). They identify that political consumers 'choose particular producers or products because they want to change institutional or market practices. They make their choices based on considerations of justice or fairness, or on an assessment of business and government practices.' Identified through the lens of political science, these are the choice behaviours of consumer citizenship practice, that are defined as *'consumer choice of producers and products based on political or ethical considerations, or both'* (Stolle, Hooghe and Micheletti, 2005, p. 246).

From this perspective, the consumer citizen is born out of acts of political consumption and acts, either individually or collectively to make market choices that 'reflect an understanding of material products as embedded in a complex social and normative context' (Stolle, Hooghe and Micheletti, 2005, citing Micheletti, 2003). Such understanding reflects the value orientation and social embeddedness that, I argue, highlights the importance of the consumer citizenship education discussed above in Chapter 3, and shows itself in post-materialist concerns for the environment, equality, human rights and sustainable development (Stolle, Hooghe and Micheletti, 2005, p. 252).

From customer to consumer citizen: hybridisation of public and private law

The increased opportunity for choice and the broad range of individual behaviours associated with the consumer citizenship practice discussed in this book also find a particular relevance in the modernisation of the public services sector.[5] Micklitz suggests that it is this modernisation process, and specifically the privatisation and liberalisation of services of general economic interest that has yielded the concept of the consumer citizen: that the consumer citizen, in law, has appeared as a consequence of a hybridisation of the public/private law divide in the triangular relationship between the state regulatory agencies, the privatised service provider and the *customer* (Micklitz, 2009, pp. 9–10, although it is acknowledged that he uses the reversed and hyphenated term citizen-consumer). Even here, the use of the word 'customer' may be seen as a 'modern' connotation in the area of public service provision, particularly with regard to the telecommunication sector, where the individual accessing such services prior to the privatisation and liberalisation initiatives was more likely to be identified as a 'subscriber'.

Services of general interest are allocated a space within the shared values of the European Union and recognised as promoting social and territorial cohesion in the wake of market liberalisation. They take their legal base from Article 14 TFEU (Article 16 EC), Article 106(2) TFEU (Article 86(2) EC) and Article 36 of the Charter of Fundamental Rights although, of these three instruments, it is only Article 106(2) TFEU (Article 86(2) EC) that enjoys direct effect. Taken together, however, these measures provide for a diverse range of public and private bodies to overcome the risk of competition rules obstructing the provision of a legitimate national public service interest. It is a risk that stems from the application of Article 101 TFEU (Article 81 EC) rules to *undertakings* and the paradox whereby vertically integrated services provided by public authorities may escape these competition rules whereas undertakings providing *the same services* may find the rules applied to a degree that threatens the provision of such a legitimate public service (Sauter, 2008). As a legal concept, such general interest services provide a resolution to this paradox through the use of public and universal service obligations that allow for proportionate restrictions to be applied to competition in the liberalised economy that mediate 'between traditional state duties towards citizens and the demands of competitive markets' (Szyszczak, 2007, p. 213).

It may be possible to distinguish services of general interest from the more specific services of general *economic* interest, as a term used in Article 106 TFEU (Article 86 EC) that refers to those commercial market services of general economic utility which the Member States subject to specific public service obligations by virtue of a general interest criterion. However, Micklitz' introduces us to a discussion of the hybridisation of the public/private law divide that is located in this same space: a space in which he suggests it is 'simply a dead end to try to distinguish between non-economic and economic' sectors, yet still a space in which the consumer citizen concept is rooted (Micklitz, 2009, p. 9). This is a construct of the consumer citizen in which the *citizen* is elevated to the status of the *consumer citizen* as a consequence of the 'extension of the entrepreneurial statutory activities' but is also reduced from the full status of the *consumer* with a complete freedom to contract 'due to the fact that the state remains involved in regulation of the public sector even after privatisation' (Micklitz, 2009, p. 9).

The traditional bilateral private law relationship, based on freedom to contract between the customer and the merchant, was superseded in those sectors that became state monopolies providing services of general interest. The incumbent service provider was obliged to contract with the customer and the legal relationship between the state monopoly and the customer switched to a public law setting, in which price was often determined by political subsidy. The subsequent privatisation of the state monopolies and the liberalisation of the services of general interest markets introduced new dynamics into the customer–service provider relationship. Privatisation brought with it the concept of a *universal service obligation* that reached 'beyond the limits set to the freedom of contract via standard terms legislation' (Micklitz, 2009, pp. 9–10) and introduced a guarantee of 'access to all, irrespective of the economic, social or geographical situation, at a specified quality and an affordable price' (Szyszczak, 2007, pp. 244–245). Whilst privatisation was accompanied by rules to prevent social exclusion, liberalisation of the services of general interest introduced competition in the provision of services and *choice* of service provider. The essential nature of this marketisation of public services attracted an amalgam of developing normative processes and the hybridisation of public and private law in *sector-specific regulation* implemented through secondary legislation that 'generally takes precedence over the competition law rules found in the primary... legislation of the EC Treaty' (Freedland, 2001, p. 141).

This is a regulatory framework in which the Commission expresses an aspiration for an active and participatory consumer citizenship practice with, suggests Micklitz, the regulatory agencies acting as 'representatives' of the consumer citizen interest (Micklitz, 2009, p. 16). It is a representative role for the regulatory agencies that the Commission has described by suggesting that

> [t]he capacity of consumers and users... to take up their rights, especially their right of access, often requires the existence of independent regulators with appropriate staff and clearly defined powers and duties. These include powers of sanction, in particular the ability to monitor the transposition and enforcement of universal service provisions. These also require provisions for the *representation and active participation of consumers and users* in the definition and evaluation of services, the availability of appropriate redress and compensation mechanisms, and the existence of a review clause allowing requirements to be adapted over time to reflect new social, technological and economic developments. (Commission, 2007e, pp. 10–11, emphasis added)

Yet, as Micklitz points out, there is no legal obligation in the secondary legislation for the regulatory agencies to uphold the rights of consumer citizens although '[t]here is a gradual movement of [EU] secondary law into that direction which might overcome... the still existing discrepancies between the role and function of the regulatory agencies in the Member States' (Micklitz, 2009, p. 16).[6]

Conclusion

This chapter has provided a definition for a developing consumer citizenship practice based on the idea of individuals acting, alone or collectively, in the role of a politicised consumer and within a market characterized within four broad sectors. Across all sectors this development is increasingly embracing consumption as a normative good although the model of consumer citizenship is still subject to limitations and threats. The basis of this model draws on a notion of citizenship established in terms of process and access: process that is variable both between and within broad market sectors and access that marks a distinction between areas of European social solidarity and areas of free market individualism.

Whilst there may be little in the Treaty that explicitly facilitates the involvement of citizens with the actual process of European decision-making, the Court has proved to be an active institution in the constitutionalisation of free movement rights and the right to non-discrimination on the ground of nationality. Where globalisation and developing technology have impacted on the nation state's capacity for autonomous action, the Court has developed economic and market-related rights for the economic citizen that have been reflected in subsequent legislation. Individualistic, active and informed consumer citizenship has been at the heart of the Unions approach, and perhaps a reaction to European economic integration in a world economy influenced by the effects of globalisation. International inter-dependence and economic convergence have been accompanied by a gradually increasing political accountability and an ever more active civil society at the EU level. Even though specific market areas may be subject to restrictions based on science rather than politics, internal and external pressures have in general resulted in a thickening of the content of market citizenship, although, the tangible aspects of this content are variable, depending on the market sector, and rely on a redefinition of the citizenship container within an EU territorial dimension.

The analysis in this chapter brought a focus to four broad and overlapping sectors within the market that each, to varying degrees and in different ways, appear to lend some legitimacy to the notion of the consumer citizen and to consumer citizenship practice. Out of this analysis has also come a new rudimentary model of the boundaries and spaces of EU consumer citizenship that helps to clarify the relationship between individuals couched in terms of access rights and choice duties, the market with its sectoral membership dimensions, and the EU with its post-national territorial dimension. The development of this model can be seen as related to structural changes in the market: changes that have seen a degree of commodification of public services with new profitable fields for both public and private investment in the public sector; changes that have seen social rights de-coupled from national citizenship and linked merely to work or residency status.

Through both negative and positive integrational initiatives the social welfare sector provides access gateways to basic compulsory welfare schemes and social assistance. Increasingly, access to, and consumption of, these welfare products is predicated on *individual rights* and *residency principles*. The development of EU citizenship in this area provides for more market focussed supplementary pensions which in turn give way to fully private pensions products and mark a tension between an area of social solidarity and the individualism of the free market. This has been fertile ground for the Court in its pursuance of the principle of non-discrimination on grounds of nationality and its 'broader objective of creating an area in which community citizens enjoy freedom of movement' (Case 66/85, para. 12).

Under the heading of 'public sector' the discussion has concentrated on education and health services. In these two key areas the Court has reflected the general enthusiasm shown by the other institutions of the EU, since the mid-1980s, for providing access to public sector services through the development of individual rights. An objective of which also appears to encourage the improvement of trust in the governance of these services through engaging individuals in the social dimensions of the internal market.

As we progress along the membership dimension of the model of EU consumer citizenship, Hirschman's theory of exit, voice and loyalty appears to have a particular resonance with the recognition, by the Commission, of the increasingly assertive consumer engaging with the services and networks of general interest sector. Not only does this sector, on the basis of Article 14 TFEU (Article 16 EC), have the potential for developing a specific 'European concept' of citizenship rights, Micklitz identifies it as the source of a new area of law that has brought about a legal basis for the concept of the consumer citizen in the hybridisation of public and private law. The broader concept of the consumer citizen, derived from the political sciences, is also identified in the discussion on political consumerism where choice, of either the producers/service providers or of products, and across all sectors of the market, becomes a channel for the exercise of responsibility based on political and/or ethical considerations in consumer citizenship practice.

5
The Relevance and Limitations of Consumer Citizenship Practice

Introduction

This book has so far discussed the economic and social aspects of a consumer citizenship practice where the importance of monitoring consumer outcomes is reflected in the Commission's 2007–2013 Consumer Policy Strategy and in the degree to which the consumer's voice, rights and expertise can be integrated into the EU's structures of 'new governance'. It has provided a discussion of the politics of EU consumer law in which the model of the consumer citizen is associated with a developing social responsibility, an increasingly assertive role, and market shaping. In this final substantive chapter my intention is to bring a focus to the *theoretical relevance* and to the *practical limitations* of this conception of consumer citizenship practice.

In its opening section this chapter addresses the issue of *how to apply* the theoretical concept of consumer citizenship practice. It achieves this through the drawing together of the normative components of consumer citizenship practice identified in this book. The resulting model is then assembled into a hierarchical framework through which the functioning of any particular sector of the market may be assessed from the perspective of the model of consumer citizenship practice that I have sought to elaborate. It is a model that emphasises the complexity associated with the concept of consumer citizenship and highlights the barriers that limit the degree to which consumer citizenship practice can reasonably be expected to achieve the freedom and responsibility reflected in the duty aspect of the ambitions of Barrington's curly headed boy and the exercise of true position and power espoused by Redfern.

The subsequent sections of this chapter then assess the effectiveness of the functioning of the energy sector within its legal and regulatory framework, as measured against the framework of the normative components of consumer citizenship practice. Energy has been chosen as a case study because of its relative importance as a market sector; it is an essential good and service in the internal market, crucial for business and domestic consumers; the results of the largely regulatory approach to liberalisation have been mediocre (Von Rosenberg, 2009) and are giving way to a more consumer rights focus in policy and legislation (Commission, 2007b); and finally, because of the particular challenges and opportunities the energy sector offers for a developing consumer citizenship practice. Further, as Mombaur has suggested, the importance of the sector cannot be overstated; and he places energy alongside 'knowledge, creativity and capital...[as] one of the fundamental necessities of humankind'; it is as central and crucial a sector as any to adopt for use as a case study (Mombaur, 2008).

The case study is divided into two sections; the first section examines the normative potential of the legal environment in the energy sector. Here, effective competition is central to policy objectives that are seeking to improve the efficiency of the sector, the security of supply and to provide for the sustainability of energy sources (House of Lords, 2008). Approached from this perspective, the energy sector lends itself to an examination of the impact of liberalisation in services of general economic interest (SGEI) on the consumer citizenship concept: a liberalisation, and associated privatisation, of what had previously been a centrally owned and managed public sector, utility and services market. Now, at the beginning of the implementation phase of a third European legislative package the sector is marked by new consumer rights (for example, universal and public service obligations); new consumer roles and relationships with new regulatory bodies (in both the control of unfair contract terms and competition enforcement), and new competitive markets (Micklitz, 2009, p. 10). As already identified in the 2nd Consumer Markets Scoreboard, the energy sector, and the retail electricity market in particular, has also raised concerns *inter alia* over the comparability of offers, of unfair commercial practices and billing transparency.

The second part of the case study acknowledges that the energy sector is experiencing significant challenges from environmental and sustainability factors that are a focus of green consumer activism and are triggering a technological revolution in energy management systems. These are areas of influence that call for a significant increase in the public's adoption of active and responsible consumer citizenship practice with regard to energy consumption/conservation, and yet qualitative research suggests there are significant barriers that stand in the way of engaging consumers with the behavioural changes necessary to achieve a positive environmental impact.:difficulties that are amplified, and demonstrated in this research, when attitudes towards energy consumption are analysed using a consumer segmentation model that divides energy consumers into groups according to their environmental values and pro-environmental behaviours.

Such consumer segmentation is commonly used as a critical marketing tool across all market sectors to help with identifying the most appropriate target market for a particular product. It also helps to define the right marketing communications strategy for relating the particular products' brand essence in a specific consumer segmented manner and forms the basis of customer relationship management (CRM). Now a normal component of business strategy, particularly in large organisations, CRM utilises technology to integrate marketing, sales, customer service and technical support activities in order to grow and retain its customer base and market share.

As a closing section to this chapter, the consumer segmentation model applied to the public's understanding of sustainable energy consumption in the home is applied to an empirical analysis of the likely impact of the roll-out of smart metering on consumer behaviour. A roll-ut associated with the EU's energy policy that intends 'to equip 80 per cent of energy consumers with smart meters by 2020... [and] to encourage European energy consumers to become active participants in how they use energy' (Smartmeters.com, 2009).

Normative components of consumer citizenship practice

An introduction to the normative hierarchy of consumer citizenship practice

In order to apply the concept of consumer citizenship practice developed in this book, this section makes the proposition that the model adheres to a normative hierarchy. This is a hierarchy that provides a functional framework for evaluating consumer citizenship practice as a factor of market functioning, by market sector. It is a tool that provides for the assessment of the extent to which consumers have the protection, information, capability and motivation to pursue their aspirations, if they have any, as market agents.

This hierarchical model of the normative elements of consumer citizenship practice is depicted in Figure 5.1 and is drawn together from the threads of arguments defining a coherent and tangible notion of consumer citizenship practice contained in previous chapters. Brought together in this way, these are threads of argument that support the notion of consumer citizenship and explain the relationships between four levels of normative influences in consumer citizenship practice. Whilst depicted as hierarchical levels, these normative influences are interlinked and interrelated such that the effectiveness of each level has dependencies contingent on both its subordinate and superior levels.

Whilst closely interlinked and interrelated, the separate levels of this hierarchy are also distinct in their normative dimensions. In its normative dimension European consumer protection law addresses the issues of how legal rules can be formulated to complete the internal market, to protect vulnerable consumers or to provide mechanisms for redress with regard to faulty or damaged goods or services. This is the legal base in the hierarchy of consumer citizenship practice that, at a minimum, makes available to individuals a framework of consumer rights to which they can appeal (see, generally, MacCormick, 2007). The second level comprises normative sources of information and their dependencies that are a necessary adjunct to consumer empowerment, even if their effect is limited by the need for the information to be understood and where, if understood, the consumer is motivated and able to act on it. At the third level, capability is used within the dual context of Amartya Sen's *capability approach* that gives normative priority to the existential features of functionings and Rawlsian principles of social justice that were discussed in Chapter 3: social justice that is dependent on structural policies to alleviate the poverty, inequality and unemployment that would exclude those affected groups from the market. This is social justice that Echávarri discusses in the context of *social capability* and the individuals' access to the capability for being self-sufficient, the capability for self respect and the *capability for agency* (Echávarri, 2003). Finally, at the highest level of the normative hierarchy, motivation is used as a label for normative behaviour that can be understood in the context of the intrinsic motivation directed by the individual consumer's sense of compliance with, and commitment to, personal and social norms, and their identification with the social groups that they associate themselves with.[1]

Dependencies, contingencies and relationships of the normative hierarchy model

In its communication on a internal market for twenty-first-century Europe the Commission identified that it was a central goal of the consumer

Level	Normative hierarchy			Features/enablers	Barriers/consequences
4	Motivation		Solidaristic and communitarian	Self-responsibility; altruism; ethical and sustainable consumption; communal interest; perceived effectiveness of action; wealth; trustworthiness of information source; 'good guilt' social trends	Capability barriers; dependency on education and/or capability factors; unwilling to act; cost; attitude–behaviour gap; information overload;
			Individualistic	Self-responsibility; personal safety; demand for quality and reduced cost; self interest; perceived effectiveness of action; wealth	Capability barriers; dependency on education and/or capability factors; unwilling to act; cost; attitude–behaviour gap
		Structural	Market	Open markets and free competition; absolute and comparative monitoring of consumer behaviours / outcomes (e.g. scoreboard and eurobarometer); access to national consumer agencies; product design; soft law in the form of industry standards and voluntary codes of quality; corporate social responsibility; non-discriminatory dignity and respect	Market distortion and market failure; competition and policy deficit; market power; inadequate unbundling in network sectors; lack of operational transparency; general consumer detriment; product design; generic delivery and consumer interface models
			Social	Access to primary social goods (rights, liberties, opportunities, powers and income and wealth); perceived individual responsibility; future focussed; able to take action; no/few personal needs conflicts with action; access to informed for a and/or social groups	Cultural barriers; little/no sense of individual responsibility; cost driven choice/no choice; present focussed; unacceptable or unfeasible goals
3	Capability	Individual	Cognitive	The exercise of informed, educated and reasoned, value guided choice; learned experience	Individual consumer detriment; false perceptions of consumer welfare; limited access to education
			Physical	Active and communicative; confidence and self assuredness; switching; complaining	Vulnerability through disability, age, language and deprivation; individual consumer detriment
			Financial	The means to choose not limited to price	Limitation of means; financial vulnerability; consumer detriment

2	Information	Product labelling and branding	Origin and content data; safety information; energy efficiency ratings; 'green' labelling; brand identification; product differentiation; informed choice	Technical terminology; pace of life; accessibility of information; dependency on education and/or capability; globalised e-commerce
		Education and public information	Market functioning indicators (scoreboard data); consumer agency awareness; confident consumers; informed choice; school's curriculum	Insufficient education opportunity and/or capability barriers; information overload
		National consumer organisations	Product comparison; representative action; popular awareness and media presence; informed choice; promotion of consumer interests	Insufficient education and/or capability to exploit information; lack of conformity between Member States
1	Protection	Empowerment	Consumer rights and redress mechanisms; consumer voice and influence; consumer agency in policy development; universal / public service rights; informed choice; trust in national consumer agencies; transparency of contract terms	Consumer irrationality and inconsistency; narrow interpretation of subsidiarity; lack of understanding and/or acceptance of self-responsibility
		Enforcement	Effective public enforcement and regulatory agencies; universal / public service obligations; transparent redress mechanisms; ADR provisions; competition authorities	Competition enforcement deficit; access to (competition) evidence; cost; globalised e-commerce; lack of awareness of enforcement processes

Figure 5.1 Normative hierarchy of consumer citizenship practice

policy strategy to *empower* all consumers, including those more vulnerable consumers with special needs or disabilities (Commission, 2007d, p. 6). This is a consumer policy strategy that was discussed in Chapter 2 and that recognises the relevance of empowered consumers as the 'motor of economic change', that through *information and education* such empowerment has the dual objective of providing consumers with the means to protect themselves and the consequential drive towards quality improvement and competition for goods and services in the market. This relationship between the first two levels in the normative hierarchy of consumer citizenship practice depicted in Figure 5.1 is explicitly extended to the fourth, *motivation*, level by the Commission's consumer policy strategy for 2007–2013 where the objective of shifting the focus of regulation 'towards citizen-focussed outcomes', is based on the provision of market tools to 'empower citizens, as consumers, to make sustainable environmental choices' (Commission, 2007a, p. 3). The broad approach of the Commission is to encourage *empowerment* and personal development through inclusive policies and services aimed at reducing dependence and supporting the autonomy and self-reliance of people such that they will be able to adopt greater responsibilities and manage their own affairs (Commission, 2001c, 2007a). It is an approach that links the *empowerment* aspect of consumer protection with both the *information* and *motivation* levels in the normative hierarchy by seeking to ensure that consumers can, through better information, be able to make 'informed, environmentally and socially responsible choices on food, the most advantageous products and services, and those that correspond most to their lifestyle objectives' (Commission, 2005b, section 4.2.4).

At the information level, consumer empowerment is supported by product information, branding and labelling that the Court recognises contains a mechanism for achieving consumer protection. However, as identified in Chapter 2, empowerment through information has already been identified as a 'contrivance of limited effect' and 'wasted on many'. Physical access to product information may be a necessary prerequisite for acquiring empowering information but it needs to be complemented with intellectual and social access in order to realise its full potential (Burnett, Jaeger and Thompson, 2008, p. 66). Again, as has already been shown, Howells has catalogued existing empirical studies in which he identifies that busy lives and the frequent need to seek out information result in few consumers taking any notice of the information provided, although some do, and, he suggests, some of these may have more reason to than others; those that do form a 'margin of active information seeking consumers [that] can have a healthy impact on the market' (Howells, 2005, p. 357). This is a margin with the cognitive capability to exercise value-guided and informed choice to push up standards for all and that connect the information, motivation and capability levels of consumer citizenship practice. A margin where information is empowering for the consumer, where information can be absorbed and where the individual is motivated and is able to act on the information.

Howells identified limitations in the normative value of information for those with busy lives and the frequent need to seek out information, and suggested that choice for all, but particularly for the poor, may merely be illusory (Howells, 2005, p. 358). Consumers do not, or cannot, always make rational and fully informed choices: consequentially, consumer detriment impinges on normative aspects of motivation and capability and justifies the introduction of consumer protection measures. In contrast, Scammell provides a far more positive commentary. As we have already identified, she sees possibilities for information and choice effectively transforming the market and the power of the consumer, relative to that of the producer, such that '[i]ncreasingly producers will have to find products for consumers, not customers for pre-designed products' (Scammell, 2003, p. 120).

For European policy makers, Europe Economics has provided a detailed report that both analyses the issues of personal and structural consumer detriment and identifies its potential use as a policy tool. *Structural consumer detriment* is identified as an economics-based concept that focuses on the loss of consumer welfare due to market or regulatory failure and that has the potential to apply across an entire market or sector (Europe Economics, 2007, pp. 40–41). In its analysis of structural detriment, the report suggests that the Commission might use the concept in the context of competition law, citing mergers and Article 101 or Article 102 TFEU (Article 81 EC or Article 82 EC) investigations; and in the '[i]mpact assessment of policies designed to improve outcomes for consumers by addressing market or regulatory failures'. The relevant benchmark for the purposes of policy assessment, the report suggests, 'is simply consumer welfare without the policy' (Europe Economics, p. 66).

In contrast, Europe Economics associates the concept of *personal consumer detriment* with a focus on negative outcomes for individual consumers, relative to some benchmark such as expectations or reasonable expectations, and the idea that some aspects of this type of detriment depend on the psychology of the person concerned. With regard to consumer welfare, the report identifies a number of aspects of *personal detriment*, providing examples of 'things which could constitute a "negative outcome" for a consumer' that include financial loss, inconvenience, loss of time, stress, low quality products and reduced real choice. Such examples are then categorised as *financial* or *non-financial detriment* and take the form of a psychological damage that is revealed through negative feelings of anger, worry or regret (Europe Economics, p. 47). These are feelings that may be associated with the counterfactual benchmark of consumer expectations (actual or reasonable), and in which 'personal detriment becomes almost identical to widely-accepted definitions of consumer dissatisfaction' (Europe Economics, p. 49). The report also highlights the complexities that may be associated with the use of 'expectations' as a counterfactual in an EU context: it draws attention *inter alia* to the lower level of consumer expectation that may be found in the newer Member States, as compared to the EU-15, who may as a consequence 'appear to suffer lower detriment even if, objectively measured, consumer outcomes are actually worse'.

The relationship between EU policy formulation, the EU's legal framework of consumer protection and the normative aspects of consumer citizenship practice proposed in this book are drawn together with a symbiotic relevance in the Europe Economics report. The report expressly identifies personal consumer detriment as 'a useful concept for policy-makers' such that through consumer protection, consumers may be provided with 'greater assurance, thus encouraging participation in the market and potentially improving market outcomes' (Europe Economics, p. 57). An assurance that may help to bring about a reduction in consumer detriment through the developing legal framework of consumer protection measures, through an increased consumer motivation and through improved capability in consumer citizenship practice. The concept of personal consumer detriment, the report suggests, 'seems particularly relevant to policy proposals which seek to ... provide a framework for well-functioning markets ... [and] [p]rotect against negative outcomes which are so severe that society is unwilling that anyone should be exposed to them' (Europe Economics, p. 58).

Consumer agency and the relevance of consumer citizenship practice

Despite the legislative provisions that provide for a general consumer protection through enforcement and empowerment mechanisms, and include protection for vulnerable consumers, their effectiveness is tempered by the individual consumer's irrational, incoherent and inconsistent role as a market actor in which he or she may seek out risk and excitement and may, or may not be fettered by moral considerations: a limiting of the normative effectiveness of European consumer protection that has also been questioned, by the EESC, and linked to a concern that too narrow an interpretation of subsidiarity could present another barrier to consumer empowerment.

Consumer protection, as the foundation level in the normative hierarchy of consumer citizenship practice outlined in Figure 5.1, is characterised by the provisions of the EU's consumer *acquis* and other legislative initiatives that provide for the empowerment and enforcement paradigms depicted in Figure 3.1 and discussed throughout this book. They are the twin channels of consumer protection that have been identified as underpinning EU consumer policy and are identified with the 'smooth functioning of markets': a 'smooth functioning' that is monitored at the EU level in the two-stage process in which the Consumer Markets Scoreboard performs a screening of consumer markets as a prelude to detailed analysis of those market sectors that are then suspected of malfunctioning.[2]

The basic indicators of *consumer empowerment* and *market malfunctioning* employed in the Consumer Markets Scoreboard measure consumer complaints, redress, switching, enforcement of consumer rights, and trust in national consumer organisations to protect individual rights: monitoring that also provides for national benchmarking data focussed on enforcement. The Commission asserts that the 'Scoreboard initiative addresses the need to be more responsive to the expectations of citizens and pay greater attention to outcomes of policies' whilst, with the EU Consumer Policy Strategy 2007–2013, it is striving to empower EU consumers and to put consumer welfare at the heart of well-functioning markets. It is an initiative in which the value of individual consumer agency in the market is recognised by the Commission, in particular, with regard to the five 'top-level' indicators identified within the Scoreboard results: complaints, satisfaction, switching, prices and safety.

The Commission acknowledges that '[g]iven the effort required to complain, each complaint is a hard fact which indicates a potential problem in the market' (Commission, 2009b, p. 3). In the year leading up to February 2008, such monitoring identified that 16 per cent of EU consumers had made a formal complaint to a trader about a problem they encountered: a measure, that by extrapolation, the Commission equates to 'around 78 million European citizens making formal complaints in one year', and a total in which a 'quarter of those consumers took the matter to a third party organisation' (Commission, 2009b, p. 3, citing Eurobarometer, 2008). The number of complaints addressed to third parties is recognised in the Commission communication as being 'just the tip of the iceberg' and dependent on factors 'such as the perceived effectiveness of complaining, the level of anxiety involved, access to the legal system and so on' that are reflected, at various levels, in the features of the normative hierarchy of consumer citizenship practice defined in Figure 5.1.

Whilst direct complaints to traders are a normal part of the market process that does not necessarily indicate market malfunctioning, the collection and monitoring of complaints has the power to shape dialogue between public authorities and business. The Commission identifies that complaints are collected by consumer authorities or complaint bodies in all Member States but, for example, in Denmark, France and the UK, where third-party consumer organisations collect and monitor consumer complaints for a wide range of policy purposes, they are able to identify 'systemic issues that cause detriment to consumers' (Commission, 2009b, p. 4). Particular attention is drawn to the role played by complaints in the regulated sectors where Member States or regulatory bodies have an explicit role in monitoring market opening and competition at retail level and where there is an increasing trend of consumers addressing their complaints to the regulatory authorities (Commission, 2009b, p. 5).

Closely related to complaints, and specifically linked to prices and customer relations management, consumer satisfaction data shows less satisfaction with services than with goods markets. The second edition of the Consumer Markets Scoreboard drew attention to the more complex contracts, consumer relations and changing consumer environment when markets are liberalised. Whilst consumers using transport experience the lowest levels of satisfaction and the greatest number of problems, overall satisfaction was also low for fixed telephony, postal services and energy (electricity and gas supply) (Commission, 2009a, p. 3). The energy sector, as one of the problematic sectors surveyed in the Scoreboard exercise, was identified as scoring particularly badly in terms of switching with only 7 per cent of consumers switching gas supplier and 8 per cent electricity provider. Price data remains merely experimental at present but indicates cross-border issues for market functioning; yet of the problematic sectors identified in the Scoreboard 'energy is the one on which consumers spent most...of their household budget' (Commission, 2009b, p. 2).

Academic analysis of the savings that consumers would require to motivate them to switch supplier, from an incumbent gas supplier to a new entrant in the UK retail energy market, highlights the significance of the *consumer detriment* reflected in low switching rates and the failures in the liberalisation process. Based on a 1998 survey of consumer choice and industrial policy Giulietti, Waddams and Waterson argue that it was most profitable for the incumbent gas supplier to set a price significantly above that of its competitors, a pricing strategy which would have meant loosing 45 per cent of the market, but that by 2004 still left the consumer in a position where 'the incumbent will find it profitable to maintain a price £8 per month above average incremental cost, since even with such a differential, around 55% of customers will remain loyal... In such an equilibrium the majority of customers, who stay with the incumbent, would pay a price around 33% above the competitive level, hardly the hallmark of a strongly competitive market' (Giulietti, Waddams Price and Waterson, 2005, p. 963).

Consumer citizenship and liberalisation of the European energy market

This section opens an illustrative case study on the European energy market with a review of the developing legal and regulatory framework that has emerged since the mid-1990s. It is a history of essentially regulatory initiatives introduced to create a competitive energy market at the European level that even the Commission admits has been of mediocre effect (Von Rosenberg, 2009). The consequential consumer issues surrounding the comparability of offers, unfair commercial practices and billing raised by the 2nd Annual Consumer Scoreboard (Commission, 2009a) are also reflective of the Commission's 2007 inquiry into the European gas and electricity sectors that identified that consumers were demanding 'more competitive offers from non-incumbent suppliers and... [regretting] the absence of pan-European supply offers' as a consequence of high levels of market concentration in some Member States (Commission, 2006e, p. 8).[3] The legal and regulatory framework has now entered a third phase with a new legislative package comprising three Regulations and two Directives that bring a renewed drive to achieve full unbundling (i.e., separation of producers, network operators and retail suppliers) and an increased consumer focus.[4]

   This section reviews these developments, from the perspective of consumer citizenship practice, through a discussion of the normative contribution made by the legislative and regulatory measures to the effectiveness of consumer protection and information and their consequential influences on consumer motivation and capability. These are legislative and regulatory measures that have proved, so far, to be inadequate for securing the market conditions in which the normative aspects of the motivational and capability levels of consumer citizenship practice can operate effectively. The failure of these measures to achieve market opening or the dissipation of market power within a competitive environment are shown instead to have resulted in a degree of consumer ambivalence and a consequential general consumer detriment. In concluding, this section discusses the potential of the new third legislative package to remove these barriers to effective consumer citizenship participation in the energy market.

Introducing the legal framework of the European energy market

It should first be stated that prior to the ratification of the Lisbon Treaty in 2009, national idiosyncrasies in energy policy were tempered only by the intergovernmental International Energy Agency, to which most EU Member States belong. With the coming into force of the Lisbon Treaty we have, for the first time, the introduction of a shared competence for the EU and the Member States in the area of energy, provided for in Article 4(2) TFEU.[5] Whilst there has, for a long time, been a Commissioner for energy, and a directorate general with the title Directorate General for Transport and Energy (DGTREN), the Commissions' energy initiatives have relied on those competencies it enjoys in the areas of the internal market, environment, competition, consumer protection, external relations and nuclear energy. Luciani suggests that the EU energy policies established in these areas have been 'profoundly influenced by institutional limitations' (Luciani, 2004, p. 110), yet such limitations have not prevented the gradual reform of the EU's internal energy market from the mid-1990s: a reform in which the state-based monopolies for energy generation (electricity), storage (gas), transmission, distribution and supply became subject to the establishment of national regulatory bodies, and the concept of market liberalisation, in the first phase introduction of common rules (Directives (EC) 96/92 and 98/30).

Positioned against a global background of liberalisation and privatisation of network industries more generally, the first phase of European energy reform was slow, protracted and uncertain. It had to overcome 'a powerful alliance of incumbent utilities and [sceptical] national governments' and, whilst the literature provides a number of interpretations of the process of liberalisation in this first phase, they all agree that the two 'common rules' Directives successfully introduced 'a new era of EU market governance': albeit a new era marked by only a minimal market opening and 'a European patchwork of asymmetric national rules' (Eberlein, 2008, pp. 75–76). The change reflected a paradigmatic shift from a monopolist and state-interventionist approach to one in which liberalised market mechanisms were to be balanced by new national regulatory structures (Cameron, 2007, p. 35). With a politically sensitive and complex background, the failure of this first-phase reform of the energy market to effectively address issues of the unbundling of products and services, of regulated third-party access and of cross-border trade through interconnected national systems in an integrated market has been well documented (for example, Eberlein, 2005; Szyszczak, 2007, particularly pp. 164–168).

Cameron identifies three particular problems that he suggests stand out in this first phase of reform: an uneven implementation of the common rules among the Member States, the use of discriminatory methods to manage network access and 'especially interconnectors', and high levels of market power of incumbent electricity and gas companies (Cameron, 2005, p. 9). The Commission recognised that development of the energy market had been 'steady but...a little disappointing' and even with recourse to 'further legislation, [the] [a]pplication of competition law, and [the] [v]oluntary negotiation of changes with the main players' the shortcomings of the first regulatory regime remained (Commission, 2004e, pp. 10–11).

In an attempt to correct the problems associated with the transition of the energy market the European Parliament and Council adopted a second package of measures on 26th June 2003. This second package initially comprised of Directive (EC) 2003/54 concerning common rules for the internal market in electricity (the Electricity Directive), Directive (EC) 2003/55/EC concerning common rules for the internal market in natural gas (the Gas Directive) and Regulation (EC) 1228/2003 on conditions for access to the network for cross-border exchanges in electricity. A further regulation was added in 2005 on gas transmission networks (Regulation (EC) 1775/2005) that formed the final part of this second round of liberalisation legislation. The second legislative package had, as its declared aim, an increase in the quantitative market opening with full liberalisation by 2007 and an enhanced qualitative regulatory environment that would bring about greater uniformity and coordinated national regulation (Cameron, 2005, p. 11). The Directives, in particular, also introduced new concepts to the energy market in the form of enhanced *consumer protection* through universal and public service obligations; 'supplier of last resort; 'green' labelling and compliance programmes' (Cameron, 2005, p. 11).

Protection and information in the European reforms for energy market opening

Consumer protection, as the foundation level of the normative hierarchy of consumer citizenship practice defined in Figure 5.1, was intended to be significantly improved with this new legislative package in both the enforcement and empowerment paradigms. From an enforcement perspective, the legal status of the National Regulatory Authorities (NRAs) had been enhanced with a more precise obligation on Member States to 'charge one or more [independent] competent bodies with the function of regulatory authorities'. In addition, the Directives provided for a minimum set of harmonising competences and functions for the regulatory authorities that improved European cooperation and coordination (Cameron, 2005, pp. 19–20).

Public service obligations were strengthened through provisions in the second legislative package that placed a series of overlapping obligations, objectives and options on Member States. Member States were *obliged, inter alia*, to ensure that the tasks of the NRAs would be independent and that the NRAs would be legally distinct from all organisations providing networks, equipment or services (Directive (EC) 2003/54, Article 23; Directive (EC) 2003/55, Article 25); to ensure a geographic universal service in electricity (Directive (EC) 2003/54, Article 3(3)), but not in gas; to ensure publication of measures taken to achieve universal and public service obligations; to ensure that eligible consumers can easily switch supplier; and to protect the final consumer, especially vulnerable consumers. The *objectives* to be followed by the Member States also included the protection of the final consumer, particularly vulnerable consumers and those living in remote areas, but extended to embrace environmental protection and security of supply issues (Cameron, 2005, p. 24). Again, in respect of vulnerable consumers and those living in remote areas, Member States are further provided with the *option* of establishing a *supplier of last resort* as a mechanism for ensuring both a geographic and social universal service in electricity (Directive (EC) 2003/54, Article 3(3)),[6] and a limited *social* universal service in gas for consumers already connected to the gas network. The notion of a *social* universal service in gas, as used here, is drawn from the obligation in Article 3(3) of the Gas Directive for Member States to 'ensure that there are adequate safeguards to protect vulnerable customers, including appropriate measures to help them avoid disconnection': as Cameron identifies, even the Commission, in one of its Guidance Notes, expressly states that 'contrary to electricity, gas supply cannot be considered a universal service' (Cameron, 2007, p. 175). Szyszczak identifies these universal service obligations as a link 'reconciling the liberalisation process and the defence of public services' in which the 'general interest becomes a *condition* of legality for the Community's legislative intervention' and 'allows the Community to show its citizens that it is responsive to individual and collective needs' (Szyszczak, 2007, p. 243, emphasis in the original).

Specific *consumer protection* measures are set out in an 'Annex A' to both the Gas Directive and the Electricity Directive that give effect to features of the normative hierarchy defined in Figure 5.1 at levels 1 and 2. Paragraph (a) of these annexes provides for consumers to have the *right to a contract* with their energy provider that specifies *inter alia* the services provided; the service quality levels offered; time to connect; the types of maintenance service offered; the means by which up-to-date information on applicable tariffs may be obtained; details of compensation and refund arrangements that apply if contracted service levels are not met (all measures providing for *informed choice*); and the method of initiating procedures for dispute settlement (measure providing for a *transparent redress mechanism*). Paragraph (b) of the annexes elaborates on the contractual relationship between the consumer and the energy provider, emphasising the consumers' *right to notice* of any intention to modify any 'conditions' of the contract and their *right of withdrawal*. These are features of *empowering* consumer protection measures that embrace informed choice and resonate with Hirschman's theory of exit, voice and loyalty that has already been associated with consumer citizenship practice. The remaining paragraphs of both annexes, paragraphs (c)–(g), reflect the inherently normative features of consumer rights and informed choice that can be identified in the consumer protection provisions for transparent information on applicable prices and tariffs; the fairness and transparency of contractual terms and conditions; unfair or misleading selling methods; nil cost switching and simple, inexpensive complaints handling procedures.

The Electricity Directive went farther than the Gas Directive in making explicit provisions obliging the Member States to ensure that final consumers received details of the contribution of each energy source to the overall fuel mix and other information that would lead them to 'reference sources, such as web-pages, where information on the environmental impact, in terms of at least emissions of CO^2 and the radioactive waste resulting from the electricity produced by the overall fuel mix' could be obtained (Directive (EC) 2003/54, Article 3(6)). The obligation to provide information by which final consumers could make energy decisions based on informed choice over issues related to sustainability and environmental pollution was reinforced in the 2006 Energy Services Directive. The Directive recognised that '[t]he end result of Member States' action is dependent on many external factors which influence the behaviour of consumers as regards their energy use and their willingness to implement energy saving methods and use energy saving devices' (Directive (EC) 2006/32, Recital 12). Acknowledging the informational obligations in the Electricity Directive, the Energy Services Directive emphasises the final consumers' role in achieving improved energy end use efficiency. A role in which the final consumer is to be motivated to make choices that are not merely economic: they are instead to be provided with information that presents them with a choice in which their active participation as an agent of change within the energy market is to be encouraged on the basis of efficiency and ecology. It is analogous to a citizenship concept of choice that has been discussed within the context of education policy whereby 'if one is part of a universe defined by a certain citizenship, then one is entitled to participate in the choices which it makes available' (Crouch, 2001, p. 125). In order to 'enable final consumers to make better informed decisions as regards their individual energy consumption' the Directive identifies that

> they should be provided with a *reasonable amount* of information thereon and with other relevant information, such as information on available energy efficiency improvement measures, comparative final consumer profiles or objective technical specifications for energy-using equipment... [and,] [i]n addition, consumers should be actively encouraged to check their own meter readings regularly. (Directive (EC) 2006/32, Recital 29, emphasis added)

This reasonable amount of information is to be 'made available to final customers in clear and understandable terms... in or with their bills, contracts, transactions, and/or receipts at distribution stations' and that encompasses current actual prices and actual consumption of energy; comparisons of current energy consumption with consumption for the same period in the previous year; where possible and useful, comparisons with an average normalised or benchmarked user of energy in the same user category; and contact information for consumers' organisations from which information may be obtained on available energy efficiency improvement measures, comparative end-user profiles and/or objective technical specifications for energy-using equipment (Directive (EC) 2006/32, Article 13).

Consumer detriment and other barriers to consumer citizenship practice

Where the directives of the second energy package were promoting the use of energy efficiency and environmental information as a mechanism to motivate end user consumers into a more active role as a market agent, the aspirations they contained for achieving a liberalised and open market were failing to materialise. The Commission referred Luxembourg and Spain to the Court for their failure to implement either of the Electricity or Gas Directives (Joined Cases C-353 & C-357/05, Case C-354/05 and Case C-358/05) whilst, on a broader front, the failure to achieve the objective of market opening was revealed through

> [s]ignificant rises in gas and electricity wholesale prices that ... [could not] be fully explained by higher primary fuel costs and environmental obligations, persistent complaints about entry barriers and limited possibilities to exercise customer choice [and] led the Commission to open an inquiry into the functioning of the European gas and electricity markets in June 2005. (Commission, 2006e, p. 2)

The inquiry based itself on Article 17 of Regulation 1/2003, on the implementation of the Treaty rules on competition, and was aimed at assessing the prevailing competitive conditions and establishing the causes of the perceived market malfunctioning. Amongst those areas that the inquiry determined needed to be addressed most rapidly were market concentration and market power, vertical foreclosure resulting from inadequate unbundling of the network and supply operations, and the lack of transparency in market operations (Commission, 2006e, p. 3, also at pp. 11 and 13). In response to such barriers, and the *general consumer detriment* posed by these issues, the inquiry suggested that a number of regulatory measures would be needed in addition to increased competition law enforcement (Commission, 2006e, p. 9). In particular, the inquiry identified a need for 'a substantial strengthening of the powers of regulators and enhanced European coordination [that] ... can provide the transparent, stable and non-discriminatory framework that the sector needs for competition to develop and for future investments to be made' (Commission, 2006e, p. 12).

The reforming ambitions of the second legislative package for the European energy market had merely 'replaced the natural monopoly under public ownership with oligopolistic markets where ownership could be either public or private' (Ugur, 2009, p. 24). Ugur's political economy perspective of the liberalisation of European network industries endorse the findings of the Commission's 2006 inquiry, and highlight aspects of the general consumer detriment that act as a barrier to the effective opportunity for consumer citizenship practice to impact on market functioning. Ugur's analysis challenges as 'optimistic' the Copenhagen Economics 2005 study, prepared for the Commission, that estimated a positive effect of general internal market liberalisation policy that had led to 'an increase of 1.9% in [consumer] welfare and 0.3% in overall employment from 1990–2001': gains, relative to base-year values in 2001 and equivalent to 98 billion Euros per year over the period between 1990–2001 (Ugur, 2009, p. 4).

The basis of Ugur's challenge to these estimates lies in the persistence of the market distortions within the liberalised sectors. Market dominance, inadequate unbundling and lack of transparency, coupled with the low demand-and-supply elasticities characteristic of networked industries, is conducive to increased mark-ups. The consumer welfare gains predicted in the literature do not, he argues, take account of the probability that such mark-ups 'may persist even if prices fall after market opening' (Ugur, 2009, p. 4). An observation that resonates with Giulietti, Waddams Price, and Waterson's 2005 analysis of the mark-up strategy of the incumbent gas supplier in the UK retail market: a strategy that has already been associated with consumer detriment and the high volume of consumer complaints about energy prices in 2004–2005 that influenced the Commission to 'ratchet up its support for energy market liberalisation by the use of competition policy' (Cameron, 2007, p. 564).

Ugur's analysis highlights the effect of general consumer detriment resulting from impaired structural capability. He argues that the 'impact of market opening on *consumer satisfaction* is expected to be *positive* as customers will enjoy lower prices and increased customer care in a competitive market environment' (Ugur, 2009, p. 9, emphasis in the original). Yet, the evidence he introduces of imperfect market opening and of only the partial removal of pre-existing market distortions led him to conclude, paradoxically, that

> it is not surprising to observe a significant degree of consumer ambivalence towards the liberalisation of network industries in Europe. The majority of network industry consumers tend to express satisfaction with respect to prices, quality and accessibility. However, when one examines the changes in the level of satisfaction against the degree of market opening over time, the findings tend to be mixed in the sense that market opening over time is associated with both

increased and decreased customer satisfaction. In addition, *the level of satisfaction with respect to access and prices tends to be higher in less liberalised sectors such as gas and electricity* compared to more liberalised sectors such as telephony services! (Ugur, 2009, p. 14, emphasis added)

In terms of the cognitive aspects of capability in the normative hierarchy of consumer citizenship practice it is *perceptions* of the welfare effects that appear significant in influencing customer satisfaction. Drawing on aggregate figures for the EU-15 in Eurobarometer data from various surveys conducted between 2000 and 2004, Ugur identifies the levels of consumer satisfaction in the electricity and gas supply sectors as measured against the performance criteria for prices, quality and accessibility. The results present an even more complex picture than the paradox above may suggest. The levels of satisfaction in respect of the three performance criteria of access, price and quality differ between the electricity and gas sectors; and from one criteria to the other. Between 2000 and 2004 '[i]n the least liberalised sector (i.e., gas supply), satisfaction with respect to prices *increased* by 8.96 percentage points whereas satisfaction with respect to access... [had] *fallen* by 9.44 percentage points' (Ugur, 2009, p. 16, emphasis added). Similarly, in the electricity sector, satisfaction with respect to prices *increased* by 9.3 percentage points whereas satisfaction with respect to access had *fallen* by 4.11 percentage points. Satisfaction with respect to quality, assessed as 'fairly good', had increased by 1.18 percentage points for electricity and 4.23 percentage points for gas supply.

   Levels of consumer satisfaction are defined in Ugur's analysis as a function of three sets of variables that include characteristics of the individual such as sex, education and political views; country fixed-effects such as GDP per head; and the market opening indicators such as public/private ownership, market share of the incumbent, ease of entry, and degree of vertical integration. His analysis of market opening indicators, as *one* of the variables of consumer satisfaction reveal another paradox: that '[o]n the one hand, smaller market share of the incumbent tends to have a positive effect on customer satisfaction with... gas supply', yet on the other hand, a 'larger freedom for new entry tends to reduce customer satisfaction in gas supply, whereas it tends to increase customer satisfaction in electricity supply' (Ugur, 2009, p. 17). A final observation by Ugur suggests that the failure to achieve sufficient unbundling 'tends to reduce customer satisfaction with respect to *all* criteria for which data is available' before he concludes that 'either the level of market opening in network industries is not optimal *or* customer information about market opening is impaired by imperfect information' Ugur, 2009, p. 17, emphasis added).

The third legislative package: encouraging an increased consumer agency?

Following the failure of the first and second legislative packages to achieve a liberalised and competitive energy market, a third legislative package with a revised set of proposals for a European internal market in energy was adopted on 13 July 2009. Comprised of Regulations (EC) 713/2009, 714/2009, 715/2009, Directives (EC) 2009/72 and 2009/73, the two new Directives, replace the second package Directives on common rules for the internal market for electricity and natural gas whilst two of the Regulations replace the provisions on conditions for access to the networks for cross-border exchanges of electricity and access to the natural gas transmission networks. The third Regulation introduces an Agency for the Co-operation of Energy Regulators (ACER) that *inter alia* has a policy objective of acting in the consumer interest: of identifying barriers to the completion of the internal market in electricity and natural gas; of providing opinion and recommendations to the European Parliament, the Council and the Commission on the measures that could be taken to remove such barriers; and of monitoring 'in particular the retail prices of electricity and natural gas ... and compliance with the consumer rights laid down in' the new Directives (Regulation 713/2009, Articles 4 and 11). How then, and to what degree, will this third legislative package further facilitate the normative stimuli for consumer citizenship practice defined in this book and/or remove the present barriers?

The second legislative package had introduced independent NRAs to oversee its implementation by the Member States and to encourage the development of a regulatory culture in the European energy sector (Cameron, 2007, p. 97). Further, at the EU level, and with a sector-specific architecture similar to that described for the networks and structures of European consumer policy governance described in Chapter 3 of this book, the Council of European Energy Regulators (CEER) and the European Regulators Group for Electricity and Gas (ERGEG) were established to facilitate co-operation between NRAs directly, and between the NRAs and the Commission. In a joint commentary from CEER and ERGEG, they identify that the aim of the third legislative package 'is to create a stable and coherent climate for investment in an efficient integrated grid and, to deliver *open and competitive single EU markets in* gas and electricity *in the consumer interest'* (ERGEG and CEER, 2008, emphasis in the original). Their factsheet summarises the consumer-specific provisions of the third legislative package as including: a new *consumer forum*; new measures for *increased consumer protection* and new duties on regulators; the objective of harmonising *the powers of national regulators and strengthening their independence* from political and commercial interests; the mandating of national regulators to ensure the *efficient functioning of their national market* and to promote *effective competition;* and, in the interest of the consumer, of developing a competitive single EU energy market, facilitated by a new EU energy agency (ACER).

The *new consumer forum* is intended to stimulate the creation of a truly liberalised retail market in which 'all EU citizens are able to benefit from competition' and is positioned as analogous to the Florence (electricity) and Madrid (gas) Forums that were established to promote market opening and competition through an informal EU level framework for the discussion of issues and the exchange of experience. Based on these intentions, the new forum is to 'focus on specific retail issues ... [in which] it should serve as a platform for all stakeholders to promote the establishment of an EU wide retail market' and provide guidance to assist Member States and the regulatory authorities in establishing clear, and gradually harmonising, market rules on competition in the retail market (Commission, 2007c, p. 18). Called the 'Citizens' Energy Forum', it is chaired by the Commission and attended by national and European consumer associations, representatives of the Member States, national energy regulators and representatives from the electricity and gas industries.

At its first three annual meetings, held each year since 2008 in London, the Forum has debated, in detail, the changing role of the regulator and the increasing role of consumers in the new legislation and has progressed a range of issues in the consumer interest. The Forum has identified 'the limited extent to which European citizens, and in some cases Member States, understood how European legislation protects their rights' (Citizens Energy Forum, 2009a). The response has been to facilitate, through Article 3 of the latest energy directives (Directives (EC) 2009/73 and 2009/72), the provision of accurate and practical *information* about local or regional retail markets through a 'Checklist' relating to energy consumer rights. Significantly, within the context of the normative hierarchy of consumer citizenship practice introduced in this book, the Forum also suggests that

[i]nformation for consumers is not enough to ensure their active participation in the market ... [that] consumers must be put back in the

driving seat with regard to the development of retail markets so that they are sufficiently empowered to make markets deliver concrete benefits. (Citizens Energy Forum, 2009a, p. 2)

The Forum has placed a particular focus on energy bills: these it identifies as a major source of consumer complaints and has asserted that '[i]n many countries, consumers are confronted with unreadable bills' (Citizens Energy Forum, p. 3). In the view of the Forum,

> an electricity or gas bill can and should be a simple and clear source of information for consumers, and the basic tool helping them to *understand how much energy they are using* as well as the *actual cost* of the energy which they have used, to *consume less* if possible, and to *compare offers* available for them on the market. (Citizens Energy Forum, p. 2, emphasis in the original)

In a tangible example of the potential efficacy of the Forum, at its first meeting, it mandated the European Commission to set up a working group on billing, tasked with developing recommendations for consumer-friendly energy bills; a working group that has already recommended templates for regular and annual bills (Citizens Energy Forum, pp. 4–5). Issues over the frequency of billing and the consumers' capacity to understand them remain, but there is also evidence of progress with this initiative and research at the Member State level is beginning to highlight the fundamental nature of some of the issues. In its 2010 status review on the implementation of the Commission's 'Good practice Guidance for Billing', ERGEG notes that in a majority of EU countries there is some activity with measures being taken, or predicted to be taken, to make bills more understandable for customers. However, the status review also identifies that

> [o]ften, knowledge of the *customers' opinion of bills* is quite limited and requires a customer-oriented approach. Only a very limited number of countries have access to this kind of data. In some Member States, further research with consumers (qualitative studies, focus groups, etc.) in this field may be necessary to be able to gain an in depth picture. (ERGEG, 2010, emphasis in the original)

Increased consumer protection provisions in the third legislative package take the form of reinforced consumer rights and better enforcement. The role of regulators is considerably extended through new duties requiring them to ensure that consumer protection measures are enforced and that customers benefit through the efficient functioning of their national market. Regulators will be involved in ensuring that the consumer has prompt access to their consumption data, and in monitoring the level and effectiveness of market opening through the active monitoring of switching rates, complaints, and any distortion or restriction of competition in the retail market (Directive (EC) 2009/72, Article 37(p) and (j); Directive (EC) 2009/73, Article 41 (q) and (j)).

The Member States are also obliged to ensure that a single point of contact be established to provide consumers with all necessary information concerning their rights; to ensure that an independent mechanism such as an energy ombudsman or a consumer body is in place for the efficient treatment of complaints and out-of-court dispute settlements; and to provide a definition of vulnerable consumers that may refer to those suffering energy poverty, and to the prohibition of disconnection at critical times. The new Directives follow their predecessors and contain specific consumer protection measures in an annex: but these latest measures are reinforced with new provisions providing consumers with the right to be properly informed of actual electricity consumption and costs, frequently enough to enable them *to regulate their own electricity consumption* and the right to a *good standard* of complaint handling by their energy service provider in which the consumer must be informed of the appropriate procedures.

Such changes should eventually strengthen the normative base for consumer citizenship practice and, to a degree, stimulate features of motivation and capability that will promote some increased consumer agency in the energy markets. To help, numerous information and educational initiatives to improve consumer awareness of efficient energy use have also been introduced with the support of the EU's Intelligent Energy Europe (IEE) programme. This is a programme that has been established on the premise that there are many untapped opportunities to encourage energy saving and to promote the use of renewable energy sources in Europe, but it is also a programme that recognises that market conditions do not always help. In order to improve these conditions the IEE programme acts as the EU's funding channel for research and project proposals that are intended to move us towards a more energy intelligent Europe. Member State-specific consumer education in energy matters is also to be found in the services section of the new 'Dolceta' web site (http://www.dolceta.eu), financed by the Commission as part of a project involving 27 countries. The 'Dolceta' project is, however, not limited to energy but offers a much broader consumer education service through online modules which focus on different consumer topics and that provide Member State-specific information and advice.

As we come to the end of this analysis of the third legislative package, it is worth noting that the new Directives contain a chapter dedicated to provisions relating to the independence, objectives, duties, powers and the cross-border regime of the national regulatory authorities. It is a chapter that highlights the Europeanisation of governance processes within the context of NRAs. Member States are obliged to guarantee the independence of the NRA such that it can 'exercise its powers impartially and transparently' (Directive (EC) 2009/72, Article 35 and Directive (EC) 2009/73, Article 39) and provide a senior representative to the new central agency entity, ACER, created by Regulation (EC) 713/2009. The proposition to create ACER, suggests von Rosenberg, 'stems from the growing awareness that the aims of EU energy policy, especially market integration and security of supply, cannot be achieved by 27 European NRAs all acting independently from each other', although, he remains sceptical of its political independence suggesting that 'Member States are, in view of the strategic importance, still unwilling to give up national sovereignty in the energy sector' (Von Rosenberg, 2008, p. 516). ACER is, however, established to provide a framework within which the NRAs can co-operate, and with the purpose of 'exercising, at Community level, the regulatory tasks performed in the Member States and, where necessary, to coordinate their action' (Regulation (EC) 713/2009, Articles 1 and 7 (3)). Notwithstanding von Rosenberg's concerns over political independence, the co-operative and co-ordinating framework provided by ACER may well facilitate the harmonisation of the *powers of the national regulators* and lead to improved regulatory functioning.

The defined objectives of the NRAs are, to work in close consultation with other relevant authorities, including competition authorities, and in close cooperation with ACER to improve structural capability through facilitating the elimination of restrictions on trade between Member States and the development of appropriate cross-border capacities to enhance the integration of national markets, and to help achieve secure, reliable and efficient non-discriminatory systems that are consumer oriented. Harmonisation of national regulatory powers, by ACER, at the EU level will be assisted by the NRAs who have a responsibility for contributing to the compatibility of data exchange processes and the Citizens' Energy Forum who have encouraged 'energy regulators to work in close coordination with both competition authorities and consumer bodies when monitoring the market and pursing anti-competitive or unfair practices' (Citizens' Energy Forum, 2009b, p. 3). There is still a long way to go before the functioning of the retail energy market can be expected to deliver real improvements for domestic consumers in an EU wide and coherent manner, but it is clear that an energetic consumer-centric policy approach exists at the EU level.

Green consumerism and the technology challenge

In the previous section the normative influences of consumer citizenship practice are recognised as being reinforced through policy, legislation and regulation with respect to the consumer protection elements of enforcement and empowerment, and with respect to the partial removal of structural barriers in the market. Informational obligations provided for in the third legislative package should also strengthen the consumers' awareness of his or her rights as a market agent; however, it appears less certain that information on energy efficiency and environmental issues provides sufficient a motivational stimulus to develop citizenship attributes in energy-purchasing consumer behaviour.

Consumer behaviour: motivation and barriers in environmental energy choices

Based on a 2007 consumer survey across ten European countries[7] Logica examined consumer attitudes towards climate change, their personal action to reduce energy consumption and the barriers to environmentally responsible behaviour. The research identified that, at least for the countries of Western Europe, the market was homogenous in terms of consumer attitudes and growing concerns over environmental issues and climate change. It also identified that there was a 'consensus across Europe that the amount of energy people use directly affects the climate ... [and that this] suggests that Europeans have started to make the link between climate change and their individual behaviour' (Logica, 2008, p. 5). Whilst environmental concerns were acknowledged as important in influencing people's behaviours in all of the countries surveyed, with the exception of Denmark, financial cost, rather that environmental cost, was identified as the strongest motivator for saving energy. GDP was also acknowledged as positively correlating with ethical buying at the national level such that 'higher income levels enable consumer decisions to be influenced more by value-based concerns, rather than purely monetary ones' (Logica, 2008, p. 7).

The Logica research explores the question of why consumer knowledge and attitudes about climate change and environmental issues frequently fail to be translated into behavioural changes but remain as a (motivational) attitude–behaviour gap that 'could be described as one of the greatest challenges facing the public climate change agenda' (Logica, 2008, p. 10). The barriers to the adoption of energy-saving consumer behaviour were identified as insufficient government incentives, investment costs and a lack of information on exact energy usage. Whether perceived or real, a lack of incentive from the national government was the most commonly cited reason for not saving energy at an overall level whilst the upfront investment costs for energy-saving goods such as solar power panels, roof insulation or double glazing were clearly identified as a barrier (Logica, 2008, p. 16). Boström and Klintman provide a link between this attitude–behaviour gap and the definition of consumer citizenship practice developed in this book. They identify that many people express willingness 'to make dramatic changes in their everyday lives in order to decrease their ecological footprint': a goal they suggest that can be partly accomplished through citizens expressing 'political concerns through more active consumer choices' and yet such 'green choices do not always represent the most inexpensive option, so the consumer who wants to buycott often pays more' (Boström and Klintman, 2008, p. 2).

It is the juxtaposition of the lack of information on precise energy use and the large amounts of information and advice on carbon emissions and environmental pollution that, in particular, leaves consumers feeling that 'they have very little knowledge about what the solutions to the problem are' (Logica, 2008, p. 17). The Logica survey draws on Eurobarometer data to identify that consumers are 'looking for more than large amounts of environmental information', that 'vague exhortations to reduce your carbon footprint are not very actionable' and, importantly, that whilst there are many organisations providing information on energy saving, consumers find it difficult to know who to trust. Here, the lack of trust combined with information overload fuels the attitude–behaviour gap whilst, at the same time, the research identifies that 'most' consumers acknowledge that individual action can make a difference: 'that energy saving begins at home' (Logica, 2008, p. 18). Referring to a study conducted in Great Britain, the Logica survey identifies that 56 per cent of consumers 'feel that unethical living is as much of a social taboo as drink driving': a social trend the report considers could be a 'catalyst behind a new syndrome, which some analysts have labelled "be good guilt"', but a social trend in which the attitude–behaviour gap is confounded by the problems of trust and information overload in the ethical energy consumption arena (Logica, 2008).

Public understanding and consumer segmentation

As a well-established marketing tool, consumer market segmentation identifies factors that vary between groups of consumers but that are homogenous within groups. Typically, such segmentation may be based on five primary variables: *geographic segmentation* based on such regional variations as climate, population growth rates and population density; *demographic segmentation* based on variables such as age, ethnicity, education, occupation, income and status; *psychographic segmentation* based on such variables as values, attitudes, lifestyle and personality; *behavioural segmentation* based on such variables as product usage rates, brand loyalty, price sensitivity and benefits sought; and, *technological segmentation* based on such variables as motivation, fundamental values and lifestyle perspective (Netherlands, 2009). In the UK, the Department for Environment Food and Rural Affairs (Defra) has commissioned research into consumer segmentation for the UK energy market. Although limited to the behaviours of domestic consumers in the UK energy market, the resulting segmentation model of major consumer groups provides a useful qualitative analysis of the public understanding of sustainable energy consumption in the home, and across which a hierarchy of pro-environmental and solidaristic behaviour was demonstrated. It is research that acknowledges that in the energy sector, and of relevance to individual and family consumption in the home, 'the scope is too broad and the issues too complex for a quantitative survey' (Brook Lyndhurst, 2007, p. 5).

The normative dimension of consumer citizenship behaviour depicted in Figure 5.1 attempts to highlight the key enablers and the barriers facing the individual consumer's effective agency in market shaping, economic achievement and social responsibility. The segmentation of consumer groups in the research commissioned by Defra introduces a further demographic dimension to consumer behaviour focussed on psychographic, behavioural and technological segmentation factors: a segmentation that identified seven major groups of consumers defined by their environmental values and pro-environmental behaviours and that endorsed earlier research. At the base of this hierarchy, the seventh of these groups was identified as 'disinterested', displaying no interest or motivation to change their current behaviours or make their lifestyle more pro-environmental and, as a group, were deliberately screened out of this research (Brook Lyndhurst, 2007, p. 3). Of the other six groups, it was the pro-environmental behaviours that most marked the boundaries between the groups and can be associated with the enablers and barriers at various levels in the hierarchy of consumer citizenship practice introduced in this book.

The report on the research identifies these six consumer groups as: *Greens*, driven by the belief that environmental issues are critical, are well educated on green issues, are positively connected to environmental arguments and feel individual responsibility for their own impact on the environment; *Consumers with a conscience*, who want to be seen as green, are motivated by environmental concerns, wish to avoid guilt about environmental damage, are focussed on making positive choices but, whilst feeling individual responsibility for their environmental impact, prioritize personal needs as more important; *Wastage focussed*, who are driven by a desire to avoid waste, have a good knowledge of waste and pollution issues, see themselves as ethically separate from the 'Greens', but whilst holding some sense of personal responsibility lack a broader environmental awareness and future focus; *Basic contributors*, who remain sceptical about the need for behavioural change, are driven by a desire to conform to social norms, have a low level of knowledge of environmental issues and behaviours and whose perception leads them to believe they lack opportunity to make a difference; *Currently constrained*, who would wish to be 'green' but believe that they are constrained by their current circumstances, that whilst they have a sense of personal responsibility are prevented from taking action by their circumstances, and who focus on a balance of pragmatism and realism; and, the *Long-term restricted*, who have little sense of personal responsibility and are limited by a number of serious life priority issues and behaviours that need to be addressed before they could consciously consider their personal impact in environmental terms (Brook Lyndhurst, 2007, p. 4 and Annex A).

The research identified that over the past twenty years the public's awareness of environmental and energy issues has increased and consumer information devices such as the energy efficiency label have become mainstream (Brook Lyndhurst, 2007, p. 8). *Product* policy initiatives for the European energy market, aimed at generating informed consumer choice for the individual and family as a mechanism for achieving improved energy efficiency, have relied on three main policy instruments and a raft of product-specific legislation. Firstly, the Energy Labelling Directive (Directive (EEC) 92/75) provided a framework for the compulsory provision of information on energy consumption for an ever-growing range of specified household appliances;[8] secondly, the Eco-labelling Regulation (Regulation (EC) 1980/2000) provided for the promotion of products with the potential to reduce negative environmental impacts; and thirdly, the Ecodesign Directive (Directive (EC) 2005/32) that established a framework for setting minimum Ecodesign requirements for energy using products.

The consumer segmentation model applied in the Defra research identified consumer responses across the six population segments as related to a set of behavioural goals linked to energy efficiency. Behavioural goals that included the buying and installing of energy efficient products and appliances, better management and usage of energy in the home, the installation of insulation products and the switching to a green energy tariff. The research identifies that the barriers associated with attaining these behavioural goals vary between the population segments; it also highlights the significant practical barriers facing policy initiatives aimed at encouraging the behaviours that have been associated with the theoretical model of consumer citizenship practice. Barriers challenging the normative potential at the information, capability and motivational levels of the hierarchy of consumer citizenship practice depicted in Figure 5.1 were emphasised in the research conclusions that found cynicism and confusion about environmental issues; the strongest behavioural driver to be cost, and a distrust of government, local authorities and 'big' business (Brook Lyndhurst, 2007, p. 40).

With regard to the buying and installation of energy efficient products and appliances the Defra research identifies that, despite the now well-established product labelling regime, it was only the Greens who factored in the energy rating on environmental grounds and who, with the Consumers with a conscience group, were the only groups with a marked knowledge of the scheme. Initial cost was by far the biggest driver when purchasing products, and particularly so for the Wastage focussed, Long-term restricted and Basic contributor groups (Brook Lyndhurst, 2007, p. 19). Similarly, whilst *all* consumer segments felt that better energy management in the home was an acceptable and feasible goal, it was identified that, with the exception of the Greens, cost was the primary motivation. Some of the Wastage focussed and Long-term restricted participants were already found to be restricting the amount of energy they use in the home to save money and were eager to know how they may reduce this amount even further, although the latter were often found to be physically restricted by the properties they lived in (Brook Lyndhurst, 2007, p. 20 and pp. 41–42).

For all participants, the Defra research highlighted two issues related to the improvement of energy management in the home that draw attention to the practical complexities surrounding the theoretical concept of consumer citizenship practice. Firstly, and with reference to earlier work, it identified that 'hardly any...participants mentioned ways to reduce energy consumption for laundry, e.g. washing at 30°C' (Brook Lyndhurst, 2007, p. 22): aA situation that, in a separate initiative, is being addressed by Defra through its association with 'The Sustainable Clothing Roadmap', an *industry initiative* involving over 300 companies and through which has come a recommendation to build 'on Wash at 30°C consumer campaigns to increase uptake *utilising the association with cost savings* [rather than ecological duty] as a consumer behaviour change lever' (Defra, 2009, p. 3 emphasis added). The second issue highlighted the relevance of product design and its association with consumer behaviour, identifying that many participants were 'unwilling to turn electrical appliances off at the power source for fear of losing valued presets, e.g. microwave clocks, alarm settings or pre-programmed radio and television channels' (Brook Lyndhurst, 2007, p. 22).

The increasingly complex environment in which consumers, differentiated by individual and structural capability parameters and motivational drivers, have to take ever more responsibility, 'notably with regard to their finance, energy, transport and healthcare choices' is acknowledged by Meglena Kuneva, the EU Commissioner for Consumer Affairs. In her e-brief to the Lisbon Council she recognises that education 'is only partly a solution due to the functional illiteracy of even educated people in dealing with some of the complexities involved and information overload' and, in the context of environmental sustainability, that the decision-making process of consumers will need to be 'better understood in order to find ways to promote "green" choices and recycling' (Kuneva, 2009, pp. 2–3).

Smart meters and the technological pressure for consumer citizenship practice

The introduction of smart meters (intelligent metering systems) for the EU internal energy market was provided for in the Directives of the third legislative package for energy (Directive (EC) 2009/72, Article 3(11) and Directive (EC) 2009/73, Article 3(8)). Annex 1(2) of both Directives requires Member States to 'ensure the implementation of intelligent metering systems that shall assist the active participation of consumers in the...market', wherever such systems could be considered economically reasonable and cost effective. Provisions that the Citizens' Energy Forum have suggested will 'benefit all market actors and assist the active participation of consumers in the retail energy market'. The Forum also welcomed ERGEG's offer to present recommendations on the regulatory aspects of smart metering and its agreement to consult consumer bodies on points of particular concern (Citizens Energy Forum, 2009b, p. 3).

The amalgamation of energy and climate policy, as a necessary precursor for meeting the EU's 20 per cent improvement target for energy efficiency, has also acknowledged the requirement for 'a major commitment at all levels from public authorities, economic operators and citizens alike' (Commission, 2008a, p. 9). A commitment associated with the Commission's observation that

> 2007 marked a turning point for the European Union's climate and energy policy…Public opinion has shifted decisively towards the imperative of addressing climate change, to adapting Europe to the new realities of cutting greenhouse gas emissions and developing our renewable, sustainable energy resources. (Commission, 2008a, p. 2)

Smart meters may have the potential to overcome some of the barriers to the adoption of energy-saving consumer behaviour highlighted in the Logica research discussed above. Yet, in addition to the challenge of the attitude–behaviour gap discussed in the same research, there is no accepted definition or common understanding of what constitutes a smart metering system (Darby, 2008, pp. 7–72): nor of the significant and diverse functionality that technology may add to smart metering within the emerging European Smart Grids Technology Platform (Commission, 2006f). At its most fundamental, a smart metering system provides the capability to measure energy consumption 'over representative periods to legal metrology requirements', to store the measured data for multiple time periods and, provides for ready access to the data by the consumer (Darby, 2008, pp. 7–72). In addition, as defined by the UK Industry Metering Advisory Group (IMAG) and identified by Darby, a smart meter will provide functionality for at least *one* of a range of technology and communications applications that may include a local display of the data in meaningful form; transfer of the data to the supplier or his agent for the purposes of billing; provision of a payment facility; provision of quality and continuity of supply data to the Distribution Network Operator; provision of a remote control capability for the interruption and restoration of specific consumer circuits or equipment, provision of a display of price signals for different time periods; and capability for remote change of tariff, debt or other rates of charging (Darby, 2008).

Analysis of news articles on the niche smart meter news website 'Smartmeters.com', over the period from March 2009 to January 2010, suggests the IMAG definition underplays the impact smart metering technology may have on consumer behaviour. Suggested to be an influence on smart grid development in Europe, the US and China, Taiwan Power, in cooperation with telecommunication and information technology companies, has established a research study in which consumers establish an 'energy budget' for their homes and where Taiwan Power will be able to send price change signals to consumers through their televisions, personal computers or mobile phones. The study is also experimenting with the use of wireless technology to allow smart meters to communicate with individual domestic appliances. Technology convergence in this area will enable energy supply companies to remotely power on and off domestic appliances through central control facilities.

European developments have seen German utility Yello Strom announce a prototype smart meter that will utilise Twitter short messaging services technology to inform consumers of their energy consumption information. Built upon Microsoft's operating system, and incorporating Web server and client application software, the Yello Strom meter can make consumption data available to consumers within 10 minutes, wherever they are. Classified by Yello Strom as an 'energy revolution', the utility operator 'is banking on the idea that broadband connections will transform how consumers use energy',[9] an idea supported by American research into the thesis that

> an alignment of personal motivations (e.g., increased involvement encouraged by timely reinforcement, achievement recognition, and a sense of belonging), and community environmental goals (e.g., reduced electricity usage and time-shifted energy use) can result in sustainable behavior change that is personally rewarding as well as socially responsible. (Reeves and Armel, 2009, Executive Summary)

It is a thesis supported by Kevin Meagher, CEO of UK energy management company Intamac who argues that sustainable change in consumer behaviour can be achieved '[u]sing broadband or mobile networks, [over which] consumers can use the internet or their mobile phones to see how much [energy] they're using – and even control their appliances – while they're away from the home' (Smartmeters, 2009b).

The potential of such technology to significantly change consumer behaviour and promote consumer citizenship practice in the new energy market clearly has a sound theoretical base. Yet, such change faces the practical limitations to consumer agency that are exposed in the Defra energy consumer segmentation model discussed above and is further challenged by the paucity of measures specifically encouraging such change in the legal framework that supports the EU's objectives for improved energy end-use efficiency.

Barriers and limitations in the new energy market

Consumer attitudes across the seven groups in the Defra segmentation model demonstrated a hierarchy of pro-environmental behaviour that starts with the Greens and gradually reduces to the Long-Term Restricted and, at the base, the Disinterested (Brook Lyndhurst, 2007, p. ii). The report also draws attention to the gap between attitude and behaviour that it suggests 'seems particularly acute in the case of energy' and that 'poses a particular challenge for policy' (Brook Lyndhurst, 2007). Participants in the Defra research generally responded favourably to the idea of smart meters, although

> some were not so sure. A few individuals regarded the smart meters as an intrusion. Others were unsure they would lead to lasting behavioural change (believing the devices may be ignored when the novelty has worn off). Some thought they had the potential to irritate consumers by constantly reminding them of their energy consumption and bills and *very few people wanted to pay for one themselves.* (Brook Lyndhurst, 2007, p. 32, emphasis changed)

Notwithstanding the capability and motivation barriers that will face consumers when presented with the technologically advanced functionality of smart meters described above, the legislative provisions for intelligent metering systems in the third legislative package for energy lack any specification for smart metering functionality. With smart meter functionality standards still to emerge, other aspects of the legal framework through which the EU is seeking to effect improvements in energy end-use efficiency is comprised of a range of directives that apply to energy services, buildings (Directive (EC) 2002/91), product labelling, eco-design, taxation (Directive (EC) 2003/96) and co-generation (Directive (EC) 2004/8). Of these, the Energy Services Directive, the Product Labelling Directive, and the Ecodesign Directive contain provisions specifically related to consumer behaviour in the energy market.

One of the aims of the Energy Services Directive (Directive (EC) 2006/32) is to 'create stronger incentives for the demand side' but it seeks to achieve this aim merely through the provision of *indicative* targets and 'mechanisms, incentives and institutional, financial and legal frameworks to remove existing market barriers...that impede the efficient end use of energy' and by creating the conditions for the delivery of other energy efficiency improvement measures to final consumers (Directive (EC) 2006/32, Article 1). Yet such *indicative* targets entail 'no legally enforceable obligation for Member States' as action to achieve such an aim is 'dependent on many external factors which influence the behaviour of consumers as regards their energy use and their willingness to implement energy saving methods and use energy saving devices' (Directive (EC) 2006/32, Recital 12). The Directive does require Member States to provide information relating to energy efficiency but the obligation is general in form and merely suggests that this 'can include information on financial and legal frameworks, communication and promotion campaigns, and the widespread exchange of best practice at all levels' (Directive (EC) 2006/32, Recitals 28 and 30). Where technology is creating flexible platforms through which consumers could actively utilise smart meter data in revolutionary ways to reduce their energy consumption the Directive is less ambitious. It requires Member States merely to ensure

> that, in so far as it is technically possible, financially reasonable and proportionate in relation to the potential energy savings, final customers...are provided with competitively priced individual meters that accurately reflect the final customer's actual energy consumption and that provide information on actual time of use. (Directive (EC) 2006/32, Article 13(1)

Motivating the individual consumer to regulate their own energy consumption is simply left reliant on billing based on actual consumption that is 'performed *frequently enough*' (Directive (EC) 2006/32, Article 13(2), emphasis added). The billing event, together with other contractual events but distinct from any real-time mechanisms, is also identified as the time when Member States are to ensure information on current actual prices, individual annual comparisons of energy consumption and contact information for consumers' organisations and energy agencies to be provided to the final consumer (Directive (EC) 2006/32, Article 13(3)).

The consumer-focussed provisions of the Ecodesign Directive (Directive (EC) 2009/125), in contrast to those of the Energy Services Directive, encourage active consumer agency in the market. It asserts that the eco-design of products 'provides genuine new opportunities for manufacturers, consumers and society as a whole' (Recital 5) and suggests that

> [i]n order to maximise the environmental benefits from improved design, it may be necessary to inform consumers about the environmental characteristics and performance of energy-related products and to advise them on how to use products in a manner which is environmentally friendly. (Recital 12)

More significantly, the Directive requires Member States to 'ensure that consumers... are given an opportunity to submit observations on product compliance to the competent authorities' (Article 3(4)) and that they are provided with 'the requisite information on the role that they can play in the sustainable use of the product' (Article 14(a)). Information is also to be provided 'on the significant environmental characteristics and performance of a product... to allow consumers to compare these aspects of the products' and, 'on how to install, use and maintain the product in order to minimise its impact on the environment and to ensure optimal life expectancy, as well as on how to return the product at end-of-life' (Annex 1, Part 2 (b) and (c)). The Ecodesign Directive goes further than providing for consumers to be supplied with information; it explicitly requires that consumers' associations, as part of civil society, must be invited to comment on self-regulatory initiatives and monitoring reports where they are adopted and that consumer organisations, along with other interested parties, shall contribute to defining and reviewing implementing measures and to examining the effectiveness of the established market surveillance mechanisms for eco-design products (Article 18).

Conclusion

This chapter has argued that components of the theoretical concept of consumer citizenship may be drawn together to establish a four-level hierarchical model that helps to explain the relationships between the normative influences in consumer citizenship practice. It is a model that reflects the primary drivers for the consumer empowerment that forms a central goal of the Commission's consumer policy strategy: a strategy, that seeks to provide for consumers to exercise 'informed, environmentally and socially responsible choices' and to encourage them to adopt greater responsibilities. The model highlights the features and enablers for consumer citizenship practice that describe the individual characteristics or behaviours of the consumer and the market; it also highlights the barriers and consequences, relevant both to the individual and the market, that limit the degree to which practical consumer agency can influence market shaping. Taken together, this chapter has argued that the normative hierarchy of consumer citizenship practice, as presented in Figure 5.1, provides a relevant and functional framework for evaluating market functioning.

Whilst personal and structural consumer detriment reduces consumer welfare in all markets, measurement of detriment is dependent on consumer expectations that may vary across the different geographical areas of the EU's internal market. As a partial counter to such consumer detriment, consumer protection measures provide policy makers with a tool for bringing greater assurance to consumers and encouraging empowered participation in the market. In particular, measures employed in the Consumer Markets Scoreboard provide objective data on market functioning and consumer empowerment and that is reflected in the value placed on individual consumer agency by the Commission.

The case study of the energy sector illustrates the challenges facing policy- and law-makers that extend beyond the normative influences of consumer protection and information and includes barriers to the development of increased consumer agency associated with normative capability and motivational aspects of consumer citizenship practice. The reform of the European energy market is taking place within a global shift towards liberalisation and privatisation of networked industries and the emergence of new regulatory structures at national and EU level. The Directives of the successive legislative packages for the EU internal market in energy have extended consumer protection and established rights that support empowerment and embrace the concept of informed choice. They reinforce the enabling, normative, aspects of consumer citizenship practice associated with consumer protection and information and carry the presumption of an increasing and positive consumer agency in market functioning. The Energy Services Directive highlights this broader role for the consumer where he or she is to be *motivated*, by information, to make choices that are not merely economic.

The market opening and liberalising ambitions of the successive legislative energy packages have yet to be fully realised such that market dominance and inadequate unbundling allow for a general consumer detriment as a consequence of impaired structural capability. Levels of consumer satisfaction are distorted and confused through a resulting ambivalence towards the market by consumers and further complicated by geographic variations in consumer expectations. Regulatory agencies at the EU level suggest that the aim of the third legislative package is to bring stability and coherence to this complex market, in the consumer interest. The legislation has provided for the introduction of the new EU energy agency (ACER) that comes with the objective of improving structural capability through harmonisation of national regulatory powers: powers that are extended through new duties requiring national regulators to enforce consumer protection measures and to supervise the consumers prompt access to consumption data and market functionality. The Citizens' Energy Forum is another product of the third legislative package and a tangible example of the increasing influential role for consumers, through consumer associations. Whilst still in its formative stage, the Forum is making optimistic statements regarding the active participation of empowered consumers as market-shaping agents, yet these are statements that fail to address the motivational barriers facing consumers in an energy market influenced by environmental issues.

Existing studies have shown through consumer segmentation models that, whilst consumer attitudes to environmental issues contain recognition of the link between climate change and their individual behaviour, there remains a significant and challenging attitude–behaviour gap that constitutes a motivational barrier to consumer citizenship practice. The segmentation model used in the Defra study highlights the practical difficulties facing policy initiatives that have the objective of promoting consumer citizenship practice in the form of increased consumer agency in market shaping. Barriers challenging the normative potential of information, capability and motivation were emphasised in the research conclusions that found cynicism and confusion about environmental issues: the strongest behavioural driver to be cost, and a distrust of government, local authorities and 'big' business.

If the optimism expressed in the Citizens' Energy Forum over the potential impact of empowered and active consumers as market shaping agents is based on changing consumer attitudes, then it is reflected in the Commission's observation that '[p]ublic opinion has shifted decisively towards the imperative of addressing climate change' (Commission, 2008a, p. 2). Structures of new governance are providing channels for the consumer voice but the prospect of engaging consumer agency with a technologically driven revolution in the energy market, centred on smart metering, smart grids and individual consumer energy data management, faces the capability and motivational barriers exposed in the Defra research. The legislative provisions of the Energy Services Directive (Directive (EC) 2006/32) reflect the difficulties facing policy and law in effecting a change between consumers' attitudes and their behaviour that would justify the Forum's and the Commission's optimism. The Directive simply acknowledges that consumer behaviour, 'and their willingness to implement energy saving methods and use energy saving devices' is 'dependent on many external factors' (Directive (EC) 2006/32, Recital 12).

Capability and motivational barriers limit the practical effectiveness of the consumer citizenship model developed in this book and slow the effective implementation of any policy objectives that encourage market-shaping activity by consumers. Yet, the Ecodesign Directive (Directive (EC) 2009/125) exemplifies the EU's desire to exploit the concept of consumer citizenship within new governance structures. The Directive requires Member States to ensure that consumers' observations on product compliance can be submitted to 'competent authorities' and explicitly identifies consumers' associations with civil society. It also scopes out a role for consumers' associations in which they must be invited to comment on self-regulatory initiatives and monitoring reports where they are adopted, to contribute to defining and reviewing implementing measures, and to examine the effectiveness of the established market surveillance mechanisms (Directive (EC) 2009/125, Article 18).

6
Reflections, Transformations and Conclusions

My purpose in writing this book was twofold. The first was to contribute to the understanding of a developing post-national citizenship through a study of the changing relationship between individuals, in their role as consumers, and the internal market. The second was to bring a study of the characteristics of newer forms of governance, and a broader understanding of the politics of European consumer law, into the mainstream of European consumer law scholarship.

To achieve these objectives this book has examined the hypothesis, based on Redfern's assertions from 1920, that within an EU context the *opportunity* for the consumer to *realise* his or her *true position and power* has never been greater. It has drawn attention to the legislative provisions for consumer protection and empowerment, and to the case law that has helped to develop aspects of access rights and non-discrimination for consumers. I have also discussed the role and the effectiveness of legal measures in such consumer affecting areas as product labelling and competition law. Yet, the approach has been to try to place this legal discourse within a practical and policy setting that has examined the relationship between citizenship and the consumer. I hope that I have gone some way to help define what we may mean by the term *consumer citizen* and to expose the nature of a developing *consumer citizenship practice*: a practice that can be characterised as those behaviours associated with the changing status of individuals in relation to the opportunities and barriers that affect their access and choice rights as market actors and the development of market related duties and obligations. If the consumer in the European internal market may be construed as one side of a coin, then the citizen is the other and a central theme of this book has argued that there exists a coherent, tangible and relevant, albeit perhaps narrow, concept of citizenship that can be associated with the notion of the consumer citizen.

This book started with the proposition that descriptive identity labels reflect the consumers improving status as an influential market actor and the paradoxical reality of an increasing vulnerability and potential for consumer detriment. The review of consumer descriptions in EU law and policy drew attention to the range of consumer identities that demonstrate a complexity that extends beyond the benchmark of the 'average consumer' found in the Court's jurisprudence. These multiple identities of the consumer are used to describe behaviours associated with consumer vulnerability and with consumer capability; they help define aspects of citizenship found in the practice of consumption and in particular those aspects of consumption that relate to environmental, social justice, rights, labour and gender issues (McGregor, 2002, p. 90).

It is also from a behavioural perspective that we find explicit recognition of the essential attributes of the 'consumer citizen': the individually or collectively active market participant who is interested in developing and improving society by considering ethical issues, diversity of perspectives, global processes and future conditions in their transactional, post-transactional and extra-transactional activities as a consumer. The term is legitimised by the increasingly blurred boundary between citizenship and consumerism and also by the way EU policy has embraced the essential nature of the economic and social aspects of consumer citizenship practice through its focus on consumer outcomes and the encouragement of policy shaping new governance networks that provide a platform for the consumers to exercise their constituent power.

In Chapter 4 the territorial and membership dimensions of consumer citizenship practice were identified in a model comprised of four broad market sectors that reflected the social welfare, public sector, services of general economic interest and the private retail markets. It is a model that reflects the transformation of the internal market in which commodification and private sector delivery of public services has brought a rights-based consumerist focus to all sectors, including those that were once exclusively state managed. It is a rights base that provides for an increasing choice for consumers in all sectors and acts as a channel for the potential exercise of responsibility as the duty component of consumer citizenship practice.

That the exercise of such responsibility and the realisation of true consumer power is limited by barriers to effective consumer protection, information, capability and motivation raises a significantly more complex set of issues than Redfern's concern of a mere failure to think and act together. The core argument of Chapter 3 was that the EU's consumer citizen has more opportunity now than he or she ever has had to voice individual and collective concerns, and to influence policy, through the networks and structures of European policy governance. Yet, the hierarchy of normative influences, identified in this research as shaping the behaviour of European citizens as they interact with the market also draws attention to the significant barriers that limit the effectiveness of consumer citizenship practice. These are the barriers of structural and individual capability that highlight a tension between the market and social values: a tension that is related to individualistic and solidaristic aspects of motivation *and* to social aspects of individual capability.

EU law provides a framework of measures that help shape all four of the normative influences on consumer behaviour, yet a better understanding of the relationships between these influences would add to the building blocks for strategic decision-making by the institutions of government and governance at the EU and national level. For it is these institutions that are offering new opportunities for consumer citizens to get involved with market shaping. Paradoxically, consumer vulnerability, in its widest sense, is increasing as, for example, technology, financial services and climate change issues combine to challenge the suitability of existing regulatory frameworks. Mobilising a research agenda to develop the understanding of the relationships between consumer motivation, capability, information and protection could draw together research interests from a variety of academic disciplines, but could include the political sciences, behavioural economics, educationalists and law, and could work with the relevant institutions of civil society, government and governance.

It was mentioned earlier in this book that the pace and diversity of change in European integration and Europeanisation had given EU legal studies an event-sensitive, or problem-centred, approach at both the systemic level and in sectoral research (Walker, 2005, pp. 590–591). But these have also been changes that have played a significant part in the transformation of the concepts and structures on which political and economic governance and markets are based. It is these same changes that have provided the foundations for the normative influences of consumer citizenship practice and through which we have also seen the transformation of the individual into the consumer citizen. For those both capable and motivated individual market actors the structures of 'new governance', in the consumer domain, provide for an internal coherence within a poly-centred structure of political authority that embraces the notion of a fragmented sovereignty, and that is evident at supranational, national and individual levels.

The new institutions and the new channels for agency that have appeared reflect movements in decision-making power away from the Member States and, upwards towards the EU; outwards towards independent regulatory agencies and enforcement authorities and downwards towards individual consumers. Changes that, within the context of independent regulatory agencies, has been argued to have produced 'a weakening of the state-*qua*-central actor although at the same time it could be seen as a strengthening of public action and effective governance *for* the people' (Schmidt, 2009, p. 205). These regulatory authorities, and the consumer agencies of civil society, are forming new networks of self-supporting epistemic communities for the sharing of new ideas and best practice that, it was suggested, are strengthening governance *for* the people and providing consumer citizenship practice with the channels for voice and influence, but that may also be increasing the 'power position' of the Commission *vis à vis* national government (Coen and Thatcher, 2005, p. 335).

Such ideas of governance are concerned with relationships, processes, networks and organisation of collective action in multi-level regimes with many centres of competing authority that have emerged, or are emerging, and that are now beginning to provide for consumer input into the policy process. Networks and structures of EU consumer policy governance have been shown to provide channels for consumer input into policy decisions, and more sector-specific market shaping through sector-specific consumer organisations. Political endorsement of consumer citizenship practice and its role in governance and policy is found in the White Paper on European Governance in which the Commission undertook to help reinforce a culture of consultation and dialogue in the EU (Commission, 2001b). Whilst such cultural changes were to be facilitated by the institutions of government at the EU level, and to a greater or lesser extent at the Member State level, this transformation of governance processes can be seen as a response to the political realities that had developed in the 1990s. Citizens had begun to engage with their political elites in a process that sought to define their rights, their access to such rights and who they were as citizens in such a way that it was suggested to be able to enshrine the constitutive elements of citizenship practice in 'a democratic surplus as citizens seek ways to be part of the constitution-building process' (Wiener and Della Sala, 1997, p. 611).

The blurred boundary between public and private authority is a characteristic of the infranational structures of EU governance in which the

institutions and organisations that shape European policy are continuing to develop to accommodate the increasingly citizenship like role
of the consumer: a role seen as essential in order to be able to meet the
challenges of the changing political and market environments that, the
Commission suggests, flow from the increasing sophistication of retail
markets, from the growth in services and liberalised services in particular, from the increasingly interlinked nature of goods and services,
from the internet, digitalisation and growth in e-commerce, and from
globalisation of production (Commission, 2007a, pp. 3–4).

This book has traced the legislative, case law and policy sources of
consumer empowerment in what has become both an enduring and
central theme of the EU's consumer policy strategy: a strategy in which
around 500 million EU consumers are considered to be central to the
three main challenges of growth, jobs and the need to re-connect with
its citizens that face the EU. The empowered consumers, it appears, have
become so integral to these issues that they have been described as 'the
lifeblood of the economy... [where] Confident, informed and empowered consumers are the motor of economic change as their choices drive
innovation and efficiency'(Commission, 2007a). As a consequence of a
new economic, social, environmental and political context, consumer
policy has been placed at the heart of the next phase of the internal
market that has the intention to shift the focus of regulation towards
citizen-focussed outcomes, to provide consumers with the means to
protect themselves, and, through consumer citizenship practice, to
drive towards quality improvement and better competition for goods
and services in the market.

We are all consumer citizens and at the same time we are all vulnerable consumers; we all engage in consumer citizenship practices
and yet we are all limited in our endeavours as good consumer citizens by structural and personal barriers. Some of us are more capable and/or better motivated to secure positive consumer outcomes
but our motives may be influenced by individualistic or solidaristic
intentions and our motivation may be limited to specific transactions
or types of transaction. Even then, structural barriers in the form of
anti-competitive commercial practices that result in market distortion or failure can lead to such general consumer detriment that even
the most capable and motivated consumers cannot resolve problems
through good consumer citizenship practice alone. To provide support
for consumers and alleviate the detriment caused by such structural
barriers the regulatory agencies, once more concerned with sectoral
competition issues of access and dominance, are being encouraged to

develop a role as the representative of the consumer citizen interest (Micklitz, 2009, p. 16).

Whilst there may be not yet be any legal obligation in the secondary legislation requiring the regulatory agencies to develop resources focussed on upholding the rights of consumer citizens we have noted Micklitz's observation that '[t]here is a gradual movement of [EU] secondary law into that direction which might overcome ... the still existing discrepancies between the role and function of the regulatory agencies in the Member States' (Micklitz, 2009). Particularly relevant across the heavily regulated and broad market sector of services of general economic interest, but increasingly so in the internal market as a whole, this 'gradual movement' of law has the encouragement of Commission policy. Support for the consumer citizen cause, the Commission recognises, 'often requires the existence of independent regulators with appropriate staff and clearly defined powers and duties ... [that] include powers of sanction, in particular the ability to monitor the transposition and enforcement of universal service provisions'. It is also the view of the Commission that provisions are required to ensure the *active participation* of consumers in the definition and evaluation of services, in the availability of appropriate redress and compensation mechanisms, and in the existence of a review clause allowing service requirements to develop over time to reflect new social, technological and economic developments (Commission, 2007e, pp. 10–11).

In the short case study of the energy sector we can see evidence of these changes taking place. The Citizens' Energy Forum, as a component of the new governance machinery in a sector-specific context, has debated, *in detail*, the changing role of the regulator and the increasing role of consumers in the new legislation. It is also an example of a new generation of policy influencing bodies that is helping to develop the discourse on consumer outcomes within the context of a consumer citizenship practice that is reliant on a complex diversity of normative influences in order to put consumers 'in the driving seat with regard to the development of retail markets so that they are sufficiently empowered to make markets deliver concrete benefits' (Citizens' Energy Forum, 2009a, p. 2).

Notes

1 Introduction: European consumer citizenship practice

1. Article 20(1) TFEU (Article 17(1) EC) introduced by the Treaty of Amsterdam 1999 following concerns that any strengthening of Union citizenship, following the Treaty of Maastricht 1993, could be interpreted as weakening national citizenship.
2. See in particular, Cases C-423/99 *Baumbast and R* [2002] ECR I-7091, para. 82; C-184/99 *Grzelczyk* [2001] ECR I-6193, para. 31, and the Opinion of AG Mazák in Case C-33/07 *Gheorghe Jipa* [2008] ECR I-5157, para. 30.
3. For a discussion embracing these issues of poly-centred authority and fragmented sovereignty see Walker, 2005, particularly pp. 592–593.
4. Excerpts from Chapter 3 and other minor elements of this book appear as an original publication of a paper by the author available at www.springerlink.com, DOI 10.1007/s 10603-009-9108-7 (Davies J, 2009).
5. Comprising, Regulation (EC) 713/2009 establishing an Agency for the Cooperation of Energy Regulators; Regulation (EC) 714/2009 on conditions for access to the network for cross-border exchanges in electricity; Regulation (EC) 715/2009 on conditions for access to the natural gas transmission networks; 2009/72/EC concerning common rules for the internal market in electricity, and Directive 2009/73/EC concerning common rules for the internal market in natural gas.
6. Annex 1(2) of both Directives 2009/72/EC concerning common rules for the internal market in electricity and 2009/73/EC concerning common rules for the internal market in natural gas.

2 From cog to cognisance: evolution of the consumer citizen

1. Preliminary programme of the European Economic Community for a consumer protection and information policy [1975] OJ C 92/2.
2. For example, Directive (EEC) 85/577 to protect the consumer in respect of contracts negotiated away from business premises [1985] OJ L 372/31; Directive (EEC) 93/13 on unfair terms in consumer contracts [1993] OJ L95/29 and Directive (EEC) 87/102 for the approximation of the laws, regulations and administrative provisions of the Member States concerning consumer credit [1987] OJ L42/48.
3. For example, Directive (EEC) 85/374 concerning liability for defective products [1988] OJ L 307/54.
4. For example, Directive (EEC) 92/59 on general product safety [1992] OJ L 228/24, and subsequently, Directive (EC) 2001/95 on general product safety [2002] OJ L 11/4.

5. Article 115 TFEU (Article 94 EC) provides 'The Council shall, acting unani-mously...issue directives for the approximation of such laws...as directly affect the establishment or functioning of the common market.'

6. Single European Act 1987, introducing Article 114 TFEU (Article 95 EC) enabling derogation from unanimity for measures aimed at approximation of the 'law, regulation or administrative action in Member States which have as their object the establishment and functioning of the internal market'.

7. Proposals included directives: to protect the consumer in respect of con-tracts which have been negotiated away from business premises; relating to the approximation of the laws, regulations and administrative provi-sions of the member states concerning misleading and unfair advertising; relating to the approximation of the laws, regulations and administrative provisions of member states concerning liability for defective products and a directive relating to the approximation of the laws, regulations and administrative provisions of the member states concerning consumer credit.

8. *inter alia*, interpretation of: Article 110 TFEU (Article 90 EC) (Case 170/78, *Commission of the European Communities v United Kingdom of Great Britain and Northern Ireland* [1983] ECR 2265); Articles 34, 35 and 36 TFEU (Articles 28, 29 and 30 EC) (Case 286/81, *Oosthoek's Uitgeversmaatschappij BV* [1982] ECR 4575 and Case 178/84, *Commission of the European Communities v Federal Republic of Germany* [1987] ECR 1227) and Article 101 TFEU (Article 81 EC) (Case 172/80, *Züchner V Bayerische Vereinsbank AG* [1981] ECR 2021).

9. The purpose of the Directive offers protection to a community broader than final user consumers; Article 2(3) of the Directive defines a 'person' as either a natural or legal person.

10. The cases referred to by the Court in this case were: Case C-362/88 *GB-INNO-BM* [1990] ECR I-667; Case C-238/89 *Pall* [1990] ECR I-4827; Case C-126/91 *Yves Rocher* [1993] ECR I-2361; Case C-315/92 *Verband Sozialer Wettbewerb* [1994] ECR I-317; Case C-456/93 *Langguth* [1995] ECR I-1737; and Case C-470/93 *Mars* [1995] ECR I-1923.

11. EURLex, Simple search, Query – Case-law: All case-law AND Title and text, search terms: average consumer who is reasonably well informed and rea-sonably observant and circumspect, 11 January 2011.

12. He includes the very young, those not educated sufficiently well to make informed choices, immigrants not speaking the language, the poor who are subject to the *mala fide* practices of credit sharks and those consumers in specific situations such as the relatives of a debtor called on to sign a guarantee.

13. Specifically in the context of the environment, Regulation (EC) 1367/2006 on the application of the provisions of the Aarhus Convention on Access to Information, Public Participation in Decision-making and Access to Justice in Environmental Matters to Community institutions and bodies [2006] OJ L 264/13.

14. For example, the explicit emphasis placed on information by the Court in *GB-INNO-BM* (Case C-362/88) para. 18: 'under Community law concerning consumer protection the provision of information to the consumer is con-sidered one of the principal requirements.'

15. For example, Bennett, 2004; Diani, 2001; Van de Donk and others, 2003; Ford and Gil, 2001; Pickerill, 2004 and Street and Scott, 2001. All cited in Baringhorst, 2005.

3 European consumer citizenship: a coherent theoretical model?

1. In arriving at this definition of the average consumer in *Gut Springenheide*, Case C-210/96, the Court also cited its earlier case law in *GB-INNO-BM*, Case C-362/88; *Pall*, Case C-238/89; *Yves Rocher*, Case C-126/91; *Verband Sozialer Wettbewerb*, Case C-315/92; *Langguth*, Case C-456/93 and *Mars*, Case C-470/93.
2. The comparison of the different notions of 'consumer in the Consumer Law Compendium is drawn from: Directive (EEC) 85/577 to protect the consumer in respect of contracts negotiated away from business premises; Directive (EEC) 87/102 for the approximation of the laws, regulations and administrative provisions of the Member States concerning consumer credit; Directive (EEC) 90/314 on package travel, package holidays and package tours; Directive (EEC) 93/13 on unfair terms in consumer contracts; Directive (EC) 94/47 on the protection of purchasers in respect of certain aspects of contracts relating to the purchase of the right to use immovable properties on a timeshare basis; Directive (EC) 97/7 on the protection of consumers in respect of distance contracts; Directive (EC) 98/6 on consumer protection in the indication of the prices of products offered to consumers; Directive (EC) 99/44 on certain aspects of the sale of consumer goods and associated guarantees; Directive (EC) 2000/31 on certain legal aspects of information society services, in particular electronic commerce, in the Internal Market; Directive (EC) 2002/65 concerning the distance marketing of consumer financial services; Directive (EC) 2002/91 on the energy performance of buildings, and Directive (EC) 2005/29 concerning unfair business-to-consumer commercial practices in the internal market.
3. Respectively, Articles 13–15 of the Brussels I Convention, now Articles 15–17 of Regulation (EC) 44/2001 on jurisdiction and the recognition and enforcement of judgments in civil and commercial matters [2001] OJ L 12/1, and Article 5 of the Rome I Convention.
4. Charter of Fundamental Rights of the European Union, OJ C 303/1 of 14 December 2007.
5. and see Shaw, Hunt and Wallace, 2007, p. 45. Also, Article 2 EC has now been repealed by the Treaty of Lisbon 2009 and replaced in substance by Article 3 TEU.
6. OJ C 303/1, Chapters III (Equality) and IV (Solidarity).
7. On the basis of the freedoms guaranteed by Articles 45, 49 and 56 *et seq* TFEU (Articles 39, 43 and 49 *et seq* EC), namely freedom of movement for workers, freedom of establishment and freedom to provide services.
8. In particular, Sen, 1985 and 1999, from Deakin, 2005, p. 3.
9. See, for a discussion of the renewal of the 'Community Method' and the Commissions monopoly of legislative and policy initiation, Majone, 2005, pp. 53–56).

10. Details of National Consumer Groups are available at http://ec.europa.eu/consumers/empowerment/cons_networks_en.htm#national
11. For a recent example see Case C-511/08 *Handelsgesellschaft Heinrich Heine GmbH v Verbraucherzentrale Nordrhein-Westfalen eV* [2010] ECR I-00000, not yet reported.
12. For example, European Performance Satisfaction Indicator, Customer Satisfaction Pan European Benchmark Report 2007 (Stockholm 2008) last accessed at http://www.epsi-rating.com/images/stories/reports/epsi_report_2007/Web_version.pdf on 28 January 2010.
13. See Commission, 2008b, p. 8, highlighting areas of failure that include: consumer empowerment; consumer detriment; the relationship between import prices and consumption prices; regulatory effect; regulatory compliance; sectoral qualitative analysis; access and affordability – particularly for essential services; and interoperability – the ability of a system or a product to work with other systems or products without special effort on the part of the consumer.

4 Boundaries of European consumer citizenship

1. For example, Case C-422/01, *Skandia and Ramstedt* [2002] ECR I-6817, concerning the tax treatment of an occupational pension insurance policy taken out by Skandia for the benefit of Mr Ramstedt with companies established in other Member States. The Court held (para. 52) 'that any tax advantage resulting for providers of services from the low taxation to which they are subject in the Member State in which they are established cannot be used by another Member State to justify less favourable treatment in tax matters given to recipients of services established in the latter State. Such compensatory tax arrangements prejudice the very foundations of the single market.'
2. See generally, Osborne and Gaebler, 1993; Bartlett, Roberts and Le Grand, 1998; Pollitt and Bouckaert, 2000, and Newman, 2006.
3. See also Szyszczak, 2007, p. 213.
4. See also, with regard to Directive (EEC) 93/13 on unfair terms in consumer contracts, Nebbia, 2007, p. 12.
5. The broad construction of the public services sector suggested here would equate to the three market sectors comprising social welfare, the public sector and services of general interest depicted in Figure 4.1. See also Picard, 1998, pp. 87 *et seq.*
6. See also Figure 3.1, where there is no empowerment arrow between the consumer and the state regulatory agencies.

5 The relevance and limitations of consumer citizenship practice

1. For a discussion of the normative aspect of intrinsic motivation, see Lam and Lambermont-Ford, 2008.
2. See the European Commission Consumer Markets Scoreboard web site, last accessed at http://ec.europa.eu/consumers/strategy/facts_en.htm#background on 9 December 2009.

3. See also Szyszczak, 2009, p. 304.
4. Regulation (EC) 713/2009 establishing an Agency for the Cooperation of Energy Regulators [2009] OJ L211/1; Regulation (EC) 714/2009 on conditions for access to the network for cross-border exchanges in electricity [2009] OJ L211/15; Regulation (EC) 715/2009 on conditions for access to the natural gas transmission networks [2009] OJ L211/36; Directive 2009/72/EC concerning common rules for the internal market in electricity [2009] OJ L211/55, and Directive 2009/73/EC concerning common rules for the internal market in natural gas[2009] OJ L211/94.
5. The International Energy Agency was established in 1974 and comprises some 28 member countries, including the USA, Australia, Canada, Japan, Republic of Korea and New Zealand; and enjoys the involvement of the European Commission (Luciani, 2004, p. 110).
6. For a discussion of the meaning of 'supplier of last resort' which is not specified in the Directive, see EURELECTRIC, 2004, also cited in Cameron, 2005, p. 25.
7. Denmark, Finland, France, Germany, Norway, Portugal, Spain, the Netherlands, Sweden and the United Kingdom.
8. Product specific legislation implementing the Energy Labelling Directive comprises: Directive (EC) 2003/66 with regard to energy labelling of household electric refrigerators, freezers and their combinations; Directive (EC) 2002/40 with regard to energy labelling of household electric ovens; Directive (EC) 2002/31 with regard to energy labelling of household air-conditioners; Directive (EC) 99/9 with regard to energy labelling of household dishwashers; Directive (EC) 98/11 with regard to energy labelling of household lamps; Directive (EC) 96/89 with regard to energy labelling of household washing machines; Directive (EC) 96/60 with regard to energy labelling of household combined washer-driers, and Directive (EC) 95/13 with regard to energy labelling of household electric tumble driers.
9. Data sourced from various email alerts of news articles provided by Smartmeters, 2009a.

References

ANEC, (2009) web pages, last accessed at, http://www.anec.org/anec. asp?rd=53342&ref=01-01&lang=en on 12 February 2009

Anton C, Camarero C and Carrero M (2007) 'Analysing Firms' Failures as Determinants of Consumer Switching Intentions: The Effect of Moderating Factors', 41 *European Journal of Marketing* 135

Aron R (1974) 'Is Multinational Citizenship Possible?', 41 *Social Research* 638

Bairoch P and Kozul-Wright R (1996) 'Globalization Myths: Some Historical Reflections on Integration, Industrialization and Growth in the World Economy', UNCTAD Discussion Paper 113, last accessed at http://www.unctad. org/en/docs/dp_113.en.pdf on 06 December 2010

Balibar É (2004) *We, the People of Europe? Reflections on Transnational Citizenship* (Princeton University Press, Princeton and Oxford)

Barber N W (2002) 'Citizenship, Nationalism and the European Union', 27 *European Law Review* 241

Baringhorst S (2005) 'New Media and the Politics of Consumer Activism – Opportunities and Challenges of Euro-Asian Anti-Corporate Campaigns', Annual Conference of the European Consortium of Political Research, Granada, last accessed at http://www.protest-cultures.uni-siegen.de/pdf/baringhorst_ecpr.pdf 15 December 2010

Barry B (1974) (reviewed work), 'Exit, Voice, and Loyalty: Responses to Decline in Firms, Organization, and States by Albert O. Hirschman', 4 *British Journal of Political Science* 79

Barry J (1996) 'Sustainability, Political Judgement and Citizenship: Connecting Green Politics and Democracy' in Doherty B and de Geus M (eds) *Democracy and Green Political Thought* (Routledge, London)

Bartlett W, Roberts J A and Le Grand J (eds), (1998) *A Revolution in Social Policy. Quasimarket Reforms in the 1990s* (Policy Press, Bristol)

Bauman Z (1992) 'Soil, Blood and Identity', 40 *Sociological Review* 205

Bellamy R and Warleigh A (2009) 'Cementing the Union: The Role of European Citizenship', last accessed at ftp://ftp.cordis.europa.eu/pub/improving/docs/ser_citizen_bellamy.pdf on 14 December 2009

Bennett L (2004) 'Branded Political Communication: Lifestyle Politics, Logo Campaigns, and the Rise of Global Citizenship' in Micheletti M and others (eds), *Politics, Products and Markets. Exploring Political Consumerism Past and Present* (Transaction Books, London)

BEUC web pages, last accessed at http://www.beuc.eu/Content/Default. asp?PageID=839&LanguageCode=EN on 12 February 2009

Bishop S and Walker M (2002) *The Economics of EC Competition Law* (2nd edn, Sweet & Maxwell, London)

Bonny S (2003) 'Why Are Most Europeans Opposed to GMO's? Factors Explaining Rejection in France and Europe', 6 *Electronic Journal of Biotechnology* 50, accessed at http://www.ejbiotechnology.info/content/vol6/issue1/full/4/4.pdf 15 December 2008

Boström M and Klintman M (2008) *Eco-Standards, Product Labelling and Green Consumerism* (Palgrave Macmillan, Basingstoke)

Bourgoignie T and Trubek D (1987) *Integration Through Law – Europe and the American Federal Experience: Consumer Law, Common Markets and Federalism in Europe and the United States* (Vol. 3, Walter de Gruyter, New York)

Bovis C (2005) 'Financing Services of General Interest, Public Procurement and State Aids: The Delineation between Market Forces and Protection in the European Common Market', *Journal of Business Law* 1 January

Bradgate R, Twigg-Flesner C and Nordhausen A (2005) 'Review of the Eight EU Consumer *Acquis* Minimum Harmonisation Directives and Their Implementation in the UK and Analysis of the Scope for Simplification', Report for the Department of Trade and Industry, URN 05/1952

Brennan C and Coppack M (2008) 'Consumer Empowerment: Global Context, UK Strategies and Vulnerable Consumers', 32 *International Journal of Consumer Studies* 306

Breton R (1995) 'Identification in Transnational Political Communities' in Knop K, Ostry S, Simeon R and Swinton K (eds), *Rethinking Federalism: Citizens, Markets, and Governments in a Changing World* (University of British Columbia Press, Vancouver)

Brook Lyndhurst (2007) 'Public Understanding of Sustainable Energy Consumption in the Home', last accessed at http://randd.defra.gov.uk/Document.aspx?Document=EV02046_6701_FRP.pdf on 14 December 2009

Burnett G, Jaeger P and Thompson K (2008) 'Normative Behaviour and Information: The Social Aspects of Information Access', 30 *Library and Information Science Research* 56

Cameron P (2005) (ed.) *Legal Aspects of EU Energy Regulation* (OUP, Oxford)

Cameron P (2007) *Competition in Energy Markets: Law and Regulation in the European Union*, (2nd edn, OUP, Oxford)

Chalmers D (2006) 'The Unbearable Heaviness of European Citizenship', 31 *European Law Review* 779

Citizens' Energy Forum (2009a) Press Release, MEMO/09/429, 30 September 2009, last accessed at http://europa.eu/rapid/pressReleasesAction.do?reference=MEMO/09/429&format=HTML&aged=0&language=EN&guiLanguage=fr on 18 November 2009,

Citizens' Energy Forum (2009b) Conclusions, last accessed at http://ec.europa.eu/energy/gas_electricity/doc/forum_citizen_energy/2009_09_29_citizens_energy_forum_conclusions.pdf on 30 October 2009

Clarke J and Newman J (2006) 'The People's Choice? Citizens, Consumers and Public Services', Paper presented to conference on *Citizenship and Consumption: Agency, Norms, Mediation and Spaces*, Trinity Hall, Cambridge, last accessed at http://www.open.ac.uk/socialsciences/creating-citizen-consumers/downloadable-papers.php on 10 December 2009

Clarke J and others (2007) *Creating Citizen-Consumers: Changing Publics and Changing Public Services* (Sage, London)

Coen D, and Thatcher M (2005) 'The New Governance of Markets and Non-Majoritarian Regulators', 18 *Governance* 329

Cohen J and Sabel C (1997) 'Directly Deliberative Polyarchy', 3 *European Law Journal* 313

Cohen J and Sabel C (2003) 'Sovereignty and Solidarity: EU and US' in Zeitlin J and Trubek D M (eds), *Governing Work and Welfare in a New Economy: European and American Experiments* (OUP, Oxford)

Commission (1985) 'Completing the Internal Market: White Paper from the Commission to the European Council' (White Paper) *COM* (1985) 310 final, 14 June 1986

Commission (1989) 'Amended Proposal for a Council Directive on the Approximation of the Rates of Excise Duty on Alcoholic Beverages and on the Alcohol Contained in Other Products' (Proposal) *COM* (1989) 527 Final, 7 December 1989

Commission (1990) 'Proposal for a Council Directive on the Harmonization of the Structures of Excise Duties on Alcoholic Beverages and on the Alcohol Contained in Other Products' (Proposal) *COM* (1990) 432 Final, 7 November 1990

Commission (1993) 'EC Education and Training Programmes 1986–1992' (Report) *COM* (93) 151 final, 5 May 1993

Commission (1995) 'The Single Market in 1994' (Report) *COM* (1995) 238 final, 15 June 1995

Commission (1996a) 'Services of General Interest in Europe [1996]' *OJ* C 281/3

Commission (1996b) 'Services of General Interest in Europe' (Communication) *COM* (1996) 443 final, 11 September 1996

Commission (1996c) 'Education – Training – Research – The Obstacles to Transnational Mobility' (Green Paper) *COM* (1996) 462 final, 2 October 1996

Commission (1999) 'The Strategy for Europe's Internal Market' (Communication) *COM* (1999) 464 final, 5 October 1999

Commission (2000) 'Services of General Interest in Europe' (Communication) *COM* (2000) 580 final, 20 September 2000

Commission (2001a) 'Integrated Product Policy' (Green Paper) *COM* (2001) 68 final, 7 February 2001

Commission (2001b) 'European Governance' (White Paper) *COM* (2001) 428 final, 25 July 2001

Commission (2001c) 'Draft Joint Report on Social Inclusion' (Communication) *COM* (2001) 565 final, 10 October 2001

Commission (2003a) 'The Implementation and Evaluation of Community Activities 1999–2001 in Favour of Consumers under the General Framework as Established by Decision 283/1999/EC' (Report) *COM* (2003) 42 final, 31 January 2003

Commission (2003b) 'A More Coherent European Contract Law – an Action Plan' (Communication) *COM* (2003) 68 final, 12 February 2003

Commission (2003c) 'Concerning Unfair Business-to-Consumer Commercial Practices in the Internal Market (the Unfair Commercial Practices Directive)' (Proposal) *COM* (2003) 356 final, 18 June 2003

Commission (2003d) 'Extended Impact Assessment on the Directive Concerning Unfair Business-to-Consumer Commercial Practices in the Internal Market (the Unfair Commercial Practices Directive)' (Staff Working Paper) *SEC* (2003) 724 final, 18 June 2003

Commission (2004a) 'On The Implementation of the Detailed Work Programme on the Follow-up of the Objectives of Education and Training Systems in Europe' (Report) *OJ* C 104/1, 30 April 2004

Commission (2004b) 'Follow-up to EESC Opinions Delivered in the First Quarter of 2004, DI CESE 165/2004' (Commission Position) (2004), last accessed at http://eesc.europa.eu/documents/follow-up/2004/suivi_avis_1t_04_en.pdf on 2 October 2008

Commission (2004c) 'White Paper on Services of General Interest' (Communication) *COM* (2004) 374 final, 12 May 2004

Commission (2004d) 'Third Benchmarking Report on the Implementation of the Internal Electricity and Gas Market' (DG TREN Draft Working Paper) (2004), last accessed at http://ec.europa.eu/energy/gas_electricity/interpretative_notes/doc/benchmarking_reports/2003_report_bencmarking.pdf on 16 November 2009

Commission (2005a) 'Report on Progress in Creating the Internal Gas and Electricity Market' (Report) *COM* (2005) 568 final, 15 November 2005

Commission (2005b) 'Healthier, Safer, More Confident Citizens: a Health and Consumer Protection Strategy' (Communication) *COM* (2005) 115 final, 6 April 2005

Commission (2005c) 'Damages Actions for Breach of the EC Antitrust Rules' (Green Paper) *COM* (2005) 672 final, 19 December 2005

Commission (2005d) 'Progress in Creating the Internal Gas and Electricity Market' (Staff Working Document – Report Technical Annex) *SEC* (2005) 1448 final, 15 November 2005

Commission (2005e) 'Damages Actions for Breach of the EC Antitrust Rules' (Staff Working Paper) *SEC* (2005) 1732, 19 December 2005

Commission (2006a) 'On the Implementation of Regulation (EC) No. 1830/2003 Concerning Traceability and Labelling of Genetically Modified Organisms and the Traceability of Food and Feed Products Produced from Genetically Modified Organisms' (Report) *COM* (2006) 197 final, 10 May 2006

Commission (2006b) 'Market Reviews under the EU Regulatory Framework: Consolidating the Internal Market for Electronic Communications' (Communication) *COM* (2006) 28 final, 6 February 2006

Commission (2006c) 'Concerning A Consultation on Action at EU Level to Promote the Active Inclusion of the People Furthest from the Labour Market' (Communication) *COM* (2006) 44 final, 8 February 2006

Commission (2006d) 'Review of the Consumer Acquis' (Green Paper) *COM* (2006) 744 final, 8 February 2007

Commission (2006e) 'Inquiry Pursuant to Article 17 of Regulation (EC) No 1/2003 into the European Gas and Electricity Sectors' (Communication) *COM* (2006) 851 final, 10 January 2007

Commission (2006f) 'European Smart Grids Technology Platform' (Community Research) (2006), last accessed at http://ec.europa.eu/research/energy/pdf/smartgrids_en.pdf on 6 January 2010

Commission (2007a) 'EU Consumer Policy Strategy 2007–2013 – Empowering Consumers, Enhancing Welfare, Effectively Protecting Them' (Communication) *COM* (2007) 99 final, 13 March 2007

Commission (2007b) 'Towards a European Charter on the Rights of Energy Consumers' (Communication) *COM* (2007) 386 final, 5 July 2007

Commission (2007c) 'Draft Proposal for a Directive Concerning Common Rules for the Internal Market in Electricity' (Communication) *COM* (2007) 528 final, 19 September 2007

Commission (2007d) A Single Market for 21st Century Europe' (Communication) *COM* (2007) 724 final, 20 November 2007

Commission (2007e) 'Services Of General Interest, Including Social Services of General Interest: A New European Commitment' (Communication) *COM* (2007) 725 final, 20 November 2007

Commission (2008a) '20 20 by 2020 Europe's Climate Change Opportunity' (Communication) *COM* (2008) 30 final, 23 January 2008

Commission (2008b) 'Monitoring Consumer Outcomes in the Single Market: The Consumer Markets Scoreboard' (Communication) *COM* (2008) 31 final, 29 January 2008

Commission (2008c) 'White Paper on Damages Actions for Breach of the EC Antitrust Rules' (White Paper) *COM* (2008) 165 final, 2 April 2008

Commission (2008d) 'On Sustainable Consumption and Production and Sustainable Industrial Policy Action Plan' (Communication) *COM* (2008) 397 final, 16 July 2008

Commission (2008e) 'Proposal for a Directive on the Indication by Labelling and Standard Product Information of the Consumption of Energy and Other Related Resources by Energy-Related Products' (Proposal) *COM* (2008) 778 final, 13 November 2008

Commission (2009a) 'Monitoring Consumer Outcomes in the Single Market: Second Edition of the Consumer Markets Scoreboard' (Communication) *COM* (2009) 25 final, 28 January 2009

Commission (2009b) 'On A Harmonised Methodology for Classifying and Reporting Consumer Complaints and Enquiries' (Communication) *COM* (2009) 346 final, 7 July 2009

Commission (2009c) 'Second Consumer Markets Scoreboard' (Staff Working Document) *SEC* (2009) 76, (Part 1), (Part 2) and (Part 3), 28 January 2009

Commission (2011a) Socrates Programme of Educational and Training Initiatives (Now Integrated into the 'Lifelong Learning Programme'), Comenius (schools sub-programme) 2.1(no date), last accessed at http://ec.europa.eu/education/lifelong-learning-programme/doc78_en.htm on 3 January 2011

Commission (2011b) 'What Is Governance', last accessed at http://ec.europa.eu/governance/index_en.htm on 2 January 2011

Commission (2011c) 'Young Consumer Competition', last accessed at http://ec.europa.eu/consumers/cons_info/eycc_en.htm on 3 January 2011

Council (1975) Resolution on a Preliminary Programme of the European Economic Community for a Consumer Protection and Information Policy [1975] *OJ* C 92

Council (1981) Resolution on a Second Programme of the European Economic Community for a Consumer Protection and Information Policy [1981] *OJ* C133/1

Council (1986) Resolution on Consumer Education in Primary and Secondary Schools [1986] *OJ* C184/21

Council (1993) Resolution of the Council and the Representatives of the Governments of the Member States on a Community Programme of Policy and Action in Relation to the Environment and Sustainable Development [1993] *OJ* C 138/1

Council (1996) Common Position 29/96 Concerning Misleading Advertising so as to Include Comparative Advertising [1996] *OJ* C219/14

Council (1999a) Resolution on the Consumer Dimension of the Information Society [1999] *OJ* C23/1

Council (1999b) Resolution on Community Consumer Policy 1999–2001 [1999] *OJ* C206/1

Council (2005) Common Position 6/2005 with a view to adopting a directive of the European Parliament and of the Council concerning unfair business-to-consumer commercial practices in the internal market [2005] *OJ* C 38E/1

Craig P and de Búrca G (2008) *EU Law: Text Cases and Materials*, (4th edn, OUP, Oxford)

Crouch C (2001) 'Citizenship and Markets in Recent British Education Policy' in Crouch C, Eder K and Tambini D (eds), *Citizenship, Markets and the State* (OUP, Oxford)

Dahl R (1994) 'A Democratic Dilemma: System Effectiveness versus Citizen Participation', 109 *Political Science Quarterly* 23

Darby S (2008) 'Why, What, When, How, Where and Who? Developing UK Policy on Metering, Billing and Energy Display Devices' ACEEE Summer Study on Energy Efficiency in Buildings, last accessed at http://www.eci.ox.ac.uk/research/energy/downloads/darby08-aceee.pdf on 6 January 2010

Davies G (2007) 'The Effect of Mrs Watts' Trip to France on the National Health Service', 18 *King's Law Journal* 158

Davies J (2009) 'Entrenchment of New Governance in Consumer Policy Formulation: a Platform for European Consumer Citizenship Practice?', 33 *Journal of Consumer Policy* 245

de Búrca G (2003) 'The Constitutional Challenge of New Governance in the European Union', 28 *European Law Review* 814

Deakin S (2005) 'The "Capability" Concept and the Evolution of European Social Policy' in Dougan M and Spaventa E (eds), *Social Welfare and EU Law* (Hart Publishing, Oxford)

Deakin S and Browne J (2003) 'Social Rights and Market Order: Adapting the Capability Approach' in Hervey T and Kenner J (eds), *Economic and Social Rights under the EU Charter of Fundamental Rights: A Legal Perspective* (Hart Publishing, Oxford)

DeBardeleben J and Hurrelmann A (eds), (2007) *Democratic Dilemmas of Multilevel Governance* (Palgrave Macmillan, Basingstoke)

Defra (2009) 'Sustainable Clothing Roadmap Presentation', last accessed at http://ec.europa.eu/environment/ecolabel/ecolabelled_products/categories/pdf/laundry/BIS%20sustainable%20clothing%20roadmad.pdf on 4 January 2010

Dehousse R and Weiler J (1990) 'The Legal Dimension' in Wallace W (ed.), *The Dynamics of European Integration* (Royal Institute of International Affairs, London)

Delacote P (2009) 'On the Sources of Consumer Boycotts Ineffectiveness', 18 *The Journal of Environment and Development* 306

Della Sala V (2001) 'Constitutionalising Governance: Democratic Dead End or Dead On Democracy?', conWEB – webpapers on Constitutionalism and Governance beyond the State, accessed at http://www.bath.ac.uk/esml/conWEB/Conweb%20papers-filestore/conweb6-2001.pdf on 19 January 2009

Diani M (2001) 'Social Movement Networks. Virtual and Real' in Webster F (ed.), *Culture and Politics in the Information Age. A New Politics?* (Routledge, London)

Díaz A (1997) Written Question No. 1094/97 to the Commission, Directive 94/62/EC on packaging and packaging waste [1997] *OJ* C373/64

Dickinson R and Hollander S (1991) 'Consumer Votes', 23 *Journal of Business Research* 1

Donohue K (2003) *Freedom from Want – American Liberalism and the Idea of the Consumer* (Johns Hopkins University Press, Baltimore)

Downes T (2001) 'Market Citizenship: Functionalism and Fig-leaves' in Bellamy R and Warleigh A (eds), *Citizenship and Governance in the European Union* (Continuum, London)

Drakopoulos S (1992) 'Keynes' Economic Thought and the Theory of Consumer Behaviour', 39 *Scottish Journal of Political Economy* 318

DTI (2005) 'Extending Competitive Markets: Empowered Consumers, Successful Businesses', last accessed at http://www.berr.gov.uk/files/file23787.pdf on 10 December 2009

Eberlein B (2005) 'Regulation by Cooperation: The "Third Way" in Making Rules for the Internal Energy Market' in Cameron P (ed.), *Legal Aspects of EU Energy Regulation* (OUP, Oxford)

Eberlein B (2008) 'The Making of the European Energy Market: The Interplay of Governance and Government', 28 *Journal of Public Policy* 73

Ebers M (2008) 'The Comparative Analysis of the Notion of "Consumer" in Community Law' in Schulte-Nölke, H, Twigg-Flesner, C and Ebers, M (eds), *Consumer Law Compendium (Comparative Analysis)*, last accessed at http://www. eu-consumer-law.org/consumerstudy_full_en.pdf on 10 November 2009

EC Bulletin (1972) 'Statement from the Paris Summit', No 10, last accessed at http://www.ena.lu/statement-paris-summit-19-21-october-1972-020002284. html on 20 January 2010

Echávarri R (2003) 'Development Theories and Development as Social Capability Expansion', Working Paper 0305, Departamento de Economía – Universidad Pública de Navarra, accessed at ftp://ftp.econ.unavarra.es/pub/ DocumentosTrab/DT0305.PDF on 4 December 2009

EESC (1990) 'On The Amended Proposal for a Council Directive on the Approximation of the Rates of Excise Duty on Alcoholic Beverages and on the Alcohol Contained in Other Products' (Opinion), [1990] *OJ* C 225/51

EESC (1996) 'On The Single Market and Consumer Protection: Opportunities and Obstacles' (Opinion), [1996] *OJ* C 039/55

EESC (1997) 'Communication from the Commission on Energy for the Future: Renewable Sources of Energy' (Opinion), [1997] *OJ* C206/41

EESC (1999) 'On the Consumer Policy Action Plan 1999–2001' (Opinion), [1999] *OJ* C209/1

EESC (2000) 'On General Product Safety' (Opinion), [2000] *OJ* C 51/67

EESC (2002) 'European Governance – a White Paper' (Opinion), [2002] *OJ* C 125/61

EESC (2003) 'On Consumer Education'(Opinion), [2003] *OJ* C133/1

EESC (2006) 'Launching a Debate on a Community Approach Towards Eco-Labelling Schemes for Fisheries Products' (Opinion), [2006] *OJ* C88/27

EESC (2008a) 'On Consumer Policy Strategy 2007–2013' (Opinion), [2008] *OJ* C162/20

EESC (2008b) 'On Eco-Friendly Production' (Opinion), [2008] *OJ* C224/1

ERGEG (2010) 'Implementation of EC Good Practice Guidance for Billing', ERGEG Status Review, Ref: E10-CEM-36-03, 8 September 2010

ERGEG and CEER (2008) '3rd Energy Package and Creating an Effective EU Agency (ACER) in the Consumer's Interest', Fact Sheet Reference No. FS-08-01

EURELECTRIC (2004) 'Report on Public Service Obligations', last accessed at http://www.unesa.es/informes_actualidad/informe_mercado_electrico_servicio_publico.pdf on 18 November 2009

Eurobarometer (1998) 48, 'Standard Eurobarometer', last accessed at http://ec.europa.eu/public_opinion/archives/eb/eb48/eb48_en.htm on 10 December 2009

Eurobarometer (2001) 55.2, 'Europeans, Science and Technology', last accessed at http://ec.europa.eu/research/press/2001/pr0612en-report.pdf on 10 December 2009

Eurobarometer (2004) Qualitative 'On Cross Border Shopping in 28 European Countries', last accessed at http://ec.europa.eu/consumers/topics/cross_border_shopping_en.pdf on 10 December 2009

Eurobarometer (2008) Special, 298, 'Consumer Protection in the Internal Market, 2008' last accessed at http://ec.europa.eu/public_opinion/archives/ebs/ebs_298_en.pdf on 10 December 2009

Europa (2009), 'Product Labeling and Packaging, Affected Product Areas and Access to the Individual Legislative Measures', last accessed at http://europa.eu/legislation_summaries/consumers/product_labelling_and_packaging/index_en.htm on 10 December 2009

Europe Economics (2007) 'An Analysis of the Issue of Consumer Detriment and the Most Appropriate Methodologies to Estimate It' Report for DG SANCO, last accessed at http://ec.europa.eu/consumers/strategy/docs/study_consumer_detriment.pdf on 23 November 2009

European Performance Satisfaction Indicator (2008) Customer Satisfaction Pan European Benchmark Report 2007, last accessed at http://www.epsi-rating.com/images/stories/reports/epsi_report_2007/Web_version.pdf on 28 January 2010

Everson M (1995) 'The Legacy of the Market Citizen' in Shaw J and More G (eds), *New Legal Dynamics of European Union* (OUP, Oxford)

Everson M (2006) 'Legal Constructions of the Consumer' in Trentmann F (ed.), *The Making of the Consumer: Knowledge, Power and Identity in the Modern World* (Berg, Oxford)

Everson M and Joerges C (2006) 'Consumer Citizenship in Postnational Constellations?', EUI Working Paper, Law No. 2006/47

Ewen S (1992) 'From Citizen to Consumer?', 20 *Intermedia* 3

Ferrera M (2005a) 'Towards an "Open" Social Citizenship? The New Boundaries of Welfare in the European Union' in de Búrca G (ed.), *EU Law and the Welfare State: In Search of Solidarity* (OUP, Oxford)

Ferrera M (2005b) *The Boundaries of Welfare* (OUP, Oxford)

Fine B (2006) 'Addressing the Consumer' in Trentmann F (ed.), *The Making of the Consumer: Knowledge, Power and Identity in the Modern World* (Berg, Oxford)

Finke B (2007) 'Civil Society Participation in EU governance', 2 *Living Reviews. Euro. Gov.*, No. 2 [Online Article], accessed at http://www.livingreviews.org/1reg-2007-2 on 16 September 2009.

Fischer S (2003) 'Globalization and Its Challenges', Revised version of the Ely Lecture, presented at the American Economic Association meeting in Washington DC, accessed at http://www.iie.com/fischer/pdf/fischer011903.pdf on 10 December 2009

Follesdal A (2001) 'Union Citizenship: Unpacking the Beast of Burden', 20 *Law and Philosophy* 313

Ford T and Gil G (2001) 'Radical Internet Use' in Dowding J H (ed.), *Radical Media. Rebellious Communication and Social Movements* (Sage, London)

Freedland M (1998) 'Law, Public Services, and Citizenship: New Domains, New Regimes?' in Freedman M and Sciarra S (eds), *Public Services and Citizenship in European Law* (Clarendon Press, Oxford)

Freedland M (2001) 'The Marketisation of Public Services' in Crouch C, Eder K and Tambini D (eds), *Citizenship, Markets and the State* (OUP, Oxford)

Gabriel Y and Lang T (1995) *The Unmanageable Consumer: Contemporary Consumption and its Fragmentations* (Sage, London)

Gamble A (1988) *The Free Economy and the Strong State: Politics of Thatcherism* (Macmillan, Basingstoke)

Gasper D (2007) 'What Is the Capability Approach? Its Core, Rationale, Partners and Dangers', 36 *The Journal of Socio-Economics* 335

Giuliano M and Legarde P (1980) ' Report on the Convention on the Law Applicable to Contractual Obligations' [1980] *OJ* C282/1

Giulietti M, Waddams C and Waterson M (2003) 'Consumer Choice and Industrial Policy: A Study of UK Energy Markets', last accessed at http://www.ucei.berkeley.edu/PDF/csemwp112.pdf on 22 November 2009

Giulietti M, Waddams Price C, and Waterson M (2005) 'Consumer Choice and Competition Policy: A Study of UK Energy Markets', 115 *The Economic Journal* (October) 949

Graham M (2000) 'Issues in Health Sector Regulation', Oxford Policy Institute Seminar Series, last accessed at http://www.opi.org.uk/publications/documents/Graham2000_000.pdf on 10 December 2009

Greenwood J (2007) 'Organized Civil Society and Input Legitimacy in the EU' in DeBardeleben J and Hurrelmann A (eds), *Democratic Dilemmas of Multilevel Governance* (Palgrave Macmillan, Basingstoke)

Hall D (2007) 'Waste Management Companies in Europe 2007' Public Services International Research Unit, University of Greenwich, a report commissioned by the European Federation of Public Service Unions (EPSU), last accessed at http://www.psiru.org/publicationsindex.asp on 22nd April 2008

Haltern U (2002) 'Pathos and Patina: The Failure and Promise of Constitutionalism in the European Imagination', conWEB – webpapers on Constitutionalism and Governance beyond the State, accessed at http://www.bath.ac.uk/esml/conWEB/Conweb%20papers-filestore/conweb6-2002.pdf on 19 January 2009

Harker M and others (2008) ESRC Centre for Competition Policy, University of East Anglia, 'Benchmarking the Performance of the Uk Framework Supporting Consumer Empowerment through Comparison against Relevant International Comparator Countries', Report prepared for BERR, last accessed at http://www.berr.gov.uk/files/file47653.pdf 10 November 2009

Harlow C (1998) 'Public Service, Market Ideology, and Citizenship' in Freedland M and Sciarra S (eds), *Public Services and Citizenship in European Law: Public and Labour Law Perspectives* (Clarendon Press, Oxford)

Harris J (1999) 'State Social Work and Social Citizenship in Britain: From Clientism to Consumerism', 29 *British Journal of Social Work* 915

Hatzopoulos V (2007) 'The ECJ Case Law on Cross-Border Aspects of Health Care', Briefing Note prepared for the European Parliament's committee on Internal Market and Consumer Protection, last accessed at http://www.europarl.europa. eu/comparl/imco/studies/0701_healthserv_ecj_en.pdf on 10 December 2009

Hayek F (1980) *Law, Legislation and Liberty: A New Statement of the Liberal Principles of Justice and Political Economy* (Routledge, London)

Heater D (1990) *Citizenship: The Civic Ideal in World History, Politics and Education* (Longman, London)

Heater D (1999) *What is Citizenship?* (Polity Press, Blackwell Publishers, Oxford)

Heldman C (2003) 'T-CAP Consumer Activism Project', last accessed at http:// web.whittier.edu/academic/politicalscience/tcap.htm on 7 December 2008

Hervey T and McHale J (2004) *Health Law and the European Union* (Cambridge University Press, Cambridge)

Hilson C (2008) 'Environmental Solidarity and the Ecological Citizen', paper presented at the Modern Law Review workshop: Seeking Solidarity in the European Union – Towards Social Citizenship and a European Welfare State?, Sussex Law School, University of Sussex, 7 May 2008

Hilton M (2003) *Consumerism in Twentieth-Century Britain: The Search for a Historical Movement* (Cambridge University Press, Cambridge)

Hilton M (2006) 'The Banality of Consumption', Paper presented to conference on *Citizenship and Consumption: Agency, Norms, Mediation and Spaces*, Trinity Hall, Cambridge

Hirschman A (1970) *Exit, Voice, and Loyalty. Responses to Decline in Firms, Organizations, and States* (Harvard University Press, Cambridge MA)

Hirst P (1997) *From Statism to Pluralism* (UCL Press, London)

Hirst P (2000) 'Democracy and Governance' in Pierre J (ed.), *Debating Governance* (OUP Oxford)

Hondius E (2006) 'The Notion of Consumer: European Union versus Member States', 28 *Sydney Law Review* 89

House of Lords (2008) European Union Committee. 'The Single Market: Wallflower or Dancing Partner', HL Paper 36-I, 8 February 2008

Howden-Chapman P and Kawachi I (2006) 'Paths to and from Poverty in Late 19th Century Novels', 60 *Journal of Epidemiology and Community Health* 102

Howells G and Weatherill S (2005) *Consumer Protection Law* (2nd edn, Ashgate Publishing, Aldershot)

Howells G (2005) 'The Potential and Limits of Consumer Empowerment by Information',32 *Journal of Law and Society* 349

Hunt J and Shaw J (2009) 'Fairytale of Luxembourg? Reflections on Law and Legal Scholarship in European Integration' in Phinnemore D and Warleigh-Lack A (eds), *Reflections on European Integration: 50 Years of the Treaty of Rome* (Palgrave Macmillan, Basingstoke)

Hurrelmann A and Debardeleben J (2009) 'Democratic Dilemmas in Eu Multilevel Governance: Untangling the Gordian Knot', 1 *European Political Science Review* 229

Incardona R and Poncibò C (2007) 'The Average Consumer, the Unfair Commercial Practices Directive, and the Cognitive Revolution', 30 *Journal of Consumer Policy* 21

Kadelbach S (2003) 'Union Citizenship' Jean Monnet Working Paper 9/03, accessed at http://www.jeanmonnetprogram.org/papers/03/030901-04.rtf on 3April 2007

Kenner J (2003) 'Economic and Social Rights in the EU Legal Order' in Hervey T and Kenner J (eds), *Economic and Social Rights under the EU Charter of Fundamental Rights: A Legal Perspective* (Hart Publishing, Oxford)

Komninos A (2008) 'The EU White Paper for Damages Actions: a First Appraisal', Doctrines, Concurrences No.2, 84, last accessed at http://www.concurrences.com/article_revue_web.php3?id_article=16485&lang=en&onglet=12 on 10 December 2009

Kroes N (2006) 'More private antitrust enforcement through better access to damages: an invitation for an open debate'(Speech) last accessed at http://europa.eu/rapid/pressReleasesAction.do?reference=SPEECH/06/158&format=HTML&aged=0&language=EN&guiLanguage=en on 10 December 2009

Kuneva M (2009) 'A Blueprint for Consumer Policy in Europe: Making Markets Work with and for People' (Lisbon Council e-brief, 2009) last accessed at http://ec.europa.eu/consumers/docs/kuneva_consumer_blueprint_en.pdf on 4 January 2010

Lam A and Lambermont-Ford J (2008) 'Knowledge Creation and Sharing in Organisational Contexts: A Motivation-based Perspective', School of Management, Royal Holloway University of London, Working Paper Series SoMWP–0801, last accessed at http://eprints.rhul.ac.uk/727/3/Lam-LF_0801.pdf on 2 November 2009

Lecca J (1990) 'Nationalità e cittadinanza nell'Europa delle immigrazioni' in WAA (Italian for various editors/authors), *Italia, Europa e Nuove Immigrazioni* (Edizione della Fondazione Giovanni Agnelli, Turin)

Lewis N (1996) *Choice and the Legal Order, Rising above Politics* (Butterworths, London)

Leys C (2003) *Market-Driven Politics: Neoliberal Democracy and the Public Interest* (Verso, London)

Logica CMG (2008) 'Turning concern into action: Energy efficiency and the European consumer', last accessed at http://www.efonet.org/index.php?option=com_docman&task=doc_download&gid=49&Itemid=41 on 7 December 2010

Lubkin G (1996) 'Is Europe's Glass Half-Full or Half Empty?: The Taxation of Alcohol and the Development of a European Identity' Harvard Jean Monnet Working Paper 7/1996, accessed at http://centers.law.nyu.edu/jeanmonnet/papers/96/9607ind.html on 10 November 2009

Luciani G (2004) 'Energy Policies in the European Union,' in ECSSR, *Risk and Uncertainty in the Changing Global Energy Market* (Abu Dhabi: Emirates Center for Strategic Studies and Research)

Maas W (2007) *Creating European Citizens* (Rowman & Littlefield, Plymouth)

MacCormick N (2007) *Institutions of Law: An Essay in Legal Theory* (OUP, Oxford)

Maduro M (2000) 'Europe's Social Self: "The Sickness Unto Death"' in Jo Shaw (ed.), *Social Law and Policy in an Evolving European Union* (Hart, Oxford)

Majone G (1994) 'The Rise of the Regulatory State in Europe', 17 *West European Politics* 77

Majone G (2005) Dilemmas of European Integration: The Ambiguities & Pitfalls of Integration by Stealth (OUP, Oxford)

Malpas and others (2006) 'Problematizing choice: responsible subjects and citizenly consumers', Paper presented to conference on *Citizenship and Consumption: Agency, Norms, Mediation and Spaces*, Trinity Hall, Cambridge.

Marshall T H (1950) *Citizenship and Social Class* (Cambridge University Press, Cambridge 1950) (Pluto, Reprinted London 1992)

McAuslan P (1981) *The Ideologies of Planning Law* (Pergamon, Oxford)

McGregor S (2002) 'Consumer Citizenship: A Pathway to Sustainable Development?', International Conference on Developing Consumer Citizenship, Norway, last accessed at http://www.consultmcgregor.com/documents/keynotes/norway_keynote.pdf on 10 December 2009

Meehan E (1993) *Citizenship and the European Community* (Sage, London)

Micheletti M (2003) *Political Virtue and Shopping: Individuals, consumerism, and Collective Action* (Palgrave, New York)

Micklitz H W (2009) 'Universal Services: Nucleus for a Social European Private Law', EUI Working Paper, Law 2009/12, accessed at http://cadmus.eui.eu/dspace/bitstream/1814/12238/1/LAW_2009_12.pdf on 24 September 2009

Micklitz HW, Roethe T and Weatherill S (1994) (eds) *Federalism and Responsibility, A Study on Product Safety Law and Practice in the European Community* (Graham & Trotman, London)

Minas R (2009) 'Activation in Integrated Services? Bridging Social and Employment Services in European Countries', 11 Working Paper/Institute for Futures Studies, Stockholm, accessed at http://www.framtidsstudier.se/filebank/files/20090611$162002$fil$24T7T4t8XJ468EVwSJdy.pdf on 29 September 2009

Mombaur P (2008) 'Preparation for the Competitive European Electricity Sector', 2 *European Review of Energy Markets* 2

Morris S and Adley C (2000) 'European GMO Regulations: A Victim of Biopolitics?', University of Limerick, last accessed at http://www.isb.vt.edu/articles/jul0008.htm on 15 December 2008

Mort F (2006) 'Democratic Subjects and Consuming Subjects' in Trentmann F (ed.), *The Making of the Consumer: Knowledge, Power and Identity in the Modern World* (Berg, Oxford)

Nebbia P (2007) *Unfair Contract Terms in European Law: A Study in Comparative and EC Law* (Hart, Oxford)

Netherlands (2009) 'Consumer Segmentation in Relation to the Social Services Sector in the Netherlands', last accessed at Http://www.docstoc.com/docs/15124896/Consumer-segmentation-in-housing-and-care-matters on 21 December 2009

Newdick C (2008) 'Preserving Social Citizenship in Health Care Markets: There May be Trouble Ahead', 2 *McGill Journal of Law and Health* 93

Newman J (2001) *Modernising Governance. New Labour, Policy and Society* (Sage, London)

Nussbaum M (2006) *Frontiers of Justice: Disability, Nationality, Species Membership* (Harvard University Press, London)

O'Leary S (2005) 'Solidarity and Citizenship Rights' in de Búrca G (ed.), *EU Law and the Welfare State: In Search of Solidarity* (OUP, Oxford)

Olsen D H (2006) 'Work, Production, Free Movement and Then What? Concepts of Citizenship in European Integration 1951–71', EUI Working Paper, SPS No. 2006/08

Olson M (1965) *The Logic of Collective Action: Public Goods and the Theory of Groups* (Harvard University Press, Cambridge MA)

Ortino M (2007) 'The Role and Functioning of Mutual Recognition in the European Market of Financial Services', 56 *International Comparative Law Quarterly* 309

Osborne D and Gaebler T (1993) *Reinventing Government: How the Entrepreneurial Spirit is Transforming the Public Sector* (Penguin, London)

Patten S (2003) *The Economic Basis of Protection* (Batoche Books, Kitchener)

Peebles G (1997) 'A Very Eden of Innate Rights of Man? A Marxist Look at the European Union Treaties and Case Law', 22 *Law & Social Inquiry* 581

Pernice I (2002) 'Multilevel Constitutionalism in the European Union', 27 *European Law Review* 511

Picard E (1998) 'Citizenship, Fundamental Rights, and Public Services' in Freedland M and Sciarra S (eds), *Public Services and Citizenship in European Law: Public and Labour Law Perspectives* (Clarendon Press, Oxford)

Pickerill J (2004) *Cyberprotest: Environmental activism online* (Manchester University Press, Manchester)

Pitt T (1985) Written Question No. 336/85 to the Commission on the Farm Price Review [1985] OJ C269/11

Pollitt C and Bouckaert G (2000) *Public Management Reform. A Comparative Analysis* (OUP, Oxford)

Powell M, Doheny S and Greener I (2006) 'In Search of the Citizen-Consumer', Paper presented to conference on *Citizenship and Consumption: Agency, Norms, Mediation and Spaces*, Trinity Hall, Cambridge, accessed at http://www.consume.bbk.ac.uk/citizenship/Powell.doc on 4 June 2008

Prosser T (2005) 'Competition Law and Public Services: From Single Market to Citizenship Rights?', 11 *European Public Law* 543

Ramonet I (2000) 'Fears of the Year' (editorial), Le Monde Diplomatique, (English edition), last accessed at http://mondediplo.com/2000/12/01fears on 10 December 2009

Redfern P (1920) 'The Consumers' Place in Society' (Co-operative Union, Manchester), last accessed at http://www.archive.org/details/consumersplacein00redfuoft, PDF link, on 4 January 2010

Reeves B and Armel C (2009) 'Serious Games and Energy Use Behavior' Precourt Institute for Energy Efficiency, Stanford University, last accessed at http://www.stanford.edu/group/peec/cgi-bin/docs/behavior/research/Serious%20Games%20and%20Energy%20Use%20Behavior.pdf on 9 January 2010

Reich N (1996) *Europäisches Verbraucherrecht* (Nomos, Baden-Baden)

Reich N (2006) 'Protection of Consumers' Economic Interests by EC Contract Law – Some Follow-up Remarks', 3 *Sydney Law Review* 28

Rinaldi E (2005) 'Consumer Education in Italy and in Europe: Themes, Tools and Trends for the Future Years' in Doyle D (ed.), *Consumer Citizenship: Promoting new responses (Vol. 1) Taking Responsibility* (Consumer Citizenship Network, Hedmark University College, Hamar, Norway)

Robeyns I (2005) 'The Capability Approach: A Theoretical Survey', 6 *Journal of Human Development* 94

Rose L (1999) 'Citizen (Re)Orientations in the Welfare State: from Private to Public Citizens?' in Bussemaker E (ed.), *Citizenship and Welfare State Reform in Europe* (Routledge, London)

Ross M (2000) 'Article 16 EC and Services of General Interest: From Derogation to Obligation?', 25 *European Law Review* 22

Rott P (2007) 'Consumers and services of general interest: is EC consumer law the future?', 30 *Journal of Consumer Policy* 49

Ruzza C (2004) *Europe and Civil Society: Movement Coalitions and European Governance* (Manchester University Press, Manchester)

Salais R (2005) 'The Capability Approach and the European Project', English revised version of a paper published in the special issue 'On Sen' in L'économie politique, last accessed at http://www.idhe.ens-cachan.fr/Eurocap/CARSalais. pdf on 10 December 2009

Sauter W (2008) 'Services of General Economic Interest and Universal Service in EU Law', *European Law Review* 167

Scammell M (2000) 'The Internet and Civic Engagement: The Age of the Citizen-Consumer', 17 *Political Communication* 351

Scammell M (2003) 'Citizen Consumers: Towards a New Marketing of Politics?' in Corner J and Pels D (eds), *Media and the Re-styling of Politics* (Sage, London)

Schmidt V (2009) 'The EU and its Member States: From Bottom Up to Top Down' in Phinnemore D and Warleigh-Lack A (eds), *Reflections on European Integration: 50 Years of the Treaty of Rome* (Palgrave Macmillan, Basingstoke)

Schulte-Nölke H, Twigg-Flesner, C and Ebers, M (eds), (2008) Consumer Law Compendium (Comparative Analysis) (2008), last accessed at http://ec.europa. eu/consumers/rights/docs/consumer_law_compendium_comparative_ analysis_en_final.pdf 10 December 2009

Scott J and Trubek D (2002) 'Mind the Gap: Law and New Approaches to Governance in the EU', 8 *European Law Journal* 1

Sen A (1985) *Commodities and Capabilities* (North Holland, Amsterdam)

Sen A (1999) *Development as Freedom* (OUP, Oxford)

Shaw J and More G (eds), (1995) *New Legal Dynamics of European Union* (OUP, Oxford)

Shaw J (1997a) 'Citizenship of the Union: Towards Post-National Membership?' Harvard Jean Monnet Working Paper 6/1997, accessed at http:// jeanmonnetprogram.org/papers/97/97-06-.html on 4 January 2010

Shaw J (1997b) 'The Many Pasts and Futures of Citizenship in the European Union', 22 *European Law Review* 554

Shaw J, Hunt J and Wallace C (2007) *Economic and Social Law of the European Union* (Palgrave Macmillan, Basingstoke)

Simon H (1986) 'Rationality in Psychology and Economics', 59 *Journal of Business* (supplement) S209

Smartmeters.com (2009) 'Taking Smart Meters Further', last accessed at http:// www.smartmeters.com/the-news/706-taking-smart-meters-further.html on 6 January 2011.

Steffek J, Kissling C and Nanz P (eds), (2007) Civil Society Participation in European and Global Governance: A Cure for the Democratic Deficit? (Palgrave Macmillan, Basingstoke)

Stein E (1981) 'Lawyers, Judges, and the Making of a Transnational Constitution', 75 *The American Journal of International Law* 1

Stolle D, Hooghe, M and Micheletti, M (2005) 'Politics in the Supermarket: Political Consumerism as a Form of Political Participation', 26 *International Political Science Review* 245

Street J and Scott A (2001) 'From Media Politics to E-Protest? The Use of Popular Culture and New Media in Parties and Social Movements' in Webster F (ed.),*Culture and Politics in the Information Age. A New Politics?* (Routledge, London)

Stuyck J (2000) 'European Consumer Law after the Treaty of Amsterdam: Consumer Policy In or Beyond the Internal Market?', 37 *Common Market Law Review* 367

Supiot A (1999) (ed.) Au delà de l'emploi: transformations du travail et l'avenir du droit du travail en Europe (Flammarion, Paris)

Swedish Consumer Agency (2011) 'About the Swedish Consumer Agency', last accessed at http://www.konsumentverket.se/otherlanguages/English/About-the-Swedish-Consumer-Agency/ on 3 January 2011

Szyszczak E (2000) *EC Labour Law* (Longman, Harlow)

Szyszczak E (2006) 'Experimental Governance: The Open Method of Coordination', 12 *European Law Journal* 486

Szyszczak E (2007) *The Regulation of the State in Competitive Markets in the EU* (Hart, Oxford)

Szyszczak E and Cygan A (2008) *Understanding EU Law*, (2nd edn, Sweet & Maxwell, London)

Szyszczak E (2009) 'Lisbon – Kyoto – Moscow: Joining the Dots?', XIX *Fordham Environmental Law Review* 287

Thoresen V (ed.), (2003) 'Consumer Education and Teacher Training: Developing Consumer Citizenship' Comenius 2.1 Project 2001–2004, Conference report, accessed at http://fulltekst.bibsys.no/hihm/oppdragsrapport/2003/03/opprapp03_2003.pdf on 12 February 2009

Tiersky R (2003) *François Mitterand: A Very French President* (Rowman & Littlefield, Plymouth)

Trentmann F (2001) 'Bread Milk and Democracy: Consumption and Citizenship in Twentieth-Century Britain' in Daunton M and Hilton M (eds), *The Politics of Consumption: Material Culture and Citizenship in Europe and America* (Berg, Oxford)

Trentmann F (ed.), (2006a) *The Making of the Consumer: Knowledge, Power and Identity in the Modern World* (Berg, Oxford)

Trentmann F (2006b) 'Knowing Consumers – Histories, Identities, Practices' in Trentmann F (ed.), *The Making of the Consumer: Knowledge, Power and Identity in the Modern World* (Berg, Oxford)

Turner B (1986) *Citizenship and Capitalism: The Debate over Reformism* (Allen and Unwin, London)

Turner B (1990) 'Outline of a Theory of Citizenship', 24 *Sociology* 2

Ugur M (2009) 'Liberalisation in a World of Second Best: Evidence on European Network Industries', MPRA Paper No. 17873, accessed at http://mpra.ub.uni-muenchen.de/17873/1/MPRA_paper_17873.pdf on 25 October 2009

Van Berkel R and Van der Aa P (2005) 'The Marketisation of Activation Services: A Modern Panacea?', 15 *Journal of European Social Policy* 329

Van de Donk W and others (eds), (2003) *Cyberprotest: New Media, Citizens and Social Movement* (Routledge, London)

Van der Mei A P (2005) 'EU Law and Education: Promotion of Student Mobility versus Protection of Educational Systems' in Dougan M and Spaventa E (eds), *Social Welfare and EU Law: Essays in European Law* (Hart Publishing, Oxford)

Van Gunsteren H (1978) 'Notes on a Theory of Citizenship' in Birnbaum P, Lively J and Parry G (eds), *Democracy, Consensus and Social Contract* (Sage/ ECPR, London)

Vigoda-Gadot E and Mizrahi S (2007) 'Public Sector Management and the Democratic Ethos: A 5-Year Study of Key Relationships in Israel', 18 *Journal of Public Administration Research and Theory* 79

Von Rosenberg H (2008) 'No Ace to Win the Trick – the Proposed Acer and Its Influence on Ec Competition Law', 29 *European Competition Law Review* 512

Von Rosenberg H (2009) 'Unbundling through the Back Door...the Case of Network Divestiture as a Remedy in the Energy Sector', 30 *European Competition Law Review* 237

Walker N, (2005) 'Legal Theory and the European Union: A 25th Anniversary Essay', 25 *Oxford Journal of Legal Studies* 581

Walker N (2007) 'Post-Constituent Constitutionalism? The Case of the European Union' in Loughlin M and Walker N (eds), *The Paradox of Constitutionalism* (OUP, Oxford)

Ward I (2001) 'Beyond Constitutionalism: The Search for a European Political Imagination', 7 *European Law Journal* 24

Warleigh A (2001) 'Purposeful Opportunists? EU Institutions and the Struggle over European Citizenship' in Bellamy R and Warleigh A (eds), *Citizenship and Governance in the European Union* (Continuum, London)

Weatherill S (1996) 'The Evolution of European Consumer Law: From Well Informed Consumer to Confident Consumer' in Micklitz H W (ed.), *Rechtseinheit oder Rechtsvielfalt in Europa?* (Nomos, Baden-Baden)

Weatherill S (1997) 'On the Depth and Breadth of European Integration', 17 *Oxford Journal of Legal Studies* 537

Weatherill S (1999) 'Consumer Policy' in Craig P and de Búrca G (eds), *The Evolution of EU Law* (OUP, Oxford)

Weatherill S (2007) 'Who is the Average Consumer?' in Weatherill S and Bernitz U (eds), *The Regulation of Unfair Commercial Practices under EC Directive 2005/29: New Rules and New Techniques* (Hart Publishing, Oxford)

Weiler J (1997) 'The Reformation of European Constitutionalism', 35 *Journal of Common Market Studies* 97

Weiler J (1999) *The Constitution of Europe* (Cambridge University Press, Cambridge)

Werhane P and others (2008) 'Monsanto Europe: Monsanto Introduces GMOs to Europe with Unexpected Results', last accessed at SSRN: http://ssrn.com/ abstract=908731 on 10 December 2009

Which? Policy report (2005) 'Which Choice? Can the Government's Choice Agenda Deliver for Everyone?' (Which?, London)

Whitford W (1973) 'The Functions of Disclosure Regulation in Consumer Transaction', *Wisconsin Law Review* 400

Wiener A and Della Sala V (1997) 'Constitution-Making and Citizenship Practice: Bridging the Democracy Gap in the EU?', 35 *Journal of Common Market Studies* 595

Wiener A (1998) *European Citizenship Practice: Building Institutions of a Non-State* (Westview Press, Oxford)

Wilhelmsson T (2004) 'The Abuse of the "Confident Consumer" as Justification for EC Consumer Law', 27 *Journal of Consumer Policy* 317

Winch D (2006) 'The Problematic Status of the Consumer in Orthodox Economic Thought' in Trentmann F (ed.), *The Making of the Consumer: Knowledge Power and Identity in the Modern World* (Berg, Oxford)

Winward J (1993) 'The Organised Consumer and Consumer Information Co-Operatives' in Keat R, Whiteley N and Abercrombie N (eds), *The Authority of the Consumer* (Routledge, London)

WTO (2006) 'Complaints by the United States, Canada and Argentina, against European Communities, Measures Affecting the Approval and Marketing of Biotech Products' (29 September 2006) DS291, DS292 and DS293, last accessed at http://www.wto.org/english/news_e/news06_e/291r_e.htm on 10 December 2009

Zellentin G (1962) 'The Economic and Social Committee', 1 *Journal of Common Market Studies* 22

Index